WISDOM OF BAT SHEVA

WISDOM

OF

BAT SHEVA

∾

IN MEMORY OF
Beth Samuels Z"L

∾

EDITED BY
Barry S. Wimpfheimer

Ktav Publishing House
Brooklyn, NY

Copyright © 2009
Library of Congress Cataloging-in-Publication Data

p. cm.
ISBN: 978-0-88125-970-4 (alk. paper)

Published by:
KTAV Publishing House
527 Empire Blvd.
Brooklyn, NY 11225
www.ktav.com
phone: 718-972-5449
orders@ktav.com

BETH SAMUELS

בת שבע בת זכריה הלוי ואיתא חנה

תשלה–תשסז • 1975–2007

ACKNOWLEDGEMENTS

A special thanks to those who contributed
articles to honor the memory of
Beth Samuels.

Three assistant editors helped to shepherd
the project from word processor to print:
Wendy Amsellem was instrumental in
soliciting contributions, Ari Tuchman
acted as an emergency style editor, and
Yanay Ofran copy-edited the Hebrew
submissions. Aliza Dzik designed the cover
and Koren Publishing Services typeset
the book. Beth's grandmother, Serita
Kolom, and Beth's aunt, Halyse Danko,
contributed the Hebrew cover artwork.

CONTENTS

Wisdom of Bat Sheva

Editor's Preface

Barry S. Wimpfheimer

As I write this introduction, it has been nearly two years since Dr. Beth Samuels was prematurely taken from us. Even as we are gaining distance from the tragedy of her death, we are still shaken by the trauma of Beth's passing and perpetually saddened by the reality of her absence. The profound nature of Beth's death has colored all aspects of the lives of her friends and family; it often leads to a form of paralysis that renders us immobile at the thought of carrying on when she cannot. Life's joys have become difficult to enjoy because we cannot share them with Beth and because they remind us of Beth's perpetual role in those joys when she was with us. This dynamic recalls the description of a group of individuals shaken by the loss of the Temple at Tosefta Sotah 15:11–14:

> When the Second Temple was destroyed, abstinents abounded in Israel who would neither eat meat nor drink wine.
>
> R. Yehoshua engaged them and said to them, "my sons, why do you not eat meat?"

They replied, "Can we eat meat when every day the daily sacrifice was offered on the altar and now it is no longer?"

He said to them, "we won't eat meat. But why", he continued, "do you not drink wine?"

They replied, "Can we drink wine when every day it was poured on the altar and is no longer."

He said to them, "we won't drink wine."

He continued, "we should not eat bread for from it they used to offer the two loaves and the showbreads.

We should not drink water for they would pour water as a libation on Sukkot.

We should not eat figs or grapes because pilgrims would bring those as first fruits on Shavuot."

The abstinents went silent.

R. Yehoshua addressed them again, "my children, [on the one hand,] no [level of] mourning could be considered excessive and [on the other hand,] one cannot [as a result] stop mourning at all, so the sages said, 'let a man lime his house and leave over a small portion in remembrance of Jerusalem; let a man prepare his feasts, but leave uneaten a small portion in remembrance of Jerusalem; let a woman accessorize but leave behind a small trinket in memory of Jerusalem."

The final period of the Second Temple was one marked by a tendency towards monasticism, part of which included abstinence from worldly pleasures. Tosefta Sotah informs us that as a result of the Temple's destruction there was a group who abstained from eating meat and drinking wine. Tosefta describes how R. Yehoshua reached out to this group and offered them counsel to console them on their loss.

The father of modern psychology, Sigmund Freud, describes two different states of response to tragedy: mourning and melancholia. For Freud, mourning is natural and healthy – a process of productively working through one's loss. But sometimes, the trauma of tragedy is so severe that the aggrieved become melancholics. Melancholia is the pathological version of mourning, the state in which the trauma of tragedy remains raw, causing the individual to act out against the loss. Melancholics, Freud tells us, are prone to extreme behaviors – behaviors that keep them in the rut of their own trauma's refusal to release them to a healthier emotional state.

The abstinents of Tosefta respond to the destruction as melancholics: the loss of the Temple is so profound for them that they cannot but reinscribe that loss every day through abstinence. How can we eat meat or drink wine, they ask, if those actions only remind us of what we had and what is lost?

R. Yehoshua recognizes this behavior as unhealthy and engages the abstinents in an attempt to console them. He listens to their reasons for meat and wine and even agrees to these practices but then points out that these practices could easily extend to others – the grip of melancholia can easily extend to other areas of one's life, allowing all of life to be entirely colored with tragedy. R. Yehoshua highlights for the abstinents that even their extreme rituals of mourning are not enough – that to be true to themselves they might have to abstain from even more. In so doing, R. Yehoshua attempts to paint the abstinents, like himself, as struggling within the confines of two poles. "[On the one hand,] no mourning would be considered excessive and [on the other hand,] one cannot [as a result] stop mourning at all." All mourning, R. Yehoshua says, is a compromise between the pain we feel that could never be satisfied in any ritual of mourning, and our need to go on with life. Rather than allowing the trauma to take over lives and inhabit all aspects of being, R. Yehoshua counsels them to follow the advice of the rabbis, making space for mourning in every aspect of their lives but continuing to live those lives.

Those of us who count ourselves as Beth's family and friends can strongly relate to the overwhelming sense of loss that the melancholic abstinents embody. We too feel that it is difficult to carry on because every activity, enterprise and emotion is colored by Beth's absence. But for us the problem is even starker than the one Tosefta describes, because Beth was also our R. Yehoshua.

Throughout her battle with cancer, Beth was the one providing strength to those of us who cared about her: it was she who shockingly managed to make even her mortal illness somehow spiritually meaningful – to find a God in cancer that she still wanted a relationship with. As I have reflected on this Tosefta text, I am struck by the fact that we are both profoundly sad because of our inconsolable loss and also in a melancholic rut because the one person who would console us and allow us to incorporate the loss productively in our lives – to work through this loss – was Beth. She was our R. Yehoshua and without her we are still melancholic abstinents seeing all of life's experiences overwhelmed by her absence.

Throughout Beth's illness and immediately after her passing, many of Beth's friends and relatives were gripped by the desire to do something – for Beth, for Ari and the girls, and for themselves. We were shaken by the loss of someone whose goodness always manifest in doing something for others into imitating that behavior. During the period of Beth's illness, I became aware of the fact that she had been editing an article about the function of numbers in Genesis. I also had read and critiqued Ari's article on Quantum Mechanics and Jewish theology during this time. After Beth's passing, I felt moved by Beth's example to edit this memorial volume that includes both Ari's article and Beth's own.

Beth was, as Ari's biographical essay demonstrates quite vividly, many things to many people. When we began this project, we thought of making a memorial volume that would include diverse intellectual contributions from mathematicians, physicists and scholars of Jewish studies. In the end we decided that the best way to honor Beth was through a volume dedicated to Torah, her first and (dare I say) paramount intellectual love.

The contributors to this volume are Beth's friends, mentors and relatives. They include rabbis, academics, scientists, physicians and lawyers. What binds us is our interest in contributing to the broadly conceived intellectual study of Torah. We can never replace Beth or forget her; this volume aims to leave over a small portion of Torah in her memory.

Introduction

Ari Tuchman

Beth Samuels touched people in a way that left them changed and made them better. Those who crossed her path in the beit midrash at Columbia University, at Drisha Institute, or in a winter camp in the Ukraine were all inspired by her; her light was contagious and indelible in a way that was neither exaggerated nor trite but rather genuinely uplifting. Her students of all ages adored her, true friends emulated her and her family simply and profoundly loved her. Everyone respected her beyond that which her age would usually warrant. Beth was not only always bursting with life and excitement but was also bursting with faith and focus. Her faith was in a loving God who listened to the cries of those in need and who taught mankind to be equally attentive to each other's cries. Her focus was on connecting to God through the pursuit of knowledge as well as through compassion to humanity.

Beth was born in Los Angeles in 1975 to Elana and Zachary Samuels. She graduated valedictorian from YULA high school and spent one year studying in Michlelet Yerushalayim LeBanot, in Jerusalem. She attended Columbia University in New York and received her BA in Mathematics with honors in 1997. At Columbia, she directed the *hevrutah* program, "Wednesday Night Learning," attracting hundreds of students to commit to serious weekly Torah learning and also was awarded the *Columbia Lion Award for Community Service*. Following graduation from Columbia, Beth enrolled in the Scholar's program at Drisha Institute in NY, in order to experience what she described as her "intellectual immersion in *gemara*." She often credited her years at Drisha, and specifically, Rabbi Dovid Silber, for encouraging creativity in analyzing Tanach narratives as well as methodological rigor in *halakha* and *gemara*. Continuing her commitment to community and spontaneity, she served as an auxiliary New York City police officer. Beth graduated from Drisha in 1999, and that summer we were married.

Beth then began her graduate work in mathematics at Yale University. She received her PhD in 2005 focusing on number theory under the guidance of Profs. Ilya Piatetski-Shapiro and Alex Lubotzky. She concurrently maintained her affiliation with Drisha and directed their High School program from 2000–2002, significantly expanding it during her tenure. While completing her doctorate, we were blessed with two children, Danelle Sophia (2002) and Natalia Meshi (2004). Our family relocated to Palo Alto, CA, and Beth began an Assistant Professorship at UC Berkeley. Beth was an active leader in women's participation in ritual, and she instituted women's prayer groups and Purim *megilah* readings. She continuously taught Torah within her community and lectured around the country as a visiting scholar. She was a gifted teacher of both Torah and mathematics, inspiring her audiences with her passion for learning and life.

Beth considered both her academic and personal milestones as intimate parts of her search for divine truth. Her research in mathematics, her devotion as loving wife and mother, her commitment to *halakha*, and her dedication to making serious Torah study accessible to everyone, were all integral in this pursuit. She believed that all knowledge enhanced her appreciation of the divine. Thus, in her YULA ten-year high school reunion booklet she began her bio with the opening line: "I continue to be impassioned by the pursuit of knowledge."

In her professional career in math, she was inspired and motivated by the aesthetic beauty of number theory. Only a few weeks before her passing, she stayed up late into the night trying to assemble a Ramanujan complex out of toothpicks, straws and construction paper. She took pride in being a woman mathematician and at a conference in Park City, Utah, the local newspaper, the Park Record, did a feature article on her as a pregnant, orthodox, mathematician. But in addition to enjoying math, intellectually and socially, she believed in its religious significance in her pursuit of truth. She wrote to a colleague of hers:

"One of the reasons I am attracted to math is that I see it as a union of the spiritual and physical worlds. We deal with theoretical (or Godly) constructs (i.e. infinite dimensions) but subject them to logic and very human reasoning. When I learned the topological homeomorphism between the circle minus a point and a straight line, I was convinced that I had insight into how God could be both one and infinite."

Understanding this topological formalism (where the infinite number line is represented as a finite circle, with the single point at the north pole representing the infinite) allowed Beth to achieve a deeper connection with God. Beth found parallels and analogies in her math that became part of her lens to view God.

Personally, Beth considered marriage as the perfect example of a human element in pursuit of the divine. She felt that the goal of marriage is to infuse physicality with holiness and is not a compromise between the material and spiritual. Beth described the profound love in our marriage as "*einah teluyah badavar,*" (independent of any external preconditions) which not only provided us endless joy and the ability to walk through life with our feet only occasionally on the ground but also created a love that was deeply religious. She believed marriage was also intended to foster community built on human compassion and kindness, *hesed*. In the program distributed at our wedding, essentially her detailed *halakhik* guide explaining the *minhagim*, customs, of the wedding ceremony, Beth writes:

> "It [marriage] is the moment where two individuals unite
> to begin an elevated existence where they are better able to
> contribute to society and to connect to God."

Motherhood presented Beth the ultimate opportunity to combine intellectual teaching with the joyful *kedusha* of kindness and compassion. She was excited by the challenge to teach about God and Torah to her children – even to a two and four year old. She taught the nightly recitation of the Shema as a dance, the Tanach narratives of Devorah and Esther as princess stories and the virtue of compassion with visits to the elderly and sick. She radiated boundless love while maintaining boundaries and discipline.

Beth viewed the path towards divine truth as a very human endeavor. But to Beth, not only was truth a pursuit which required immersion in the physical, subjective world, of academia and motherhood, but truth was in fact inherently defined by humanity. Beth believed that through prayer, human words can influence the divine plan. She recognized *halakha* as the process of ascertaining God's will with regard to human action. She taught that truth in *halakha* emerges as a synthesis of a divine framework and the reality of human imperfection. Beth deeply loved this concept of *halakhic* truth. It both empowered and challenged her. It allowed her to believe that God's presence in this world could be increased and that inequalities and injustice could be fixed. Even more importantly, it motivated Beth to strive for a partnership with God.

In understanding this partnership, Beth particularly appreciated the example of *rosh ḥodesh*, the new month, in which the beginning of each month is sanctified entirely through the actions of a *beit din*, a Jewish court, and the testimony of two witnesses. Although the dates of the holidays are abstractly ordained by God, practically determining these dates and thus the timing of applicable *halakhot* for a given festival is defined by human action. In an essay entitled "Women and Rosh Ḥodesh," Beth writes that *rosh ḥodesh* was traditionally given to women as a minor holiday, with some communities even mandating that women refrain from work. She explains:

"A major theme of *rosh ḥodesh* is our responsibility in taking an active role as partners with God in creation...

It is appropriate that the women's reward be related to the day which symbolizes empowerment of the people to create a Godly world. In Egypt, the women took active steps in creating a Jewish nation. Through the Tabernacle, the women voluntarily created a mini-spiritual world where God could dwell amongst them. The women were eager to settle the land of Israel and create a holy society as a model for the other nations. The women refused to participate in the major sins of the Golden Calf and the evil spies' report of the land. They continuously stood firm in their commitment to God.

Each *rosh hodesh* we should allow ourselves to feel renewed by a commitment to God, morality, and spirituality. We should be reminded of our responsibility to be partners with God in moving the world in the right direction."

Beth Samuels was always bursting with excitement to continue this partnership, and she recognized that her pursuit of knowledge was fundamental to it. However, Beth taught by the way she lived that the essence of *halakhic* truth cannot be achieved as only an intellectual endeavor. Beth taught that the power of human action to define truth carries with it the injuction to celebrate human subjectivity through acts of *hesed*. Beth was a *hesed* activist, always looking for quiet opportunities to bring comfort to others through gentle compassion, hospitality and charity.

Her search for the balance between truth and human subjectivity is reflected in the charter traditionally assigned to the *Sanhedrin*, the supreme legislative body in Jewish law. In tractate *Sanhedrin* (37a), the *Sanhedrin* is described with the poetic but vague philosophical charter of being a "*sugah bashoshanim*," a fence of roses. To explain the phrase's connotation, Avot d'Rabbi Natan (11,3), provides three interpretations. The first suggests that "*suga bashoshanim*" refers to *zadikim*, the righteous. The second explains that it refers to the *hakhamim*, the wise and learned, and the third, the *talmidim*, students. These combined characteristics of righteousness, wisdom and learning describe the nature of an ideal, legislative fence that defines and enforces *halakhic* truth.

A fence protects what is inside from external influence but can also preclude influencing the outside. A fence of roses offers some protection, however, it recognizes that the risk of exposure to influences is vastly outweighed by the imperative to teach and learn from the outside. This embodies the role of the *zadik*, to engage in *tikun olam*, the betterment of the entire world. It is not sufficient merely to protect a small enclave from encroaching darkness. While an iron fence is static and unyielding, a fence of roses is unafraid to grow and change and to be influenced by its surroundings. It is secure in its beliefs and boundaries. It can learn from humanity in defining *halakha* and can teach the world without compromising its values. This describes the *talmid* and the *ḥakham*, who are encouraged to learn from everyone, "*eizehu ḥakham halomed mikol adam* (Avot 4:1)" (who is wise, he who learns from everyone).

Beth was the embodiment of a *sugah bashoshanim*. She was a strong fence, and steadfastly defined her borders. She was practical, logical, mathematical, and unyielding in her respect for Torah, *halakha*, morality and truth. She would not compromise what she believed was beyond compromise. But she was always growing and radiating and was unafraid to learn from the outside world as well as to cast her brilliant light upon it. Beth was traditional as a mother yet was a revolutionary for change in the woman's role in Judaism and math and the world. She engaged in discussions on *halakha*, on God and on truth with both sides of the fence. With those very much on the outside, whom she met through Lights-in-Action, YUSSR, at various math conferences, or even at the supermarket, she was always considerate and was uniquely talented at making everyone feel that his or her opinion mattered. To those closer within, she was respectful and knowledgeable, engaging traditional communities who were less used to serious *halakhic* discussions with a beautiful fence of roses.

An impermeable fence mistrusts both the outside as well as those it protects. The boundary is obeyed because there is no choice. A *sugah bashoshanim*, however, requires faith and belief in humanity. It requires ideals to be upheld because they are true, not because they are forced. It also requires the belief that the people it is protecting are inherently good and desire truth. This is the perspective of the righteous, the ability to be "*dan lekaf zekhut*," to see good in everyone. Like the fence of roses, Beth deeply loved humanity, and was driven to try to see the good. She believed that true *hesed* is likewise based on faith in humanity, recognizing that one can only be sensitive to those who are viewed as equals. Beth's practice of *hesed* was predicated on empathy, not sympathy.

While an iron fence repels people from its boundary and prevents discussion, a fence of roses attracts with its beauty and encourages communication. A *ẓadik* can only do *hesed* if received by others; a *ḥakham* can only teach, and a *talmid* can only learn from those who will be engaged. This charter of the *Sanhedrin*, to define *halakhic* truth with knowledge strengthened by a closeness to humanity, was also Beth's goal.

Her wisdom, *Ḥakhmat Batsheva*, was her understanding of how to live a life embodying these traits of a *sugah bashoshanim*. Like the fence of roses, Beth pursued *halakhic* truth with both reverence for the divine and compassion for humanity. She pursued *hesed* not only in parallel with her search for truth but as a critical component. The articles in this memorial volume attest to the intellectual pursuits that were the foundation of her immersion in knowledge and truth. However, her true legacy was in teaching us to integrate such knowledge with a life of *hesed*.

A Literary Study of Numbers in Genesis

Beth Samuels *z"l*

N umbers represent the intellectual building blocks of our world, laying the foundation for both practical and philosophical pursuits. Scientific equations require numerical validation and quantified measurements to provide meaning in understanding the universe. Even the consonance and harmony in musical chords have been discovered to be related to numerical harmonics.[1] Historically, from the time of the Pythagoreans (500 B.C.), numbers have also had significance as abstract concepts in addition to being simply quantifiers. The Pythagoreans developed a detailed number symbolism that attributes a distinct characteristic to each digit. In their theory, "one," the generator of all other numbers, represents reason; "two," the first even or female number, signifies opinion; "three," the first odd or male number, denotes harmony by joining one and two; "four" represents justice, from the squaring of accounts, etc. This perspective upholds the centrality of numbers not only in the physical world but in the spiritual world as well. It is no surprise that the Pythagorean motto was "All is number."[1]

Given this significance of numbers to the human condition, it is natural to assume that numerical approaches can also play an important role in illuminating fundamental ideas contained within the Torah. While numbers given in the text may occasionally appear superfluous at first glance, with further exegesis their importance can be uncovered. There are various ways to study the numbers found in Genesis, each reflecting the awareness that numbers are more then just arbitrary dates, years, quantities, or measurements. The modern Biblical scholar U. Cassuto (d. 1951) analyzes the years mentioned in the genealogical passages of Genesis (chs. 5,11) in his *Perush al Sefer Bereishit*.[2] He notices the pattern of sixty and seven in the years listed and compares these numbers with those found in Canaanite mythology from the same period. He suggests that the seemingly arbitrary numbers subscribe to a trend common in other cultures of that time.[3] *Gematriya* is another method of numerical interpretation that considers numbers as representing words with the corresponding numerical value. For example, the *midrashic* collection *Gen. Rabbah* (43:2) explains that when Abraham is described as gathering 318 men with him to battle (Gen. 14:14), he is actually only taking his servant Eliezer, whose name has the numerical equivalent of 318.[4]

In this work, I apply a literary-thematic approach to examining numbers that are interspersed throughout the narratives in Genesis. By viewing the Torah as a divine masterpiece in which every single word is deliberate, each number must also be recognized as being significant. Numbers serve as key words, signifying underlying themes that link together stories. The creation story at the beginning of Genesis in which numbers first appear introduces unique characteristics associated with each number. Subsequent stories are in turn analyzed by focusing on the numbers and their associated qualities to provide deeper insight into the narrative themes. This article concentrates on analyzing the numbers "one," "two," and "three" and applies their thematic representations to the stories of Adam and Eve, the tower of Babel, the Patriarchs, and Joseph and his brothers.

Introduction

The creation story with which the Bible begins provides the critical text for defining numerical themes:

> *And God said, "Let there be light," and there was light. And*
> *God saw the light, that it was good; and God divided the light*
> *from the darkness. And God called the light "day," and the*
> *darkness He called "night;" and there was evening and there*
> *was morning; **one** day. (Gen. 1:3–5)[5]*

The first specific creation on Day One is that of light. Considering that the sun, moon, and stars are not created until the fourth day, many commentaries interpret this light as a spiritual illumination.[6] Rashi (R. Shlomo Yitshaki d. 1105) quotes from *Gen. Rabbah* 3:9 that the text deliberately describes the day as *ehad*, one, and not *rishon*, first, which would have been grammatically consistent with the language used for other days. The usage of the word *ehad* emphasizes God's "one-ness." God was one and alone on this day; neither the angels nor any other thing existed. The *midrash* in *Pesikta Zutrati* explains that the word *ehad* is used as a reflection of how Israel in the future will describe God in the "Shema" prayer: "the Lord is our God; the Lord is one" (Deut. 6:4). While God's one-ness is the obvious basis for monotheism, it also reinforces that the entire world emerged from a unified and holy place. Based on these perspectives, the number "one" is introduced as representing spiritual illumination, godliness, and unity.

> *And God said, "Let there be a firmament in the midst of the*
> *waters, and let it divide water from water." And God made*
> *the firmament and divided the waters which were under the*
> *firmament from the waters which were above the firmament;*
> *and it was so. And God called the firmament "heaven," and*
> *there was evening and there was morning, a **second** day.*
> *(Gen. 1:6–8)*

On Day Two, God separates the upper and lower waters. Day Two is the only day on which God does not comment, *"ki tov,"* it was good.[7] Several opinions in explanation are offered in *Gen. Rabbah* 4:8. According to Rabbi Yohanan, hell is created on this day, and according to Rabbi Hanina disagreement is created. In contrast to Day One, Day Two brings something separate from godliness into this world. Day Two divides the upper sphere and the lower sphere, allowing for evil to emerge. Day Two presents the first description of our world as we know it: a world filled with tensions between opposing forces, upper and lower, spiritual and physical, and good and evil. According to this reading, the number "two" represents division, tension, and ungodliness.

> And God said, "Let the waters under the heaven be gathered together to **one** place, and let the dry land appear," and it was so. And God called dry land "earth," and the gathering together of the waters, He called "seas;" and God saw that it was good. And God said, "Let the earth bring forth grass, herb yielding seed, and fruit tree yielding fruit after its kind, whose seed was in itself after its kind;" and God saw that it was good. And there was evening and there was morning, a **third** day. (Gen. 1:9–13)

On Day Three, God gathers the waters from Day Two and directs them to "one place," a place of one-ness, thereby creating dry land and vegetation. God controls the tension of Day Two by reconciling it with the holiness of Day One. The results are a permanent, solid foundation with the first sprouts of life. This is the only day where twice God comments "*ki tov*," it was good (Gen. 1:10,12).[8] Day Three is the balance of the proper combination of singularity and plurality, godliness and worldliness. According to this reading, the number "three" represents balance and the process and preparation leading to reconciliation. Day Three also marks the end of the initial stage in the creation process as Days One, Two, and Three lay the preparatory foundation for Days Four, Five, and Six.[9]

I will now analyze select narratives in the book of Genesis, focusing on passages where the numbers "one," "two," and "three" appear. I apply the characteristics associated with these first numbers to demonstrate that these numbers provide an exegetical tool to interpret larger themes within the narrative.

Adam And Eve

> And the Lord God took the man and put him into the Garden of Eden to till it and to keep it. And the Lord God commanded the man saying, "Of every tree of the garden, you

*may freely eat, but of the tree of the knowledge of good and evil, you may not eat of it; for on the day that you eat of it, you will surely die." And the Lord God said, "It is not good that the man should be **alone**;[10] I will make him a helper opposite him." (Gen. 2:15–18)*

God does not want Adam to be alone as one in the world. The *midrash* in *Pirkei deRabbi Eliezer* (ch. 12), explains that God rationalized, "I am *yeḥid*, one and only, in my world, and Adam is *yeḥid*, one and only, in his world. I don't reproduce, and Adam does not reproduce. Over time other creations may think that Adam is the Creator; therefore, it is not good for Adam to be alone. I will make him a helping mate opposite him."[11] Ultimately, only God is one. Adam was initially created as one and alone, and in this way Adam, unlike the animals, was created in the likeness and image of God. However, Adam is not God and is not intended to be God, and therefore cannot remain as one. Adam has a different purpose in life, to pursue godliness, which can only be fulfilled with a partner.

And out of the ground the Lord God formed every beast of the field and every bird of the air and brought them to the man to see what he would call them; and whatever the man called every living creature that was its name. And the man gave names to all cattle and to the birds of the air, and to every beast of the field, but for the man there was not found a helper opposite him. (Gen. 2:19–20)

While Adam is still alone, he acts like God; he names creatures the way God does in the original six days. By naming the animals, Adam distinguishes himself from them and dominates over them. Yet when Adam watches the animals he relates to their attachment to a mate. Adam, who, like them, is also from the ground, wants a partner. Rashi, quoting from *Gen. Rabbah* 17:5, comments on the verse in Gen. 2:20 that Adam petitions God, "All these animals have a counterpart, but I don't have a counterpart!" In response, God immediately remedies the situation in the next verse.[12] Perhaps, God also brought forth the animals to demonstrate to Adam that while he is above them, he also has much in common with them. While he initially was created as one, and therefore possesses some divine characteristics of one-ness, his physical being yearns to be two.

> And the Lord God caused a deep sleep to fall upon the man and he slept, and He took **one** of his sides, and closed up the flesh in its place. And of the side, which the Lord God had taken from the man, he made a woman and brought her forth to the man. And the man said, "This is now bone of my bones and flesh of my flesh; she shall be called Woman because she was taken out of Man." That is why man leaves his father and his mother and cleaves to his wife, and they become **one** flesh. (Gen. 2:21–24)

God takes "one of his [Adam's] sides" or ribs to create the woman. Interpreting the word "one" not as a modifier but rather as the central element in the verse, we can understand that God takes away one-ness from Adam. From this point on, humanity consists of two forms, male and female. Adam is no longer one, like God. However, man and woman have the challenge and the opportunity to become "one flesh" again. One-ness becomes a goal, not an assumed state of being. Through *deveikut*, cleaving, representing both a physical and spiritual union, man and woman can become one and become close to God. The concept of *deveikut* is also used to describe our relationship with God, "And you who cleave to the Lord, your God, are all alive today" (Deut. 4:4).[13] When Adam sees his partner, he gives her the name "*Ishah*," a version of his own name. Before the sin, even though Adam and his wife are separate beings, they still have the same name. They are fundamentally the same unit with great potential to exist in a state of one-ness, both with each other and with God.

> And the **two** of them were naked, the man and his wife, and they felt no shame. Now the serpent was craftier than all the beasts of the field, which the Lord God had made; and he said to the woman, "Has God said that you should not eat from any tree of the garden?" And the woman said to the serpent, "We may eat of the fruit of the trees of the garden. But of the fruit of the tree which is in the midst of the garden, God has said, 'You may not eat of it, nor may you touch it, lest

you die.'" And the serpent said to the woman, "You will not surely die. For God knows that on the day you eat of it, your eyes will be opened and you will be as gods, knowing good and evil." And when the woman saw that the tree was good for food, and that it was a delight to the eyes, and a tree to be desired to make one wise, she took of its fruit and did eat, and gave also to her husband with her. (Gen. 2:25 – 3:6)

By referring to Adam and his wife using the word "two," the text foreshadows an ungodly tension. Adam and his wife are beginning to view themselves as divided, and are no longer perceiving themselves as the single spiritual unit towards which they should be striving. Nevertheless, before the sin, no clothing is needed to separate or cover them. They still consider each other's bodies as their own. Radak (R. David Kimhi d. 1235) comments on Gen. 2:25 that before eating from the tree, their sexual impulse was just as strong (or weak) as any of their other desires, such that they were not embarrassed by these organs. He adds that they had not had intercourse yet because their sexual passion wasn't powerful enough. We see that before the sin, even sexuality did not distinguish between man and woman. It would have been natural to consider each other as part of the same one-ness.

However, their separation continues after the snake convinces the woman to disobey God. The text refers to the snake's craftiness as "*arum*," using the same word that describes the nakedness of Adam and his wife. On this observation, *Gen. Rabbah* 18:10 explains that the snake sees Adam and his wife having relations in public and desires her. This opinion reinforces the tension and separation between Adam and his wife; the snake is able to consider Adam's wife as sufficiently separate from Adam as even to be capable of having intercourse with another. He engages her separately in conversation, thereby further removing her from her husband and also attempts to contradict Adam's words to her. God had previously told Adam, before the woman was created, that he was prohibited from eating from a certain tree. We may infer that Adam told his wife about this commandment, perhaps with the additional restriction of even touching the tree. However, the snake suggests that this prohibition extends to all of the trees. The snake also entices the woman by telling her that she can be like God.

He distorts the idea of becoming one with God into undermining God's uniqueness. This opposition to God can only come from a place that is unholy and ungodly, which occurs while the woman and man are separate as two. Nevertheless, even when acting individually, the woman and man are partially united. It would be impossible for one to sin without the other. Since both of their fates and missions are unified, the woman gives the fruit to her husband immediately after she eats from the tree. In some respects they are always one, even as they act like two.

> And the eyes of the **two** of them were opened, and they knew that they were naked; and they sewed fig leaves together and made themselves loincloths. And they heard the voice of the Lord God walking in the garden in the wind of the day, and the man and his wife hid themselves from the presence of the Lord God amongst the trees of the garden. And the Lord God called to the man and said to him, "Where are you?" And he said, "I heard your voice in the garden, and I was afraid because I was naked, and I hid myself." And He said, "Who told you that you were naked? Have you eaten from the tree, of which I commanded you not to eat?" And the man said, "The woman whom you gave to be with me, she gave me of the tree and I did eat." (Gen. 3:7–12)

Immediately after the sin, Adam and his wife are again referred to with the number "two." By eating the forbidden fruit, they have left the one God and have transformed their reality. They can no longer be one with God as they could before. They now see their separateness and are embarrassed by that which distinguishes them from one another. They want clothing to protect and divide them.[14] Trying to hide from God further demonstrates their desire to be out of God's dominion. After God confronts Adam, Adam immediately blames his wife. He thereby indicates his perception that she is separate from him and in conflict with him. He also subtly blames God by reminding God that this is "the woman whom you gave me" (Gen. 3:12).

The woman in turn blames the snake for her sin, yet all three are held responsible for their own actions. God administers a distinct punishment to each, even treating the man and woman separately. The snake is punished by becoming the most cursed of all creatures, destined to live on its belly eating dust and possessing a permanent animosity towards women (Gen. 3:14–15). The woman is punished with pain in childbearing and with the desire to be with her husband who will rule over her (Gen. 3:16). The woman will never contemplate a relationship with any other creature; she will be beholden to men, which prevents their separation from becoming too severe. Yet the relationship will have hardships, especially in products of sexuality. As Adam's punishment, the land will sprout thorns and thistles and require much work from men to produce food. God reminds Adam that he is from dust and will return to dust (Gen. 3:17–19). By sinning, Adam separates himself from the spiritual aspect of his being and more closely identifies with his earthly component.[15]

> *And the man called his wife's name "Eve"(Havah) because she was the mother of all living. And the Lord God made for man and for his wife coats of skin, and clothed them. (Gen. 3:20–21)*

After the sin, Adam gives his wife a new name that is different from his, whereas previously they shared the same identity. Adam names her after the reference of childbearing described in her punishment. He recognizes that this is a fundamental feature that distinguishes between men and women; it is a characteristic which warrants granting his wife her own name. When God presents them clothing, God further separates their bodies. God recognizes their new divided state and assists them as they are. Yet, God still refers to them as man and his wife. God does not mention the woman's new name, Eve, hinting that even after the sin there is still hope of uniting the two with each other and with God.

> *And the Lord God said, "Behold, the man is like **one** of us, knowing good and evil, and now, what if he sends out his hand and takes also from the tree of life and eats and lives forever. Therefore, the Lord God sent him out of the Garden of Eden to till the ground from where he was taken. So He*

> *drove out the man and He placed the cherubs at the east of*
> *the Garden of Eden and the bright blade of a revolving sword*
> *to guard the way to the tree of life. (Gen. 3:22–24)*

The phrase "*hayah ke'eḥad mimenu*," (Gen. 3:22) literally "was like one from us" is difficult to translate. Rashi quotes from the Aramaic translation, *Targum Yonatan*, that God is indicating that in terms of knowing good and evil, Adam is one and only in the lower world like God is one and only in the upper world. This explanation is consistent with Rashi's interpretation on the verse "it is not good for man to be alone," (Gen. 2:18)[11] both explanations indicating that God is continuously struggling with the uniqueness of Adam. In *Gen. Rabbah* 21:5, R. Brekhiah suggests that God says, "As long as there was only Adam, he was as one, but when [God] took his side from him, it led him to sin to know good and evil." In other words, as long as Adam was alone, he was one with God. Then after he was split into two, his nature was susceptible to sin. When Adam was initially one like God, he belonged in the Garden of Eden, the place of holiness. But after he was split into two and, more importantly, acted like two distinct beings separate from each other and separate from God, he and his wife could no longer inhabit a place where God walks. Adam and Eve, acting as two, were thus destined to live outside of Eden. They had the potential to live united even as two separate beings, but their division overwhelmed them and led them to sin.

> *And the man knew Eve his wife, and she conceived and bore*
> *Cain saying, "I have acquired a man from the Lord." (Gen.*
> *4:1)*

After the expulsion from Eden, the next chapter opens with hope. The fruit from the Tree of Knowledge gives Adam the ability to "know" his wife. Adam and Eve unite and have children. The verse refers to the woman as both Eve and as "his wife." She is separate from Adam but also connected to him. She balances both identities. Together, they live in a world of duality and tension but recognize that they still can unite and bring godliness into their lives. By acknowledging that her child is "from the Lord," Eve demonstrates the centrality of God in the world, even outside of Eden.

The numbers "one," representing godly unity, and "two," connoting ungodly division, play a central role in the narrative of Adam and Eve. Initially Adam is likened to God, by being "alone," and therefore having elements of divine unity. Even after his one-ness is taken from him, Adam and his wife have the opportunity of becoming "one flesh" again, where they can spiritually unite together and with God. However, they separate from each other and from God through their sin. This is first reflected in the text when the "two of them" are likened to the snake, by all being called *arum*. After the sin, their "two eyes" are opened, and they hide from each other and from God. When they were "one like God" they belonged in the Garden of Eden. Now as a divided pair, their fate is exile. Their goal of uniting together and with God is now more difficult but still possible.

Tower of Babel

*And the whole earth was of **one** language and of **one** speech. And it came to pass as they journeyed from the east that they found a plain in the land of Shinar, and they dwelt there. And they said to one another, "Come let us make bricks and burn them thoroughly;" and they had bricks for stone, and slime had they for mortar. And they said, "Come, let us build us a city and a tower, whose top may reach to heaven, and let us make us a name, lest we be scattered abroad upon the face of the whole earth." And the Lord came down to see the city and the tower, which the children of men were building. And the Lord said, "Behold the people is **one**, and they have all **one** language; and this they begin to do; and now nothing will be withheld from them, which they have schemed to do. Come let us go down and there confound their language that they may not understand one another's speech." So the Lord scattered them abroad from there upon the face of the earth, and they ceased to build the city. Therefore is the name of it called Babel; because the Lord did there confound the language of all the earth; and from there did the Lord scatter them abroad upon the face of the earth. (Gen. 11:1–9)*

After the "re-creation" of the world following the flood, a new sin is described which textually resembles Adam and Eve's. Thematically, both stories begin from a place of one-ness, which is followed by separation and then exile. This parallelism is further reflected by the similar sentence structures as seen in verses Gen. 3:22 and 11:6. Both verses use the words, *hen* (behold), *eḥad* (one), and *ve'ata* (and now). Ramban (Nachmanides d. 1270), commenting on Gen. 11:2, acknowledges that according to the literal reading of the verses, the motivation of the people seems to be the desire to live united, afraid that they will scatter apart. However, he challenges this naïve understanding by focusing on their explicit desire "to make a name" for themselves. In Sanhedrin 109a, we are told that this generation is directly rebelling against God by attempting to build a tower high enough to confront and defeat God. Ramban notices that these people are referred to as *"benei ha'adam,"* children of Adam and are thus similar to him. Just as the snake convinces Adam and Eve to eat from the tree in order to know as much as God does and thereby undermine God's uniqueness, here too, the generation of Babel uses their one-ness to challenge God. They are of "one language" and "one speech," unified in thought and expression, the elevated qualities that distinguish humans from animals.[16] One-ness in this narrative represents unity in those divine characteristics found in man, which have the potential to be used to achieve closeness with God. However, the inhabitants of Babel are not united with God; they want a new name and a new identity to dominate God. As a result, God must take away their one-ness and divide them in speech and throw them scattered from Babel. This is the same treatment God had bestowed on Adam; God had divided him into two and then had exiled Adam and Eve from Eden.[17]

From this story we learn that while the goal of humanity is to unite together to serve God, this is a task with room for great corruption. The distinction between wanting to be like God and wanting to be God must remain clear. Like Adam and Eve, the generation of Babel used their uniqueness to oppose God, instead of to connect with God. God punishes them by taking away their one-ness, further separating them from each other and from God.

Abraham and Isaac

Throughout the rest of Genesis, true one-ness with God is only obtained in the context of the covenant with God. The word "one" appears at the most critical moments when the patriarchs solidify their unique covenantal relationship with God.

> *And it came to pass after these things, that God did test Abraham and said to him, "Abraham;" and he said, "Here I am." And he said, "Take your son, your **only** son (yehidkha), Isaac, and go to the land of Moriah, and offer him there as an offering, on **one** of the mountains that I will tell you."* (Gen. 22:1–2)

Instead of writing "on a mountain" or "on the mountain," the Torah chooses to describe the mountain with the word "one." The text also indicates that Isaac is *yehid*, the one and "only son" of Abraham. The root of the word *yehid*, only, is the same as *ehad*, one. While Ishmael is also a son, he is not an heir to the *brit*, the covenant with the one God. The episode of the Binding of Isaac is the final test that demonstrates Abraham's complete faith in God and serves as the transmission of the covenantal blessing from Abraham to Isaac. It is befitting that it should take place at a sight of one-ness with a son of one-ness. A. Ibn Ezra (d. 1167), comments on Gen. 22:2 that this one mountain is the future place of the Holy Temple, the place where God will dwell on Earth.[18]

> *And Abraham rose up early in the morning, and saddled his donkey, and took **two** of his young men with him and Isaac his son, and broke up the wood for the burnt offering and rose up and went to the place of which God has told him. On the **third** day, Abraham lifted his eyes and saw the place afar off. And Abraham said to his young men, "Stay here with the donkey, and I and the boy will go yonder and prostrate ourselves and come again to you."* (Gen. 22:3–5)

After God commands Abraham to sacrifice his only son with Sarah, the son that God has previously promised would inherit the blessings, Abraham immediately prepares himself. Rashi comments (Gen. 22:3) that Abraham gets up early from excitement to expedite his fulfillment of the commandment; He saddles his own donkey out of his love for

God and takes the two young men, Ishmael and Eliezer.[19] Quoting from *Tanhuma*, Rashi further indicates that the reason God delays showing him the mountain for three days is to remove any doubt as to whether Abraham would have followed this commandment if given time to ponder his actions. According to Rashi, Abraham passes this test without hesitation or ambivalence.

By focusing on the significance of the numbers "two" and "three" in this narrative, an alternate reading emerges. God's request for Abraham to kill his son is extremely disturbing and contradictory to everything God had previously told Abraham. God is testing Abraham's obedience despite logic and parental love. How could a compassionate God who disdains pagan human sacrifices ask Abraham to slaughter his son? How could the God who promised him that Isaac would inherit now order him to cut off his line? Abraham's response in taking two lads indicates that he is feeling an inescapable tension and a disharmony with God, as the number "two" symbolizes. Abraham requires three days to resolve this conflict. He needs a day to contemplate one side, another day to understand the second side, and then a third day to balance the two positions. Only after three days is Abraham prepared and ready to see the place and leave his tension and two lads behind. The number "three" represents the reconciliation process that Abraham requires in order to achieve perfection in his faith and observance.

After Isaac is bound and Abraham raises his hand in the air ready to sacrifice, an angel from heaven intercedes.

> *And an angel of the Lord called to him out of heaven and said, "Abraham, Abraham;" and he said, "Here I am." And he said, "Don't lay your hand upon the lad, and don't do anything to him, for now I know that you fear God, seeing that you have not withheld your son, your only **one** from me." (Gen. 22:11–12)*
>
> *And the angel of the Lord called to Abraham out of heaven, the second time, and said,*
>
> *"By myself have I sworn," says the Lord, "because you have done this thing and have not withheld your son, your only **one**, that I will exceedingly bless you and I will exceedingly multiply your seed as the stars in the heaven and as the*

*sand on the sea shore, and your seed will possess the gate of its enemies. And through your seed, will all the nations of the world be blessed, because you have listened to my voice." So Abraham returned to his young men, and they rose up and went together (as **one**) to Be'er Sheva, and Abraham dwelt in Be'er Sheva. (Gen. 22:15–19)*

Abraham passes this final divine test and is confirmed to be a man who fears God and who does God's will. Twice, Isaac is called *yehidkha* (your [Abraham's] only one), the one whose line will inherit the blessing and be unified with God. At the end of the narrative, the text indicates that they went together, *yahdav* (as one). Abraham and Isaac have attained the ultimate one-ness with each other and with God. It is worth noting that only Abraham's descent from the mountain is mentioned and not Isaac's.[20] The *Midrash Hagadol* commenting on Gen. 22:19 suggests that Isaac spent three years hidden in the Garden of Eden. After such a life-altering experience, Isaac has truly achieved one-ness, and therefore is able to dwell with God. However, immediately after this, the text focuses on finding Isaac a mate, a second half required to help bring the light of God to the rest of the world. He must become one with his mate in order to provide proper descendents to whom he can pass on the covenant.

Jacob

*And the sons struggled within her, and she said, "If this is so, why am I thus;" she went to inquire from God. And God said to her, "**Two** nations are in your womb, and **two** peoples will be separated from your loins; and one people will be stronger than the other people; and the older will serve the younger." And when her days to be delivered were fulfilled, behold, there were twins in her womb. And the **first** came out red, all over like a hairy garment, and they called his name Esau. And after that, his brother came out, and his hand took hold of Esau's heel, and he called his name Jacob; and Isaac was sixty years old when they were born. (Gen. 25:22–26)*

God informs Rebecca that her sons will father "two nations" and "two peoples." Their essence is to be defined by the characteristics of the number "two," constantly divided and struggling with each other. Their fighting in the womb will continue throughout their days and even will be inherited by their descendents. Esau's conflict with Jacob becomes a war against God.[21] While Esau is born first, Jacob is specifically not called the "second" since he will not be characterized by two-ness. In fact, Jacob later buys the birthright from Esau for the price of lentils, and he tricks his father into bestowing upon him the blessing intended for Esau.

> And when Esau heard the words of his father, he cried with a great and exceeding bitter cry, and he said to his father, "Bless me too, father."...And Isaac answered and said to Esau, "Behold, I have made him your lord, and all his brothers have I given to him for servants; and with corn and wine have I sustained him. What should I do now for you my son?" And Esau said to his father, "Do you only have **one** blessing, my father? Bless me too! O father." And Esau raised his voice and wept. And Isaac, his father, answered and said to him, "Behold your dwelling will be of the fatness of the ground and of the dew of the heavens above. By your sword you will live, and you will serve your brother; and when you will have dominion, you will break his yoke from your neck."
> (Gen. 27:34, 37–40)

After Esau discovers that he has been tricked, he begs his father for "one blessing" too. While Isaac gives him a blessing, it is not the blessing of one-ness that Esau seeks, which would have given him domination and connected him to the one God. Esau will thus be subordinate to Jacob. However, there will be times when Esau will break from his brother's yoke and will rule himself. This blessing reinforces the strife between Esau and Jacob, which is echoed in Esau's admitted intent to kill his brother (Gen. 27:41).

> And these words of Esau her elder son were told to Rebecca, and she sent and called for Jacob her younger son and said to him, "Behold, your brother Esau comforts himself by proposing to kill you. Now, my son, listen to my voice, get up and flee to Laban my brother's house in Haran. Stay with him for

> *several (aḥadim) days until your brother's fury turns away.*
> *Until your brother's anger turns away from you and he for-*
> *gets what you have done to him, then I will send and fetch*
> *you from there. Why should I be bereaved of the **two** of you*
> *in **one** day?" (Gen. 27:42–45)*

In fear for her son's life, Rebecca asks Jacob to travel to her brother's house and dwell there for *yamim aḥadim*, "several days," or literally "days of one-ness." She is afraid that she will lose both her sons on "one day." [22] Rebecca understands that their war over who dominates will continue. Both want the power and right of the one *brit*. Influenced by her earlier prophecies, Rebecca is adamant that if Esau takes any portion of the covenant, it will become corrupted, and they will both die. She recognizes that she will lose her two opposing sons in this fight over the one God. She sends Jacob away for *yamim aḥadim* to spend his days establishing his own relationship with God. Only then will he be ready to confront Esau. Before Jacob leaves, Isaac gives him another blessing, bestowing upon him the spiritual blessings of the covenant of Abraham. Esau, on the other hand, marries the daughter of Ishmael, symbolizing their shared fate as the son who receives some blessing but does not inherit the main covenant.

After the Binding of Isaac, where Isaac had become one with God, the Torah had focused on Isaac's need to find a partner in order to continue his pursuit of one-ness and to bear a proper descendent. Recall Rashi's opinion that parents become "one flesh" through their children (Gen. 2:24). Here too, after Jacob receives the blessing of one-ness, the Torah describes his experiences in marrying and then in having children. Jacob is only ready to leave Laban's house and confront Esau after Joseph, the first child from his beloved wife Rachel, is born.

Jacob first sends messengers to Esau, who report that he is approaching, accompanied by an army.

> *Then Jacob was greatly afraid and distressed, and he divided*
> *the people that were with him and the flocks and herds and*
> *the camels into **two** camps. He said, "If Esau comes to **one***
> *camp and smites it, then the camp which is left will escape."*
> *(Gen. 32:8–9)*

Jacob continues to feel the tension of conflict with his brother, reflected in his "two camps." He wants to make amends with his brother and put an end to their feud, but he cannot get too close to his brother and risk violating the family covenant. He divides his camp into two, fearing the direct confrontation with Esau. Esau wants to obtain the inheritance of one-ness, by attacking "one camp," the one-ness of Jacob's camp. Jacob's only salvation would be to run away with the other one camp and keep the covenant to himself.[23]

After preparing for war, Jacob prays to the God of Abraham and Isaac for assistance. He then arranges peace gifts for Esau.

> *And he delivered them into the hands of his servants, every flock by itself, and he said to his servants, "Pass before me and put a space between each flock." And he commanded the **first** one saying, "When Esau, my brother, meets you and asks you, 'Who are you? And where do you go? And whose are these before you?' Then you will say, 'They belong to your servant, to Jacob, as a present to you my lord, and behold he is behind us.'" And so he commanded the **second** and the **third** and all the flocks that followed, saying, "In this manner should you speak to Esau when you find him." (Gen. 32:17–20)*

Jacob prepares himself for the encounter with his brother. The text mentions by number explicitly three flocks of animals that Jacob sends as a present to Esau before meeting him. He is hoping that these gifts will convince Esau that his intentions are amicable. The three flocks provide the allotted time for both Esau and Jacob to balance their antagonistic feelings toward each other and prepare for their confrontation and potential reconciliation, as the number "three" suggests.

> *And he rose up that night and took his **two** wives and **two** maidservants and eleven sons and passed over the ford of Yabbok. And he took them and sent them over the wadi and sent over that which he had. And Jacob was left **alone**, and there wrestled a man with him until the breaking day. (Gen. 32:23–25)*

In the same way that Abraham and Isaac left the two lads before they approached the one mountain, Jacob separates from his "two wives" and "two maidservants" before confronting the man alone. He reconciles his familial tensions, both those relating to his wives and those pertaining to his brother. He is ready to demonstrate his complete faith in and allegiance to God. Separate from his family, Jacob must be one and alone while defending his covenant with God.[24] The *midrash* in *Gen. Rabbah* 77:1 explicitly comments that Jacob was one and alone the same way God is one and alone (Isaiah 2:11, 17). At this moment Jacob is most closely united with God and connected to His one-ness. The *midrash* in *Gen. Rabbah* 77:2 further explains that his opponent is the angel of Esau. This is where the spiritual battle between the two brothers ensues.

After an intense struggle throughout the night, the next morning Jacob remains undefeated by his adversary and his name is changed to Israel. He no longer is the person who tricked his way into the blessing, as the name Jacob suggests (Gen. 27:36). He is now the man who fought with other men and with godly beings and prevailed, as the name Israel connotes (Gen. 32:29). His strength in dominating over Esau unifies him closer with God. Jacob succeeds in establishing a unique direct relationship with the one God, while defeating his profane opponent at the same time.

Throughout the stories of the patriarchs, the number "one" symbolizes godly unity, and is a reference to the special covenant with the one God. "Two" connotes ungodly tensions that occur between the chosen and the not chosen siblings. "Three" represents the final reconciliatory process, which resolves all familial and theological challenges, thereby enabling the establishment of a unique covenant with God. Abraham receives the blessing and imparts it to his one son Isaac on the one mountain where the binding of Isaac occurs. They leave behind their covenantal threats and conflicts symbolized by separating from the two lads. They journey for three days to prepare themselves and reach reconciliation in forming a new relationship with God. Similarly, before confronting Esau, Jacob sends three enumerated flocks of animals as gifts to him, attempting to reconcile their relationship. This is the final preparation for the encounter. Jacob parts from his two wives and two maidservants indicating that he has resolved his familial and theological conflicts. Ultimately, when Jacob is alone he prevails over the angel of Esau and in the process acquires a new name and a deepened union with God.

Joseph and His Brothers

Sibling rivalry is a common theme in all of the families in Genesis but especially in Jacob's house. Previously, the covenantal blessing was passed down to only one son, and the other children were expelled from the family. With this precedent and Jacob's visible favoritism towards Joseph, Jacob's other sons have cause to fear that they will be banished from the *brit* as well. Joseph reinforces their doubts by revealing his self-aggrandizing dreams, which cause his brothers to despise him.

> *And when they saw him afar off, even before he came near to them, they conspired against him to kill him. And they said* **one** *to another, "Here this dreamer comes. And now let us kill him and throw him into* **one** *of the pits, and we will say that an evil beast devoured him, and we will see what will become of his dreams." (Gen. 37:18–20)*

> *And they took him and cast him into a pit and the pit was empty; there was no water in it. And they sat down to eat bread, and they lifted their eyes and behold a company of Ishmaelites came from Gilead with their camels bearing gum balm and ladanum, going to carry it down to Egypt. (Gen. 37:25–26)*

Joseph's brothers try to eliminate him from the family by throwing him into "one of the pits." Their goal is to destroy Joseph and his unique status. Ironically, this act also exalts him. By giving him a near-death experience at the hands of relatives in a place described as one, the brothers liken Joseph to Isaac on the one mountain and to Ishmael under one bush.[25] This experience strengthens Joseph's connection to the one God. Upon Judah's suggestion, the brothers decide to sell Joseph as a slave to a caravan of Ishmaelites. They are attempting to subject Joseph to Ishmael's fate of banishment from the covenant and temporarily succeed as Joseph is exiled to Egypt.

Not surprisingly, the number "two," which connotes ungodliness, is central in a narrative describing idolatrous Egypt. Pharaoh has "two servants" and "the two of them" have dreams (Gen. 40:2,5). "Two years" later, Pharaoh has two dreams himself (Gen. 41:1, 5). Although Egypt is a land which is fundamentally opposed to God, Joseph begins to introduce them to the one God. After the butler and baker have their dreams on "one night" (Gen. 40: 5), Joseph asks them, "Do not interpretations belong to God?" (Gen. 40:8) Similarly, Joseph tells Pharaoh that instead of having two dreams like he thought, "the dream of Pharaoh is one; God has declared to Pharaoh what he is about to do" (Gen. 41:25). Joseph is successful in enabling the Egyptians to recognize God through him.

> *And Pharaoh said to his servants, "Can we find such as this, a man in whom is the spirit of God?" And Pharaoh said to Joseph, "Since God has shown you all this, there is none so intuitive and wise as you." (Gen. 41:38–39)*

Unfortunately, although Joseph teaches the Egyptians about God, his relationship with Pharaoh initially leads to mutual influence. Once Joseph "was made to ride in the second chariot" (Gen. 41:43) and he becomes second to Pharaoh, he too is influenced by Egypt's evil tendencies. Whereas Isaac and Jacob's parents were involved in finding them wives to ensure a holy union, Pharaoh chooses Joseph's wife. Joseph has "two sons" (Gen. 41:50) of his own, and he names his first born "Menasheh," explaining "God has made me forget my toil and my father's house" (Gen. 41:51). He thanks God for enabling him to disregard his covenantal family. However, by the time Joseph has his next son, his proper allegiances have been restored. He calls his younger son "Ephraim," because "God has made me fruitful in the land of my affliction" (Gen. 41:52). Joseph no longer considers Egypt his true home.

When the ten brothers travel to Egypt to buy food, they justify their journey to their brother Joseph, the viceroy of Egypt, whom they do not recognize.

> *"We are all **one** man's sons; we are true men; your servants are not spies." And he [Joseph] said to them, "No, but you*

> *have come to see the nakedness of the land." And they said,*
> *"Your servants are twelve and we are brothers, sons of **one***
> *man in the land of Canaan, and here the youngest is this day*
> *with his father and **one** is no more." (Gen. 42:11–13)*

The brothers refer to both their father and missing brother Joseph using the word "one." Jacob is the last patriarch who united with God in the covenant, and the brothers do not know who will inherit the blessing in their generation. Perhaps they feel that their treatment of Joseph disqualified them from deserving any reward and believe that Joseph will return to inherit the one blessing which belongs to him.

Joseph next accuses his brothers of being spies.

> *"Send **one** of you and let him fetch your brother and you will*
> *be kept in prison that your words may be proved, whether*
> *there be any truth in you, or else by the life of Pharaoh you*
> *are spies." And he put them all together in custody for **three***
> *days. And Joseph said to them on the **third** day, "This do and*
> *live; I fear God. If you are true men, let **one** of your brothers*
> *be bound in the house of your confinement, and you go carry*
> *corn for the famine of your houses, but bring your youngest*
> *brother to me, so shall your words be verified and you shall*
> *not die." (Gen. 42:16–20)*

In response to his brothers' description of him using the number "one, "Joseph also refers to his brothers with the number "one." He orders them to "send one" back home to bring Benjamin, and then later he keeps one bound in Egypt, while allowing all the others to return home. Joseph understands that they will all partake in the godly blessings of their family. Whether Joseph's scheme involving his brothers is to punish or to play with them, to help them fully repent, to determine how they presently feel towards him, or to actualize his earlier dreams, in any event, he does not abandon them. He demonstrates that he cares about his brothers and wants ultimately to unite with them. Joseph uses "three days" to reconcile the tension with his brothers and to prepare for his treatment of them. He also gives them three days to contemplate their situation.[26] Just like after three days of travel Abraham proves that he fears God on Mount Moriah, here too after three days Joseph assures his brothers that he fears God and can be trusted. Joseph continues to test his brothers' faith in God and in their faith in him. He changes his plan and sends the remaining nine brothers instead of the original one brother to fetch Benjamin and keeps only one brother in Egypt. He thereby hints to them that they will all be part of the one covenant.

The brothers continue to refer to Joseph using the number "one" (Gen. 42:32), even in Judah's final speech entreating Joseph to free Benjamin (Gen. 44:28). Ultimately, in response to Judah's leadership, Joseph reveals his true identity to his brothers, and the entire family reunites with Jacob and the rest of the family traveling down to Egypt.

As this narrative concludes, and Joseph brings his two sons to Jacob (Israel) for a blessing (Gen. 48:1), Joseph has not resolved which son should be considered the first born due to a closer connection to the one God. "And Joseph took the two of them, Ephraim in his right hand toward Israel's left hand, and Menasheh in his left hand toward Israel's right hand; and he presented them to him" (Gen. 48:13). Jacob crosses his hands to place his right hand of the head of Ephraim, the son whose naming reflected Joseph's longing for one-ness. Thereby, Jacob instructs against the corrupting influence of the two-ness of Egypt in his grandchildren. Nevertheless, both of his grandchildren, Ephraim and Menasheh, become tribes of the Israelite people.

> *And Israel said to Joseph, "Here I die. And God will be with you and return you to the land of your fathers. And I have given you **one** portion (shekhem) above your brothers that I took from the hands of the Emorites with my sword and with my bow." (Gen. 48:21–22)*

Joseph receives an extra one portion above his brothers. Each brother becomes one tribe, while Joseph becomes one extra tribe. The brothers were correct in assuming that Joseph was special. While Reuben is the first born son of Jacob, Joseph, the first born to Rachel, receives the spiritual double portion.[27] However, they were mistaken in assuming that Joseph would become the sole inheritor of God's covenant, since all the brothers do receive a portion.

Conclusion

Numbers, which appear interspersed throughout the narratives of Genesis, are more than just quantifiers. Each possesses an inherent characteristic, which informs its surrounding story. The personality of the first three numbers can be determined by the description of the first three days of creation. Since God's radiance exists alone on Day One, the number "one" connotes spiritual unity and godliness. On Day Two, God divides between the upper and lower waters. "Two" represents physical tension, the drive that moves away from God. On Day Three, God directs the water from Day Two into one place, reconciling the physical and spiritual pulses, preparing for life on earth. "Three" symbolizes the process and preparation for resolving divine conflicts.

Applying these numerical symbols, we can better view the creation of Adam and Eve as a paradigm for the religious challenges of humanity. Adam is created as one, in the image of God, but also in a physical form from the dust of the earth. Consequently, God takes one-ness from the body of Adam by introducing Eve. In the form of two, Adam and Eve are separate from God, but still have the potential of uniting into one flesh and to transform their physical bodies into godly manifestations. However, they perceive themselves fundamentally as two distinct beings, and therefore violate their ideal one nature and sin against their one God. Since their spiritual one-ness did not dominate their existence, they no longer can remain in the Garden of Eden. The struggle between being a distinct physical and spiritual person while also being united with a partner and with God is the foundation of the human experience. Reconciling this tension in pursuit of godliness is a life-long goal and process.

Outside of Eden, during the generation of Babel, society grapples with this same conflict. The people corrupt their divine characteristics of one-ness and oppose God. Consequently, God divides their language and location, further removing them from the one-ness of God.

Throughout the remainder of Genesis, God's unity, seen through the number "one," manifests itself in the covenant with the patriarchs. Abraham and his one son Isaac unite with God on the one mountain in the Binding of Isaac episode. Jacob takes the "one blessing" away from Esau and later defeats his godly opponent, receiving the name "Israel," while he is one and alone. Jacob's sons refer to Joseph as their one brother, indicating their belief that he will be chosen to inherit the covenant from Jacob. Ultimately, all the brothers become tribes of Israel, but Joseph does receive an additional one portion.

The number "two" alludes to conflicts and tension, primarily in the transmission of the covenant.[28] Abraham and Isaac separate from the two lads who represent challengers to the inheritance. Jacob and Esau are referred to as two nations and two peoples, eternal enemies battling for dominion over God's world and for God's blessings. Rebecca laments the fear that these two opponents will die in one day over their heavenly feud. Jacob divides his camp into two and separates from his two wives and two maidservants to address his familial tensions that could jeopardize the fulfillment of his covenantal role before confronting his brother. A process of three appears as the patriarchs prepare for their ultimate connection with God. Abraham and Isaac travel for three days before they see Mount Moriah, and Jacob gives Esau three enumerated flocks of animals as gifts, as they resolve their tensions and prepare for their spiritual encounters. Joseph also requires three days to reconcile his feelings toward his brothers and prepare his scheme, which ultimately reunites his family and establishes the People of Israel. The numbers beyond three can also be studied in a similar fashion to enhance the narratives and add a richer dimension to the central themes.[29]

The Torah is a brilliant divine masterpiece, which teaches truths of the human condition and lessons in morality through attention to its subtle details. By utilizing additional methods for interpreting the Torah, one can gain a deeper understanding.

NOTES

The research for this article was completed during my years studying in the Talmud/*Tanakh* program at Drisha (1997–1999). I am forever indebted to Rabbi Nathaniel Helfgot and Rabbi Dovid Silber for teaching me how to learn *Tanakh*. Many of the ideas in this article are inspired by them and some are surely theirs.

1.	C. Boyer, *A History of Mathematics* (New York: John Wiley and Sons, 1991).

2. U. Casuto, *Perush al Sefer Bereishit* (Jerusalem: Hebrew University Press, 1953). See sec. 4, ch. 11, v. 10–32.

3. For example, sixty is a common base in ancient Mesopotamian cultures (sexigesimal system), possibly due to its large number of integer factors. See also note 1.

4. The six Hebrew letters in Eliezer's name are each assigned a numerical value, and these values are then totaled: *aleph=1, lamed=30, yud=10, ayin=70, zayin=7, resh=200.*

5. English translations of biblical verses are based on: *The Jerusalem Bible*, trans. H. Fisch (Jerusalem: Koren Publishers Jerusalem LTD, 1998).

6. Rashi explains that this light is reserved for the righteous in the world to come (Hagigah 12a).

7. See for ex. Gen. 1:4.

8. *Gen. Rabbah* 4:6 explains that since the position of the water created on Day Two was not completed until Day Three, the first "*ki tov*" refers to the creation of the previous day.

9. Day Four expands the light of Day One with the sun, moon, and stars. Day Five provides the birds and the fish, the life occupying the heavens and waters of Day Two. Day Six produces the animals and humans, the habitat of the dry land of Day Three. See also note 29.

10. The word *levado* (alone) denotes the same one-ness as *eḥad* (one) since being alone requires the presence of no other. In contrast, the word *rishon* (first) directly implies the presence of others to follow. The distinction between "two" and "second" is therefore not significant, both indicating the existence of two.

11. Rashi modifies the opinion given in *Pirkei deRabbi Eliezer*, by writing that God's concern was that the other creations would say that there are two deities: God who is alone in the upper world without a partner, and Adam who is alone in the lower world without a partner. The medieval commentator R. Ovadya Seforno (d. 1550), explains that Adam's purpose in being created in the likeness and image of God will not be fulfilled if he needs to occupy himself alone with the necessities of life.

12. *Gen. Rabbah* 17:5 explains that God waited to create Adam's partner until he asked for her, anticipating that Adam would later blame her for causing him to sin.

13. Rashi, commenting on the verse in Gen. 2:24 explains that "one flesh" refers to the child created by the two parents. In the child, the parent's flesh literally becomes one. Ramban disagrees with Rashi's interpretation by arguing that according to Rashi, the offspring of animals would also be one flesh. Ramban claims that when Adam called his wife,

"bone of my bones, flesh of my flesh" (Gen. 2:23), he was articulating a desire to be with her permanently. This eternal longing defines the *deveikut* as fostering a spiritual union into one flesh. Seforno affirms that in all their actions, they will behave as though the two are one flesh, as they aim to attain the perfection of the purpose of their creation.

14. Radak explains that after eating from the tree, a sexual desire was aroused in them that they could not restrain. They were embarrassed that part of their bodies was out of their control. This punishment is *midah keneged midah* (measure for measure), since they demonstrated by sinning that they were no longer under God's control.

15. The earth and humanity are inextricably linked. When humanity sins, the earth suffers, but when humanity obeys God, the earth is rewarded. Examples include the punishment of Cain (Gen. 4:11) and the flood brought as punishment to Noah's generation. The verses in Deut. 11:13–21, which comprise the second paragraph of the "*Shema*" prayer, demonstrate how the prosperity of the Land of Canaan depends on the obedience of the Israelite people to God.

16. See Rashi (Gen. 2:7).

17. The division of Adam into two people, male and female, is not considered by God to be a punishment, as seen by the description of them as being "one flesh" after their division but prior to their sin. This initial division does not detract from their one-ness. Only God's treatment of them as two separate entities in response to their sin parallels the punishment given to the people of Babel.

18. It is interesting to note that Lot and Ishmael are also saved from life threatening situations by angels at places described with the number "one." While Lot is defending his angel guests, the Sodomites call him "the one" who came to live with them and judge them (Gen. 19:9). The angels save Lot from this immediate abuse and then from the city's total destruction. In the narrative of Ishmael, he and his mother, Hagar, are wandering and weak in the desert, when Hagar "throws the boy under one of the bushes" (Gen. 21:15). An angel shows Hagar a well of water, enabling both to survive. As a relative and a child of Abraham, Lot and Ishmael receive elements of God's special relationship, even in perpetuity. For example, Ruth the Moabite is a descendent of Lot's and is the source of the Davidic line. Also, God explicitly tells Abraham that God will bless Ishmael and make him into a great nation as well (Gen. 17:20–21). However, the covenantal line will flow directly through the one son Isaac. Although in each case the number one represents a closeness with God, there are varying degrees of closeness.

19. According to Rashi, (Gen. 22:3) these two lads are Ishmael and Eliezer, both of whom were considered heirs to Abraham before Isaac was born.

20. *Gen. Rabbah* 56:20 explains that Isaac immediately went to study at the Yeshiva of Shem and Ever. Ibn Ezra argues that Isaac's descent should be inferred from the mention of Abraham's. He adamantly contests the view that Isaac actually dies and then later comes back to life.

21. Amalek, Esau's grandson, is the first to attack the Israelites after the redemption from Egypt. Amalek's nature denies the providence and existence of God. We are thus commanded to eradicate the memory of Amalek, the enemy of God (Deut. 25:19).

22. On the verse in Gen. 27:45, Rashbam (Rabbi Shmuel b. Meir, d. 1174) explains that if Esau kills Jacob, then other relatives will kill Esau to avenge Jacob's death. Rashi adds that Rebecca foresaw by the divine spirit that her two sons would die on the same day. Ibn Ezra suggests that in their battle, they might end up killing each other.

23. Ramban (Gen. 32:9) claims that this is an allusion to the way the descendents of Esau will treat the Jews. They will only afflict segments of the Jewish population at a time. When one king in one part of the world persecutes Jews, another king in another country will be merciful. This ensures Jewish survival.

24. Rashi (Gen. 32:25), quoting Hulin 91a, explains that Jacob was alone because he had forgotten some small vessels on the other side of the water and went back to get them. Ramban claims that Jacob chose to be alone by instructing his family to cross the water without him. Seforno comments that Jacob was traveling in the back of his family directing them and ensuring that nothing was left behind. He happened to be far enough back and alone when the man appeared.

25. See note 18. There are many other literary similarities between the Ishmael and Joseph narratives. For example, both characters wander (Gen. 21:14; 37:15), neither have water (Gen. 21:15; 37:24), both are thrust out of the family (Gen. 21:14; 37:28), and both marry Egyptian women (Gen. 21:21;41:45). One critical difference is that Joseph's expulsion is only temporary.

26. *Gen. Rabbah* 91:9 argues that God does not allow righteous people to suffer for more than three days, so Joseph let them go on the third day. This is seen in the stories of Jonah, Esther, and David as well.

27. *Gen. Rabbah* 97:9 states that this extra portion, *shekhem*, includes the city of Shekhem itself in which Joseph is buried.

28. The number "two" also appears in all of the stories of sexual conflict

in Genesis. The "two brothers" of Ham cover the nakedness of their father, Noah (Gen. 9:20–25). "Two angels" are accosted by Sodomites while trying to save Lot (Gen. 19:1, 5–8), and the "two daughters" of Lot seduce him after the destruction of their city (Gen. 19:30–33, 36). The "two brothers" of Dina attack the city of Shekhem after her rape (Gen. 34:1–2,13–16,25).

29.   "Four" is the first in the next set of numbers and connotes bringing godliness (and light) into our world on a communal level. The relationship between the numbers "one" and "four" is conveyed by the description of a single river which flows out of Eden "and branches into four streams" (Gen. 2:10). The Torah also enters the world after forty days and the Israelites enter the Land of Canaan after forty years. Four couples, Adam and Eve, Abraham and Sarah, Isaac and Rebecca, and Jacob and Leah, are buried in Kiryat Arba. These couples were the conduits for bringing God's light into the world. "Five" represents the lower level of blessing, as represented by the reproduction of the lower forms of creations, the birds and fish. This level of blessing sustains nations that are lacking morality. For example, Abraham begins his request from God to save and bless Sodom in the merit of "fifty righteous people in her midst" (Gen. 18:23). Joseph secures "one fifth" of the people's property for Pharaoh, which is a blessing to the Egyptian leader (Gen. 47:24). "Six" is reflected in the creation of Adam, who represents the balance between earth and godliness. It represents the higher level of physical blessing which sustains those pursuing oneness. For example, Jacob worked "six years for the cattle" of Laban, in order to acquire physical wealth (Gen. 31:41). The physical blessing connoted by the number "six" is in turn elevated in holiness through its interaction with "seven." The bible commands a six day work week to acquire physical prosperity, followed by rest on the seventh day for spiritual sanctification (Exod. 20:9–10). Similarly, the land is worked for six years and then remains fallow on the seventh, the *shemitah* year (Exod. 23:10–11). A Hebrew slave works for six years and goes free on the seventh (Exod. 21:2). The physical world requires a spiritual soul, which is created in the form of *shabbat* on Day Seven. "Seven" elevates the physicality of those who disseminate the spirit of God to the rest of the world. *Shabbat* also has the potential to bring the world back to one-ness and back to God. Thus the number "seven" is linked to the number "one." For example, Jacob offers to work "seven years" to marry Rachel to form a holy union, and "in his eyes the seven years went by like *yamim aḥadim*," days of one-ness (Gen. 29:20). In addition, one

requires seven days after significant events in life, to fully reconcile physical events with a relationship with God's one-ness and to emerge more deeply united with God and with the community. Thus, Jacob celebrates his wedding for seven days (Gen. 29:27–28) and Joseph mourns Jacob's death for "seven days" (Gen. 50:10), both practices which remain prevalent today.

Quantum Mechanical Divine Providence and Rational Prayer

Ari Tuchman

In memory of Beth Samuels, z"l, whose love
of God and humanity motivates this endeavor.

I. Introduction

The pursuit of rational religious belief requires balancing the logic of empirical reality with the emotion of spirituality and tradition. Although these forces of human cognition describe very different methods of awareness, they are not inherently contradictory. Like any religion, Judaism inevitably mandates certain postulates that are beyond the scope of scientific proof, but it is critical to recognize that Judaism need not require an acceptance of realities that are directly in contradiction to scientific laws. Thus, a rational scientific doctrine can be constructed to be consistent with religious philosophy.

Often however, proponents of an empirically consistent theology relegate the role of the divine to an abstract concept rather than an interactive presence between man and the universe. They are motivated to do so, in part, by their seemingly rational assumption that miraculous, providential intervention would violate the perfect predictability of physical law. They prefer to define God's presence purely as a paradigm to which one is obligated to connect, "*bekhol derakhekha da'eihu*," (in all your endeavors you should know Him) (Prov. 3:6). Since this theology can be consistent with the demand for the strict performance of all commandments as well as the observance of a general ethical code, its adherents may successfully achieve closeness with a non-intervening God. Nevertheless, this theology is both viscerally and traditionally problematic. Intrinsically, it precludes a relationship with a personal God. Furthermore, this attempt at reconciling science and religion contradicts fundamental tenets of Judaism such as miraculous divine providence,[1] and it negates several direct biblical examples[2] of the bi-directional relationship between man and God.[3] Accordingly, a "spiritual rationalist" is left with a seemingly irreconcilable tension between the desire, need and precedent for a responsive and interactive God and the conflicting belief that such miraculous interaction is not possible within a scientific universe.

Although this apparent conflict between objective scientific thought and divine personal intervention manifests itself throughout nearly all aspects of the theological domain, it is perhaps most clearly present in the context of prayer. Here, this tension is not merely academic, but rather determines the practical parameters of prayer. Specifically, does rational theology limit prayer to an objective endeavor that does not allow for personal requests?[4] Is the point of prayer simply to heighten awareness of God's greatness and induce humility and gratitude for His presence? Or is it possible to be scientifically rational and still pray for divine intervention within the very same scientific laws that define the basis of one's rationalism?

In this essay, I address these questions by challenging the intuitive assumption that all events are bound by the causality of experiential physical law. Specifically, I explain that a universe bound by natural law does not, in fact, have definite, predictable causality. While according to classical physics causality is sacrosanct, quantum mechanics, a revolutionary view of the physical world developed and proved over nearly the last century, illustrates otherwise. I explore the theological ramifications of this quantum theory and demonstrate how quantum mechanics allows God to operate within the laws of physics, while also maintaining a providential relationship with the individual. I illustrate how divine observation can effect change within the context of quantum mechanics.

It is important to remember that the intention of this essay is not to explain how God interacts with the universe but rather to present an analogy for how to *think* about how God interacts with the universe. This analysis further illustrates that one does not have to abandon rational science to allow room for theology in general and divine intervention specifically. On the contrary, one can use science to enhance one's appreciation of God,[5] *"ha'ahavah hi kefi hahasagah,"* (one's love for God is commensurate with one's knowledge and understanding) (Guide III:51).[6]

II. *Divine Providence and Natural Law according to Rabbinic Tradition*

The Aristotelian concept of divine eternal perfection[7] is prominent in medieval Rabbinic descriptions of God's interaction with mankind and the universe. Nachmanides, (d. 1270) in his commentary on the verse, *"hatsur, tamim pa'olo,"* (the Rock [God] whose actions are all perfect) (Deut. 32:4), explains that all actions that emanate from God are perfect and complete and will never change for eternity.[8] Maimonides (d. 1204), in *The Guide for the Perplexed,* espouses this view of divine universal perfection in the context of his description of ex-nihilo creation. He explains, "Now the works of the deity are most perfect, and with regard to them there is no possibility of an excess or a deficiency. Accordingly they are of necessity permanently established as they are, for there is no possibility of something calling for a change in them" (*Guide* II,28). The world, having been created perfectly by a perfect creator with a perfect set of physical laws, cannot deviate from that perfection. Changes in nature would therefore be coterminous with a change in the will of God as it pertains to the physical world. Furthermore, although God, according to Maimonides, does have the power to deviate from His natural law, doing so would undermine the perfect relevancy of the Torah to the physical world. Whereas the Torah is a blueprint for how mankind is to interact with the physical world, any deviation in that world necessarily invalidates the perfection of the blueprint. Similarly, whereas God also has the power to change mankind's nature, such as by removing the evil inclination, He never has nor will, for doing so would violate the eternality of the Torah's relevancy for humanity (*Guide* III:32).[9] Divine perfection, as well as perfection of the divine Torah, both require immutable natural law.[10]

However, paradoxically, Rabbinic sources also attest to divinely influenced timely deviation from that same perfection. Immediately after positing nature's immutability (*Guide* II:28), Maimonides presents an exception which supports the opposite view, asserting that God does sometimes cause changes in natural law (miracles) in order to instill fear and faith in mankind.[11]

This conflict between the immutability of natural law and the recognition of divine providence is similarly found in Maimonides' *Mishneh Torah*, when he discusses, for example, the appropriate *halakhic* response to tragic events. Although perfection precludes miracles which deviate from divinely perfected physical law (*Guide* III:15), Maimonides explains that *halakha* dictates that we pray, precisely when we need a miracle to circumvent the normal, natural course of events (*Hil. Ta'anit* 1:1). However, this time speaking from a rationalist perspective, Maimonides next describes the requirement to accept the inevitability of tragic events governed by "*minhago shel olam*" (the world behaving according to its expected laws) (*Hil. Aveilut* 13:11) and, for example, to not grieve excessively over the death of a loved one. Natural law dictates the presence of certain unavoidable realities, and thus to grieve excessively represents a failure to recognize the governing laws of physics. Then, once again returning to the voice of his religious persona, Maimonides simultaneously warns against attributing the causality of *all* events to a set of physical laws devoid of direct divine intervention. He insists on the *halakhic* obligation to recognize God's hand in a tragedy or hardship rather than to believe that an event is "*nikro nikreit*," entirely a random act of happenstance (*Hil. Ta'anit* 1:3). For Maimonides, a worldview that considers *all* events, both communal as well as for each individual, as *nikro nikreit*, fails to recognize the presence of God in our lives and thereby leads to a path of cruelty.[12] He further explains that recognizing that fate is the result of divine providence[13] motivates one to turn to God. One has both the right and obligation to pray for miraculous, divine intervention to ameliorate the hardship, while at the same time recognize that scientific causality is unavoidable. And so the challenge remains:

how can one find rational permission to pray for intervention without betraying one's belief in a perfect, unchanging God?

Maimonides attempts to reconcile these conflicts by explaining that precluding the possibility for changes in natural law specifically refers only to *permanent* changes in natural law (*Guide* II:29). He explains that the statement traditionally attributed to King Solomon, "*ein kol ḥadash taḥat hashemesh*," (there is nothing new under the sun) (Eccles. 1:9), precludes only *new* creations. However, *temporary* deviations from physical law do not constitute such *new* creations. Thus, according to Maimonides it is acceptable and logically consistent to pray for temporary deviations in the perfect system, since it is acceptable for them to occur. Nevertheless, it is difficult to overlook the fact that a temporary deviation still does denote a deviation. Perfection does not tolerate imperfection, even temporarily, and as such it appears that Maimonides' apparent "reconciliation" requires further analysis.[14]

Maimonides also offers an alternative solution, that does not require positing any temporary deviations, which builds on the opinion expressed in the *midrashic* collection *Gen. Rabbah* 5:4. The *midrash* states that miracles were built into the physical properties of the universe. During the six days of creation, God commanded that the sea would eventually part for the Jews, as He did in similar fashion with all other natural phenomena that were destined to exhibit future miraculous behavior.

R. Yehudah Halevi (d. 1141) similarly struggles to reconcile science and miracles in his work, *The Kuzari*, and expands on this *midrashic* concept, to develop his "pre-integration" theory (*Kuzari* 3:73). He quotes the *mishnah* from Pirkei Avot 5:6 that states that miracles, such as the mouth of the earth that swallowed Korach and the mouth of Bilam's donkey that spoke, were created "*bein hashmashot*," during the mystical sunset of the sixth day of creation. He explains that miracles are preordained and pre-integrated within physical law.

In the *Commentary on the Mishnah* on this *mishnah* in Pirkei Avot, Maimonides repeats his opinion that miracles are temporary and very infrequent. He also parallels R. Yehudah Halevi's interpretation that miraculous behavior was written into physical law from the beginning. Maimonides explains that other miracles not explicitly enumerated in this *mishnah* were created in the day of creation relevant to the miracle. For example, the miracle pertaining to the parting of the Red Sea was created on day two, pre-integrated in the physical laws of water. Maimonides explains that these exceptional events were preordained at the time of the creation of natural law and therefore are technically inherent in natural law. However, they are miraculous in their timing (*Guide* II:29) since these exceptions could not have been predicted to occur when they did, despite having all available scientific knowledge of the present state,[15] i.e. the state immediately preceding the miraculous occurrence.

The pre-integration theory of miracles does allow for the interpretation of communal historical events such as the parting of the Red Sea as being miraculous, without tainting the perfection of physical law by requiring *new* creations. It is not logically nor theologically inconsistent to claim that God preordained the Exodus from Egypt and its accompanying miracles at the time of creation as part of a macroscopic plan for the Jews and humanity. However, on an individual basis, any preordained miracle would only be possible if its repercussions were also consistent with a pre-creation divine plan. In the narrative in which Moses prays for Miriam's recovery from leprosy (Num. 12:1–14), itself a miraculous punishment ostensibly for slander, a pre-integration theory would be forced to posit that both Miriam's sudden illness as well as Moses' prayer were coincidental to both of their actions and words. The text rejects this possibility, since although Miriam's illness is only implicitly a punishment, God explicitly replies to Moses' prayer for forgiveness and healing, and God mitigates the punishment by limiting its duration to seven days. Similarly, in the example of King Ḥizqiyyahu's miraculous recovery from terminal illness in response to his prayer to God (Kings II, 20:5), a pre-integration interpretation would further require consideration of his prayer as coincidental to his recovery.[16]

Traditionally, divine providence for the individual is dependent on prayer for intervention as well as on penitence and good deeds to merit God's response.[17] Therefore the possibility for personal divine intervention is determined by the actions and character of the individual. But if divine intervention were entirely preordained, there would be no role for the individual's free will nor his ability to repent.

Thus there is no allowance within R. Yehudah Halevi's theory for an individual's actions or prayers to matter, and as such, any prayer asking for divine intervention still lacks a rational justification.

A modern scientific approach at explaining phenomenon portrayed biblically as miracles is similar to the pre-integration theory in its shortcoming in explaining the timing of the events in response to human causes. References to strong tides or winds to explain the parting of the Red Sea (Exod. 14:21), an earthquake to explain the Earth's swallowing of Korah's sympathizers (Num. 16:31–32), or even the summer solstice to explain the unsetting sun in the battle at Giveon (Josh. 10:12), do provide a palatable scientific explanation of how an event occurs within natural law. However, the mere stipulation of scientific conditions which could potentially yield such an event is not a justification for how a miracle is actually natural. Miracles are not described biblically in a temporal vacuum but rather occur at the precise time required to offer salvation or punishment. Scientific explanations of miracles simply shift the mystery of miracles from the details of the events to the timing with which they occur.[18] Therefore, the role of these scientific explanations within a religious framework is to present how a miracle could have happened at all, not how it could have happened when it did and in response to which conditions. However, answers to these latter questions are exactly what are required to motivate and justify rational prayer.

Justifying the Rabbinic concept of prayer from a rational perspective first requires analyzing the parameters for such prayer, specifically in the context of miracles and deviation from natural law. The *mishnah* in Berakhot 54a discusses what constitutes an invalid prayer: "*hatso'eik lesheʾavar, harei zo tefilat shav,*" (one who cries out over the past is uttering a worthless prayer). It is considered a foolish and wasteful act, not an act of devotion and piety, to pray for the reversal of events that have already happened. Praying for the gender of a baby in an already pregnant woman is not faith but futility. Hearing a scream and then praying that it didn't come from your home is without merit.[19] The general principle espoused by the *mishnah* is simply that one may not pray for events that have already transpired to have transpired differently. Alternatively stated, one is not permitted to pray for the reversal of time.

However, if Maimonides' *temporary* exception clause for miracles were taken literally, that a miracle is any rare and temporary deviation from normal physical law, then why would a prayer for time reversal be futile? If natural law dictates time's forward progression, let a temporary deviation reverse time's arrow in order to respond to one's heartfelt prayer only to then immediately revert upon completion of the miracle. Time travel should be a miracle like any other that one is permitted to pray for in periods of great distress. While intuitively one might feel more disturbed by time reversal than a lesser-perceived deviation from natural law such as beneficial rain, there is no salient distinction here between degrees of deviation of natural law. A prayer for any degree of deviation violates physical law, and thus, if any temporary deviation is allowed then all possible deviations should be permitted as well. This unavoidable conclusion from Maimonides' temporary theory lies in direct contrast to the *mishnah*,[20] which constrains the nature of deviations that one may pray for. In the *Mishneh Torah*, Maimonides himself presents this *mishnaic* principle as being the *halakha*, the practical Jewish law.[21] This apparent logical inconsistency for Maimonides requires reconciliation.

An additional description of the *halakhic* limitations to prayer is found in Sanhedrin 110a. Rava explains that Moses appears to be praying for a new creation of "*gehinom*" (hell), in order to punish Korach and his followers. The Talmud concludes that since this would be in violation of the principle of "*ein kol ḥadash*," (nothing new under the sun can ever be created), Moses must have only been asking for a change in the behavior of an already existing *gehinom*. Thus the Talmud accepts that a phenomenon may behave differently in quantity or color from that expected but does believe the emergence of entirely new phenomenon to be possible.

Collectively, the Rabbinic passages summarized above explicitly illustrate both the existence of discourse on the theological paradoxes of divine perfection and intervention as well as an attempt to reconcile them. However, these attempts at reconciliation should be viewed through a generic lens, which reveals both the motivation and fundamental requirements common to all approaches. Specifically, the discussion in Sanhedrin when understood in combination with the *mishnah* in Berakhot, presents this traditional paradigm for prayer:

**One is permitted to request miracles from God
that can be understood within natural law.**

This need not mean specifically that a miracle was preordained during the seven days of creation but rather that the ability for natural law to behave in certain unexpected ways was preordained. This generic paradigm is consistent with both Maimonides' various explanations as well as with conditions presented in Berakhot 54a, if we assume that time reversal is not one of the unexpected, yet possible behaviors that were written into natural law from the beginning. What is missing, however, from this paradigm as presented in the traditional texts, is a rational justification that avoids the logical inconsistencies inherent in both the "temporariness" and "pre-integration" theory of miracles as delineated above.

Before attempting to reconcile the conflicts between miraculous divine intervention and scientific laws, it is important to emphasize Maimonides' own recognition that future advances in science can illuminate religious truths. Maimonides is explicitly cognizant of the imperfection of his own scientific knowledge in determining what is possible or impossible within natural law but nevertheless illustrates that such a distinction does exist (*Guide* III:15).[22] Interestingly, he leaves it to philosophers, scientists and mathematicians to determine what specifically falls into the realm of the impossible and not to Rabbinic tradition to determine this. He further explains that God has decided to make such natural impossibilities likewise impossible for Himself as a result of His decision to bind Himself by physical law. One example that Maimonides gives concerns the mathematical claim that it is impossible to construct a square with a diagonal equal in length to one of its sides, an impossibility that evidently would extend to a square created by God as well. Maimonides wonders whether, in fact, this is an absolute incontrovertible truth, or whether one has the intellectual freedom to contest this specific claim.[23] He longs for a way to confidently distinguish between scientific proof and imagination-based reasoning, recognizing that future science may deviate from contemporary knowledge.

It is with this Maimonidean encouragement that it becomes imperative for us to isolate the core of Maimonides' philosophical and religious theses from the science that inspires it (as was done above for the sources from Sanhedrin and Berakhot). Just as Maimonides' discussion in *Hil. Yesodei haTorah* (ch. 4) is not rendered moot by the presence of more than four natural elements, so too is his view of miracles not compromised by limitations due to perceived Aristotelian truths of physical law. Maimonides' explanation of miracles as temporary deviations is offered to resolve an apparent conflict and does not constitute an essential component of his view, nor does it need to be taken literally. The fundamental tenets of Maimonides' philosophy of miracles can be extricated from this doctrine of temporariness that is perhaps biased by his Aristotelian influences. The core components of Maimonides' thesis reduce to an operational definition for miracles:

1. Miracles are extremely rare.
2. Miracles are intrinsic to the laws of physics.
3. Miracles do not change fundamental laws of physics.
4. Miracles are the will of God, expressing His direct involvement with humanity and the physical world.

Any scientific explanation of miracles that is consistent with the above principles, or at least not contradictory to them, would therefore be welcome in providing reconciliation between Aristotelian perfection and interactive divinity. While the final tenet lies beyond the scope of modern science (though not in contradiction to modern science), quantum mechanics offers an approach reconcilable with the first three. Similarly, quantum mechanics provides a rational justification for the traditional paradigm of prayer described earlier. Quantum mechanics provides a scientific methodology and logic for reconciling these theological paradoxes faced in Rabbinic literature, while simultaneously arriving at conclusions that preserve the essential theological truths mandated by traditional Rabbinic literature.

III. *Brief Background of the Relevant Principles of Quantum Mechanics*

Classical physics describes each object by an exact reality, in which complete knowledge of its properties as well as complete knowledge of its environment can predict with certainty its evolution in time. Although complete knowledge may be extremely difficult to ascertain, it is nonetheless possible in principle. For example, if a ball with a perfectly known mass, velocity, spin, charge, etc. is thrown up in a universe in which the properties of all other potentially colliding particles as well as gravity, wind resistance, etc. are perfectly known, then the exact trajectory for all times can be calculated. In this classical worldview omniscience of present conditions uniquely determines future evolution. Furthermore, once all present conditions are determined, even if they are unknown to the observer, the future is determined.

Certainly we do speak of statistical probabilities in classical physics when describing the behavior of an ensemble of objects. We predict one's probability of recovering from an illness, the odds of being in a car accident and countless other things. However, these statistics have meaning only for a large population and not for a single specific individual. We are forced into such a collective description precisely because we do not have omniscience of all the relevant details. If we did, then classically we would not have to rely on general probabilities to predict outcomes, but rather could calculate them exactly on an individual basis.[24] For example, perfect knowledge of how a specific cancer affects a specific person would enable us to know exactly what their outcome would be.

Quantum mechanics, in complete contrast to the intuitive, classical description, describes reality as being not uniquely defined. Most transparently on a microscopic level,[25] an object can be fully described by a possible combination of several, even infinite, simultaneously existing states. For example, an atom's location is partially localized in one central place, but the atom has a non-zero probability of being found in a location extending to the ends of the universe.[26] In this example, all of space is divided into infinitesimal units with each unit representing a distinct location and having an assigned weight. This property, referred to as "superposition," represents one of the fundamental principles of quantum mechanics, which has no parallel in the classical world.[27] A superposition state has multiple terms that taken together comprise the object's *wavefunction*. Each term in the wavefunction has a probability coefficient that determines the fractional weighting that it contributes to the overall description. However, unlike a classical probability, this coefficient does not describe the chance that a given component is actually the correct one to describe the object's reality. The description of the object's reality is the *entire* wavefunction, including all terms. Thus a quantum arrow can be in a state described by an arrow both up and down at the same time, each with an arbitrary probability coefficient, as long as the square of the sum of the coefficients is equal to one. (The probability is the coefficient squared.) The wavefunction description of the reality of a quantum arrow could be, for example, .577 up + .816 down, assuming for simplicity that the arrow can only have up and down components and not full rotational freedom.[28] The most famous example of such a superposition state is a 'Schroedinger-cat,' which can be both alive and dead at the same time.[29]

In understanding the distinctions between classical and quantum realities, even on the superficial level, it is imperative to recognize that superpositions are 'And' statements not 'Or' statements. Thus, the quantum arrow is not either up Or down, it is both up And down. Classically, we could look at an ensemble of arrows and state that a chosen arrow has a ⅓ chance of being up and a ⅔ chance of being down. This would be a classical description of a statistical ensemble and would not indicate anything novel about the description of reality. Rather the description would indicate a lack of complete knowledge. A classical arrow with a probability distribution has a definite value, which happens to be unknown to the observer at a specific time. Quantum mechanically, however, a single arrow has a reality described by a wavefunction that has components that are both up And down. A quantum arrow has multiple simultaneous values and thus, even perfect knowledge of its existence would not reduce the number of discrete states describing its reality.

As a scientific rather than philosophical theory, however, quantum mechanics must reconcile its descriptions with physical observations. Although it has been proven experimentally in a laboratory setting countless times for small particles like atoms and photons, quantum mechanics must also reconcile its claims with observed macroscopic reality outside of the laboratory. Specifically, a large object like an arrow has always been measured pointing in only one direction at a time. While a single valued arrow is a perfectly valid quantum state and is not in conflict with quantum mechanics, the fact that an arrow is never observed in a multi-valued state presents the possibility for contradiction.

This apparent conflict between laboratory quantum mechanics

and "real world" observations is the subject of current experimental and theoretical research but is generally resolved by positing that some mechanism occurs which converts the quantum state to a known classical state. Before, or possibly even while, the arrow is being observed this mechanism "collapses" the quantum arrow superposition into a single classical direction.[30] This process, referred to as *wavefunction collapse* or *collapse* for the remainder of this paper, describes the generic phenomenon by which a quantum mechanical superposition projects onto a specific, singular discrete state as observed in the classical world. Thus, after this collapse there is only one remaining state describing the observed classical reality. Furthermore, all information of the other states and their relations to each other in the original superposition has been lost, resulting in what is referred to as a "decohered" state. While the particulars of this collapse event and ensuing decoherence are experimentally unknown, it is experimentally clear that such an event can be triggered by observing the system. Observations can be understood as interactions between some external system and the quantum system under study. For the purpose of this paper, all interactions with the wavefunction of interest that lead to its collapse can be divided into two categories: interactions with the environment and intentional measurements. Although both of these mechanisms are due to interactions of the system in question with something external to that system the salient distinction here is that only the latter reflects an intended event.

Environmentally induced wavefunction collapse and ensuing decoherence is a consequence of interactions of background particles or fields with the object in question. Any particle or field in the universe could potentially be the cause of the collapse, and it in turn may depend on the random outcome of a previous collapse. Therefore, the exact cause and timing of the event can be random and unpredictable, and its outcome is never knowable, even in principle. When such a destructive interaction takes place, the object can no longer exist in its superposition, and it is randomly assigned a discrete state based on the probability coefficients of the initial wavefunction. This process does not assume any conscious observer or any conscious desire for its occurrence.

Measurement, on the other hand, is by definition intentional. Though the conscious observer need not know the measurement outcome, he willfully causes the measurement to take place at a desired time. This process also collapses the wavefunction in an unpredictable fashion based on the probability amplitudes of the initial superposition.[31]

For those new to this language of quantum mechanics an additional example is in order that illustrates the collapse event. If a classical card is chosen at 'random' from a deck, each possibility is equally statistically likely before its identity is known, since perfect knowledge of the exact preparation of the deck and the cognitive processes of the chooser are unavailable. This, of course, does not mean that the unknown card is partially a four of hearts and partially a queen of clubs etc., but rather the card has an exact, but as of yet unknown, value. Turning over the card simply illustrates what the reality of that card had been all along. On the other hand, quantum mechanics explains that a quantum card can actually be in a state described by probability amplitudes of all possible card outcomes. Thus, an unknown card could be, for example, 50% black And 50% red, before it is observed. Intentionally turning over the card is now a quantum mechanical measurement that causes the superposition to collapse. This act of revealing the card could alternatively be caused by an unintended wind. In both cases, the action which flips the card, unlike the classical action, does not simply reveal what the state of the card had been but rather forces the quantum nature of the card, previously existing as both red And black, to collapse into a single color.

There are several repercussions of the reality described above, only a few of which are relevant to our discussion. The *first* is that an object such as an atom, if measured, could possibly be found anywhere in the universe. Although it has an overwhelmingly large probability of having its wavefunction collapse to a specific location, there is a non-zero probability that it will be found in a very unlikely place.

Superpositions do not necessarily have equal probability amplitudes for all components included in the sum. In fact, in most relevant applications of quantum superpositions, there are one or more most likely outcomes in the event of collapse. Thus, if a billion such decoherent collapses were necessary to evolve from a microscopic electron state to a long-lived physical observable, the probabilistic outcomes of the collapse would all but guarantee that only the most likely event would ever occur. Imagine a phenotype for an n gene system with dominant red and recessive black, where the probability to choose black is 1% for each draw. The 1% probability of success (black phenotype) for the initial draw becomes something astronomically small as the number of required measurements increases (as $.01^n$). Nevertheless, the possibility of successive collapse processes yielding black is not exactly zero if attempted in enough systems. It is only effectively zero within the time available since the creation of the universe. This is crucial to note as it provides within natural law the possibility for exceedingly unlikely events to occur.

The *second* critical point is that complete information of a state after the quantum superposition has collapsed and decohered cannot uniquely reproduce the initial superposition state. Once decoherence occurs and a final state emerges which behaves classically, the initial state cannot be traced back even with full knowledge of all environmental and measurement factors.[32] An infinite number of initial superpositions, with different probability amplitudes for different discrete components could yield identical final observed results. The argument can be recast in reverse to reveal that omniscience of a quantum superposition state as well as environmental parameters do not allow absolute knowledge of the eventual collapsed quantum state.

The *third* relevant point is that a measurement of a superposition state that collapses the wavefunction cannot cause the wavefunction to collapse to a chosen discrete state with complete certainty. However, since the specific time of the measurement can be determined, the wavefunction evolution can be steered, which allows a simple measurement to serve as a powerful tool in affecting the evolution of a state.

The effect of a carefully chosen measurement on a final state can be seen by examining a typical sequence used in interferometry. Interferometry refers to a metrology technique that interferes particles along two similar paths in order to be sensitive to slight differences between the paths.[33] For simplicity, the sequence, defined as Sequence I, is broken down into its basic steps:

1. An atom with two discrete energy levels is assumed to begin residing fully in its lower state.
2. The atom is then exposed to a light beam which causes the

initial state to evolve into a superposition state, with the atom described as being 50% in the upper state And 50% in the lower.[34]

3. The atom is exposed to a second such light pulse that now causes the superposition state to evolve into a state where the atom is 100% in the upper level.

4. The atom is measured and found to be in the upper level.

In this sequence, the outcome is certain due to knowledge of the initial state and its subsequent precise manipulation with interacting light pulses. Thus the final observed state of the atom is always found to be in the upper level.

Let us now imagine that there is an additional measurement step performed on the atom between steps 2 and 3. Thus the five steps which comprise Sequence II are now:

1. An atom with two discrete energy levels begins in its lower state.

2. The atom is then exposed to a light beam which causes the initial state to evolve into a superposition state, with the atom described as being 50% in the upper state And 50% in the lower.

3. The atom is measured and since any measurement collapses the superposition,[35] the atom cannot remain simultaneously in both its upper and lower levels and thus must randomly collapse to one level, where each level has equal probability of being chosen.

4. Regardless of which level the atom chooses in the previous step, the light pulse interaction (step 3 of Sequence I) will now return the atom to an equally weighted superposition of both levels.

5. The atom is measured once again, but this time the measurement will sometimes force the superposition to choose the upper and sometimes the lower level.

Simply by adding a step where the atom is observed, we have taken a certain outcome and changed it. We could not force the atom to be in the lower level at the end of the sequence, but we did increase this possibility from 0% to 50%.

The *fourth* issue is that the line dividing what constitutes the pre-collapsed quantum world and the collapsed, observed classical world is not clearly drawn.[36] Quantum interference effects are continually being observed for larger and larger particles beginning with photons, and progressing to neutrons, large molecules (Bucky balls),[37] and even collective ensembles of millions of atoms in the form of Bose-Einstein Condensates.[38] Furthermore, even fabricated solid state devices, such as SQUIDS,[39] have demonstrated the ability to support quantum superposition states for measurable times. The boundary beyond which collapse and decoherence instantaneously prevail has been systematically pushed further and further into the macroscopic regime for longer and longer times. Thus modern physics cannot define at what point quantum superpositions cease to have practical relevancy due to collapse times asymptotically approaching zero.

Every actualization of an observed event requiring a macroscopic time scale is inevitably due to innumerable events that precede it, each described by a shorter, microscopic time scale. Thus, a particular superposition may be short lived but still survive just long enough to influence its immediate environment. It is conceivable that such nested processes could allow quantum superposition effects to influence events, possibly even at the level of effecting human cognition and experiences.

IV. *Reconciling Divine Providence and Natural Law through Quantum Mechanics*

These lessons from quantum mechanics can now be applied to the problem at hand of understanding the relationship between natural law, miracles and prayer. Specifically, I explain how an event never before experienced within natural law can still occur within natural law. I address how God's watchfulness can affect future outcomes in order to achieve these unlikely events or miracles within the structure of physical law. I also provide a rational distinction between miracles for which one is permitted to evoke God's watchfulness through prayer and those that are considered foolish and futile for which to ask. Finally, I explain how this framework allows for a rational prayer for divine intervention on an individual basis and justifies the paradigm for such prayer.

Recall that a quantum mechanical description of reality includes superpositions of states, some of which have extremely small, though non-zero probability coefficients. Therefore, intrinsic in natural law is the possibility for highly unlikely events to occur. Turning to how these events are actualized, I draw analogies by equating environmentally induced wavefunction collapse and decoherence with the normal course of events, "*olam keminhago noheig*," (the world behaves according to its expected laws) (*Hil. Malakhim* 12:1). On the other hand, collapse and decoherence due to an intentional measurement is equated with divine observation.

Beginning with a discussion of environmental collapse and decoherence alone, let us consider a world evolving according to the probability amplitudes within each quantum superposition. In such a scenario macroscopic phenomenon will follow the expected probabilities of experiential life.[40] Cause and effect reign supreme, people grow accustomed to what is perceived as normal behavior, and classical science appears to predict nearly everything. However, even within this unguided collapse picture, scientifically statistical projections will occasionally fail miserably due to the very nature of quantum reality. Science merely predicts probability and not possibility, and therefore, very occasionally, events occur which are highly unexpected probabilistically, thereby falling outside of a parameter range that defines intuitive human expectations. These events must be extremely rare, when viewed over all of time, since they are bound by the probability amplitudes in the relevant superpositions. However, such events do not represent violations of natural law but rather exist as a remote possibility within the superposition description of reality. These rare events are random occurrences, events of happenstance (*nikro nikreit*), and do not reflect any direct divine involvement. Their timing would not usually coincide with human circumstances that would cause them to be perceived as miracles, although this too could occur very rarely. Thus, very occasionally, a random event could be misconstrued as a divine miracle. Several notable physicists, such as Freeman Dyson, attempted to explain perceived miracles in this context.

On the other hand, we have shown above that timely observations (intentional measurements) can also affect an outcome. In our earlier thought experiment (Sequences I and II) where we analyzed the interaction of light pulses and measurements with an atom containing two energy levels, we found that, by simply adding a step where the atom was watched while keeping all other parameters identical, we drastically changed the outcome. If we indulge in a dramatic macroscopic analogy of this phenomenon where we equate the upper energy level with death and the lower with life, then the two scenarios demonstrate the role of a divine observation. In the absence of divine intervention the outcome is essentially certain death (Sequence I, step 4), however a timely divine measurement offers a 50% chance of life (Sequence II, step 5). Divine intervention, expressed as a passive observation, does affect outcomes. Outcomes of these measurements can be highly unlikely scenarios, and these unlikely events are steered by precisely when the observations take place. The more unlikely the phenomenon, the more miraculous, yet it is still consistent with natural law.

Although it is impossible to speculate as to the nature of a divine observation which causes a miracle, Maimonides instructs that God does not require any instrument or action to perform anything but rather effects change by His will alone (*Guide* 1:23). Thus, according to Maimonides, God's will to make quantum mechanical measurements is, in essence, the measurement device. A divine observation is based on the premise of divine omniscience of the rules governing physical law but does not presuppose a divine action outside of those rules. The possibility for observation is inherent in a quantum mechanical description of the universe. Therefore, it does not violate natural law for God to observe when it might help most, and it follows that a person, therefore, has both permission and a religious obligation to pray to God for a providential observation.[41]

However, a prayer to God for intervention, requesting any action other than an observation, such as for an additional force in the interferometer sequence analogy above, would be equivalent to praying for a new creation and would thereby require deviation from natural law.

This emphasizes a central distinction between the quantum mechanical definition of divine miracles described above and the statement that miracles are simply *highly unlikely* events within natural law. A scientific explanation of biblical miraculous phenomenon must not only be able to write equations whose solutions describe the event (as one could write hydrodynamic equations modeling the parting of a sea) but must also explain the event in the context of prior conditions, both regarding the physical environment as well as any individual prayer or action. Short of relying entirely on coincidence, a random statistical description of miracles necessitates a new creation outside of natural law, since, a new creation refers to both phenomenon never seen before as well as to phenomenon not allowed for a given set of preconditions. However, quantum mechanics requires only an observation in order to induce the collapse of a superposition state, potentially into a highly unexpected state. Thus a quantum mechanical divine observation can occur at a specific moment without altering physical law but still profoundly altering physical events. This permits miracles to occur within a scientific system both in the context of a global set of natural laws and also in the context of local time and individual-specific conditions.

The concept of praying for God simply to watch us has now been shown to be scientifically compatible with a quantum mechanical framework.[42] It is interesting to recognize that the concept of God as observer is also manifest in both biblical sources of prayer as well as throughout Jewish liturgy. Its presence in the liturgy reflects the Rabbinic struggle, as introduced in the first section of this essay, with the concept of prayer for active, divine interaction. Biblical examples can likewise be interpreted as attempts to guide human theology towards an understanding of miraculous, divine intervention as occurring through passive observation. For example, the priestly benediction implores God to turn His face towards us, "*yisah Hashem panav eilekha*," (Num. 6:26) in order to observe us. When an Israelite brings his first fruits to Jerusalem he prays, "*hashkifah mim'on kodshekha… uvarekh et amecha*," (look down upon us from your exalted place of dwelling…and bless your people) (Deut. 26:15). We pray to God to guard over us "*shomer Yisrael*," (the observer of Israel) and we implore, "*habita, ve'anenu be'eit tsarah*"(watch us and answer us in our time of difficulty).[43] These images, which were intended as simply an affirmation of the passive, observatory nature of God's intervention, can now be understood as a request for God to help us by measuring the quantum, microscopic building blocks through His observation in a timely fashion. We pray for God to favorably affect the macroscopic outcome in a way different from that which would most likely occur in the presence of environmental collapse.

Since quantum mechanics is by definition probabilistic, a divine measurement does not offer an absolute guarantee of behavior outside of the norm, only an increased probability for it. Practically speaking, it is of course conceivable that God could induce sequential measurements such as to render a favorable outcome with probability asymptotically approaching 100% – but never exactly 100%. Thus, it is possible, albeit improbable, that even the prayers of the most righteous would appear to have been unanswered. The probabilistic nature of collapse and decoherence, even that due to measurement, allows for the otherwise theologically problematic concept of *tsadik verah lo*, when misfortune befalls the righteous. In our quantum picture, a *tsadik* has a vastly improved probability of being protected from evil, but this probability is never exactly 100%.[44] Although God has omniscience,[45] the nature of quantum superpositions and their collapse dictate that complete knowledge of a physical system prior to its collapse does not uniquely determine its outcome.

It is important to emphasize that this quantum mechanical structure, which allows behavior outside of the norm to occur, is relevant only as long as the superposition wavefunction has not yet collapsed and decohered. Once a wavefunction collapses, the superposition ceases to exist and with it disappears the ability to strategically steer an outcome. There is no longer a relevant concept of probability, only reality. Thus, with a quantum mechanical view of miracles, prayer for intervention before collapse is a valid prayer. The future is not determined as long as collapse has not yet occurred. However, after collapse and decoherence, the prayer is invalid, as in the case of an existing fetus whose gender has already been determined though remains unknown.[46] It is for this reason that praying for a reversal of time is invalid. Recall that our knowledge of the collapse event's occurrence as well as its outcome is irrelevant. Fate is determined, even before it is known, once it is knowable, at the time when irreversible collapse and decoherence has occurred. *Gezar dineinu*, the divine decree of our fate, can be changed only before collapse and decoherence occur.[47]

One might be motivated to draw the analogy that praying for a miracle is equivalent to praying for the tail of a classical, statistical bell-shaped curve. However, as we have seen previously, this analogy is flawed because from this classical perspective a card has been chosen but simply has not yet been flipped. Although we do not know its identity, it has been determined. Even though we do not know the outcome, we would in such a classical picture still be faced with the logical paradox of entreating God to change the reality of an event that has already occurred. We may not pray to God to change an already determined reality even if unknown to us, for this explicitly violates the principles of "*tso'ek leshe'avar,*" (screaming for the past), and engaging in "*tefilat shav,*" (futile prayer) as seen above in Berakhot 54a. Quantum mechanically, however, we pray that God, through timely measurements, steer the final outcome of our fate towards one of the several states that comprise the superposition wavefunction before it has collapsed and decohered. We recognize that multiple potential outcomes exist in the superposition, and while some have very small probability coefficients, they are all possible. Since miracles are essentially highly improbable outcomes of decoherence and collapse processes, the smaller the probability coefficient the greater the miracle for which we pray.

In turning to God, one obviously cannot always know when a collapse process has occurred to irreversibly seal the very fate we pray to circumvent. Therefore, the *halakha* gives permission to pray for divine providence in all instances that are at least ambiguous as to the role of collapse and decoherence.[48]

v. *Conclusion*

In Tractate Shabbat 156a, Rav explains that the Rabbinic idiom, "*ein mazal leYisrael*" (random luck does not determine the fate of Israel) reflects God's promise to Abraham that his children would not be bound by the random happenstance of fate and luck. Using the quantum mechanical language introduced, this idiom reflects the recognition that unintended environmental collapse mechanisms are not uniquely responsible for all events in this world; God also has the ability to observe and thereby generate a wavefunction collapse at the exact moment He sees fit. As Maimonides describes in *The Guide* III:17, a ship may accidentally go down, but it is not accidental that a particular man was onboard and another was not. While admittedly, this example blurs the distinction between unlikely events that occur for reasons beyond our control, and those events that occur precisely because of our actions and decisions, the message is the same. We live in a world in which divine intervention can occasionally affect the wavefunction collapse and decoherence processes for individuals or individual events, yet on a global level averaged over time, statistical outcomes still prevail.[49]

Although quantum mechanics can provide an explanation for miraculous intervention within the structure of natural physical law, it obviously cannot explain why God chooses to intervene or make measurements when He does. The laws of quantum mechanics also offer no explanation in addressing the question of how to live in such a way that God may be more likely to project a favorable measurement for the individual. This is strictly the realm of religion, and Jewish theology does offer some guidance.[50] In describing the nature of divine providence (*Guide* III:17), Maimonides explains that the concept of divine providence in natural law applies only to humanity. Furthermore, the benefit attainable from divine providence is commensurate with one's degree of human perfection (*Guide* III:18). This recognition motivates the need for all prayer, even that which is not connected to a specific request. The very act of meditation on the divine, the awareness of God's greatness and omnipotence, brings one closer to God. This Maimonidean view can be seen from a quantum mechanical perspective, where closeness to God brings one's life more closely under God's measurement scrutiny. Alternatively, abandonment of God, or belief only in happenstance, leads to God's abandonment of his people to a fate of happenstance, "...*vehalakhtem imi bekeri, vehalakhti af ani imakhem bekeri...*" (but if you treat me as happenstance, then I will treat you with happenstance) (Lev. 26:23–24). [51]

Certainly, we cannot know the causal mechanism of any particular misfortune nor can we ascertain if a tragedy is actually a punishment when viewed from the perspective of a larger divine plan. Just as misfortune can arise from an environmental collapse it could also occur due to direct, intended divine observation such as in the example of Miriam's leprosy (Num. 12:10) and countless other biblical examples of God's punishing decrees. However, the recognition that divine observation allows a life's trajectory to deviate from that expected due to environmental collapse and decoherence provides a rational justification within a scientific framework for prayer requesting divine intervention. This recognition therefore also mandates the obligation and necessity for prayer. The examples given earlier, in which Moses' and Ḥizqiyyahu's individual prayers evoke their desired response, set the bar extremely high for what level of closeness to God merits a divine observation. Nevertheless, these examples demonstrate that such closeness is at least in principle achievable, and therefore its pursuit is neither irrational nor in vain.

Traditional theology argues that God watches more closely over those who follow in His path *"eini Hashem el tsadikim,"* (the eyes of the Lord are upon the righteous (Ps. 34:16)). Quantum theology argues that by watching more closely, God can choose the exact moment to make intentional and hopefully favorable measurements. Quantum mechanics provides the "spiritual rationalist" the rational ability to believe that God can answer prayers and the spiritual motivation to pursue closeness with God.

NOTES:

I am thankful to Gaya Bernstein, Maya Bernstein, Mayer Bick, Yanay Ofran, Rana Samuels, David Santiago, Zvi Septimus, Daniel Silverberg, John Stockton, Stan Sussman, Alan Tuchman and Barry Wimpfheimer for numerous helpful suggestions. I am also indebted to Shera Aranoff Tuchman for continuous feedback and advice.

Above all, I honor and remember my wife Beth Samuels, *z"l*, with deep sadness but eternal love and gratitude. Her love, ideas, inspiration, encouragement and challenges over the past nine years have immeasurably contributed to the development of this quantum theology as well as its specific presentation in this essay. Her ability to find holy meaning in everything life offers and to pursue truth through compassion, Torah and mathematics has profoundly motivated this work. I have dedicated this essay to her memory, since these ideas, much like all of myself, have grown as a product of our beautiful and holy years together.

1. Nachmanides, in his commentary on Exod. 20:2, (the first of the Ten Commandments), explains that God refers to Himself as the Lord who took Israel out from Egyptian slavery in order to emphasize that the foundation of all belief and acceptance of God's Torah hinges on the recognition that freedom from Egypt occurred with divine providence, *"behashgaha mimeno yatsu."* For a discussion of this commentary see for ex., H. Lookstein, "Tefillin and God's Kingship," *Tradition*, 4 (1961): 66–78.

2. Anecdotal examples such as God's relationship with Abraham, Isaac and Jacob as well as legal/ethical examples such as the prohibition against oppressing the poor ("If he [the oppressed] cries out to me, I

will hear, for I am merciful" (Exod. 22:26)) are direct biblical illustrations of the numerous examples of God's responding to an individual's plea. Although, philosophically, one is free to interpret these biblical examples metaphorically, religiously it is difficult if not impossible to reconcile such readings with millennia of Rabbinic teachings (see for ex. note 1).

3. M. Maimonides, *The Guide for the Perplexed* (Chicago: Univ. of Chicago, 1963), III:17. Subsequent references will be given in parenthesis in the text.

4. I. Leibowitz, *Judaism, Human Values, and the Jewish State* (Cambridge: Harvard Univ., 1992). See also I. Leibowitz, "The Spiritual and Religious Meaning of Victory and Might," *Tradition*, 10 (1969): 5–11.

5. M. Maimonides, *Mishneh Torah, Hil. Yesodei haTorah*, ch. 2. Subsequent references will be given in parenthesis in the text.

6. The thesis of this essay is presented primarily in the context of a Maimonidean theology. Clearly, many other Jewish theologians both ancient and modern have addressed similar issues such as divine absoluteness in relation to human affairs and the related role of prayer (see for ex. M. Buber, *I and Thou* (New York: Charles Scribner's Sons, 1970) pp. 130–132, 180–182 and E. Berkovitz, *God, Man and History* (Jerusalem, Israel: The Shalem Center, 2004) pp. 58–67.)

7. Aristotle, *Metaphysics* XII:7.

8. Unlike Maimonides, Nachmanides is unconcerned with any possible tension between his belief in divine perfection and the immutability of natural law. For example, Nachmanides comments on Ex. 13:16, "… *nisim ein bahem teva uminhago shel olam*" (miracles are not natural and not bound by natural course of events). (See also his commentary on Lev. 13:47 and Num. 16:30) In his commentary on Ex. 16:6, however, Nachmanides conveys a reluctance to accept cavalier departure from natural law explanations of biblical events. He describes the apparent miracle of abundant fowl in the desert as falling within natural law. Furthermore, he believes that the miraculous *manna* was created at sunset on the sixth day. We will see below in the opinion of Rabbi Yehudah Halevi in *The Kuzari*, that connecting miraculous events to this sunset period is one approach taken towards reconciling divine perfection with immutable natural law. This approach might be indicative of Nachmanides' belief as well. Nachmanides (Deut. 11:13) also states that miracles with either good or bad consequences, only occur to either *tsadikim gemurim* or *resha'im gemurim*, either the purely

righteous or completely wicked. He believes that everyone else in the middle is bound by "*minhago shel olam,*" (the world behaving according to its expected laws).

9.   I. Twersky, *Introduction to the Code of Maimonides* (New Haven: Yale University Press, 1980), 390.

10.   The importance of immutable natural law in the biblical cannon is found, for example, in the book of Jeremiah. Jeremiah's prophecy recounts God's declaration that He controls the natural elements such as the sun giving light in the day and the stars illuminating the night (Jem. 31:3–35). He continues that "*im yamushu hukim haeleh milifani… gam zera yisrael yishbotu,*" (If these natural laws should change before me [God], then the seed of Israel shall be extinguished).

11.   Maimonides does argue that many perceived miracles, such as the sun standing still during Joshua's battle at Giveon (Josh. 10:12), represent merely the appearance of deviation from natural law rather than an actual deviation (*Guide* II:35). However, while this example does not violate an Aristotelian sense of divine perfection, it is brought specifically in contradistinction to those supernatural miracles performed by Moses which do deviate temporarily from natural law. Furthermore, Maimonides' belief in supernatural miracles is unequivocal in his explanation of how creation in time, 'ex-nihilo', as opposed to a universe having been in existence eternally, allows for miracles which explicitly deviate from natural law (*Guide* II:25).

12.   The verse in Deut. 25:18 recounts the Amalekite nation's attack on the nation of Israel as, "*asher karkha baderekh*", ([Amalek] *happened* upon you on your way). Rashi, (R. Shlomo Yizhaki d. 1105) on this verse, explains that the word "*karkha*" denotes a *mikreh* (happenstance). This verse reflects the Amalekite general worldview of total happenstance, which presents an existential threat to an ethical society (Beth Samuels, public lecture at Hebrew Institute of Riverdale, 1999. See also B. Samuels, *A Literary Study of Numbers in Genesis*, note 21, published in this volume).

13.   The principle that fate can be (though not necessarily always is) a result of personal divine interaction is expressed in Exod. 21:13, "*vehaElohim ina leyado*", (and the Lord gave [the deceased] to his hand), in reference to an accidental killing. This verse explains that one is not executed for killing someone inadvertently and offers an explanation that this accident occurred with God's guidance (see Rashi's commentary on this verse). This explanatory clause cannot be intended to exonerate the killer, since he is nevertheless exiled, but is rather reinforcing the

presence of God's hand in what might otherwise be perceived as a random happenstance.

14. Admittedly, my teacher (Harvard University 1994–97) Prof. Rabbi I. Twersky, z"l, was accepting of Maimonides' attempt at reconciliation through the doctrine of "temporariness," (and I am fairly certain he was not relying on a quantum mechanical interpretation). Nevertheless, Prof. Twerksy, on several occasions, did ask my opinion on the scientific validity of Maimonides' assumptions, specifically pertaining to *Hil. Yesodei haTorah*, and I am thus encouraged that he would be open to this essay's interpretation.

15. However, complete knowledge of physical law established at the instant of creation would suffice to predict miraculous phenomenon.

16. As in the previous case with Miriam and Moses, it is possible to alternatively argue that King Ḥizqiyyahu's recovery was preordained before creation to be specifically contingent on his prayer. In Gen. 20:7 and 20:17, God's healing of Avimelekh contingent on Abraham's prayer even seems to illustrate that such a paradigm may occasionally exist. However, it is illogical to extend such an interpretation to all future individuals. Such an extension would require an infinite number of initially posited deviations from natural law which can be triggered by prayer, to be specifically preordained for every future individual. This argument would invalidate any set of physical laws through its accompanying infinite set of exceptions.

17. See Rosh Hashanah 17b–18a for a discussion on prayer and good deeds reversing a divine judgement. In the High Holiday *mahzor* (prayer book), we find the refrain, "Penitence, prayer and charity can overturn the evil decree."

18. Regarding the "miracle" at Giveon, one may logically argue that Joshua simply knew when and where to plan his battle with the Amorites in order to take advantage of the summer solstice, and thus a scientific justification need not rely on coincidence to explain the event's timing. Similarly, it is conceivable that Moses knew when and where low tides would allow crossing through the Red Sea and planned the escape route from Egypt accordingly. However, this "human planning" interpretation of miracles is difficult, if not impossible, to extend to all biblical miracles, such as the Egyptian plagues, the likes of which had never been seen, or the recovery of King Ḥizqiyyahu, which was a direct divine response to an individual's prayer.

19. See Berakhot 60a for a discussion of the *mishnah*.

20. In his *Commentary on the Mishnah* on Berakhot 54a, Maimonides

explains that the central point of this *mishnah* is that one may not pray to undo what has already been decreed, "*davar shekevar nigzar.*" It is also unclear from this explanation what determines when the decree is considered to have occurred or what logic dictates the inability to pray after a decree (see notes 46 and 47). For example, Maimonides explains in *Hil. Ta'anit* that one is obligated to pray even after an enemy has attacked (1:1) or after one is already ill (1:9).

21. *Hil. Tefilah* 10:22–26. This opinion is also that presented in the *Shulhan Arukh* O.C. 230:2.

22. Maimonides also points out that his limited knowledge in non-scientific issues as well, such as Sabean religious practices and historical details of the Edomite kingdoms, limits his ability to explain the reasons for various mitzvot and passages in the Bible (*Guide* III:50). While it is logically obvious to the modern reader that imperfect scientific or historical knowledge can compromise the accuracy of an interpretation, such a recognition is not often found in Rabbinic literature.

23. In fact such a diagonal might be possible if one considers a non-Euclidean geometric space or relativistic length contraction along the axis of the diagonal. Obviously, such concepts like Riemannian geometries (Riemann d. 1866) popularized by Einstein's general theory of relativity in the 1920's were not available to Maimonides. However, Maimonides' questioning of the science of his time is a direct appeal to future advances in science to help determine the categorization of possible and impossible, which in turn carries theological implications.

24. In a classical world there is no such thing as pure randomness. Even random number generators are mathematically only pseudo-random, often derived from complicated algorithms that manipulate a computer's internal timing.

25. The distinction between microscopic and macroscopic quantum mechanics is blurred throughout this essay but is justified for our purposes in the fourth summary point below.

26. This is the DeBroglie wavelength associated with an atom, whose spatial extent depends on the atom's mass and velocity. Heisenberg's uncertainty principle states that two observables (properties) which are related in a specific way through commutation relations cannot be simultaneously known to perfect accuracy. (These are referred to as conjugate variables, which do not commute). Thus if the position of an object is known very precisely, its momentum is described by a superposition of several momentum possibilities.

27. Discussion of the required coherence aspects of a quantum mechanical superposition is beyond the scope of this background summary.

28. I assume discreteness, in contrast to continuity, in most examples herein for purposes of clarity. Discreteness implies that energy levels, photon number, angular momentum, spin, charge and other physically measurable quantities exist in well-defined states where only integer multiples of specific values are allowed. These discrete objects, initially referred to as quanta, determine the fundamental units which combine to describe the observed macroscopic reality. Thus a quantum clock would always appear digital as compared to a classical clock which would be analog. It should be noted, however, that not all quantum observables are in fact discretized due to the lack of specific boundary conditions. Position and momentum are examples of such continuous variables as seen above in the discussion of an atom's spatial DeBroglie wave.

29. The famous Schroedinger Cat example, refers to a *"geddankin,"* or thought experiment proposed by E. Schroedinger in 1935:

    > *A cat is placed in a sealed box. Attached to the box is an apparatus containing a radioactive atomic nucleus and a canister of poison gas. This apparatus is separated from the cat in such a way that the cat can in no way interfere with it. The experiment is set up so that there is exactly a 50% chance of the nucleus decaying in one hour. If the nucleus decays, it will emit a particle that triggers the apparatus, which opens the canister and kills the cat. If the nucleus does not decay, then the cat remains alive. According to quantum mechanics, the unobserved nucleus is described as a superposition (meaning it exists partly as each simultaneously) of "decayed nucleus" and "undecayed nucleus"* (excerpt from Wikipedia entry on Schroedinger Cat).

    While introduced by Schroedinger as a paradox to illustrate the missing variables "problem" of quantum mechanics, the resulting state of a cat being in a superposition of living and dead has become the catchphrase in modern quantum mechanics for a macroscopic superposition state.

30. This Copenhagen interpretation (N. Bohr and W. Heisenberg 1927) of wavefunction collapse, assumed throughout this paper, presumes that a quantum mechanical wavefunction collapses during an irreversible event which destroys all information of the original superposition,

thereby leading to complete decoherence. An alternate view is that interactions simply entangle the system with the environment (possibly the entire universe in an open system) such that local observations cannot distinguish phase coherence between discrete states in a superposition. According to this view, to a local observer an object simply appears to behave classically. This philosophical debate has theoretical ramifications as to whether or not information of the initial quantum superposition is always irretrievably lost to the universe, although practically speaking it is certainly lost in any realistic experiment. However, what is most critical for this paper is that both approaches recognize that a local quantum superposition instantaneously ceases to exist after the wavefunction is simply observed (by either an intended or environmental interaction).

31. The outcome of a measurement depends on the basis in which the measurement takes place. Any measurement could in principle be carried out in an orthonormal basis where the superposition is one of the basis states. Although practically this is not feasible for most laboratory experiments, an omniscient observer could measure the superposition without causing collapse and decoherence. Since a priori knowledge of the superposition state is required to conduct such a measurement, no new knowledge would be gained through it.

32. There are some simple experimental exceptions to this irretrievable loss of quantum information upon collapse which require that the initial superposition state is "entangled" with another system. The second system essentially stores the quantum information of the first system after the first system's wavefunction collapses. This concept of entanglement forms the basis for phenomenon such as quantum teleportation. For a complete discussion of entanglement see, M. Nielsen and I. Chuang, *Quantum Computation and Quantum Information* (Cambridge: Cambridge Univ. Press, 2000).

33. For a general overview of some basic techniques see, N. Ramsey, *Molecular Beams* (London: Oxford Univ., 1963).

34. This is referred to as a $\pi/2$ pulse. The effect of a $\pi/2$ light pulse on a superposition state depends on the relative phase between the two probability coefficients, driving it either entirely to the upper or lower level. See P. Berman ed., *Atom Interferometry* (New York: Academic Press, 1997).

35. We ignore the possibility of a quantum non-demolition (QND) measurement. We are further assuming that the measurement does not cause the wavefunction to evolve in ways other than simply inducing its collapse.

36. E. Joos et al., *Decoherence and the Appearance of a Classical World in Quantum Theory* (Berlin: Springer, 2003).

37. M. Arndt et al., "Wave-particle Duality of c60 Molecules," *Nature* 401 (1999): 680–2.

38. M. Andrews et al., "Observation of Interference Between Two Bose Condensates," *Science* 275 (1997): 637–41.

39. C. van der Wal et al., "Quantum Superposition of Macroscopic Persistent Current States," *Science* 290 (2000): 773–7.

40. I directly apply principles of quantum mechanics to examples of macroscopic phenomenon in the interest of clarity. As noted before, it is still not scientifically determined where to draw the line between the microscopic quantum world and our collapsed and decohered macroscopic world. Furthermore, the effect of microscopic decoherence on eventual macroscopic observables is open to debate.

41. One could potentially reconcile this quantum mechanical view of miracles with Maimonides' doctrine of temporariness by extracting the principle of Maimonides' philosophy from its scientifically outdated details. At least from the perspective of an observer (albeit not from the perspective of natural law), miracles would appear temporary since their deviation from a most likely outcome is a temporary deviation when considered in the context of the mean. If human observation and intuition expect a constant and well defined parameter range for an event, then any event that lies within that range could be considered to be following the permanent guidelines. An event outside of those experiential boundaries would be assumed to have temporarily violated the norm. Of course, from quantum mechanics' perspective, this is not a temporary deviation in natural law, just a collapse to a state with a low probability coefficient. Alternatively, Maimonides' language of temporariness can be applied to a rare event that occurs specifically due to a divine measurement representing a temporary deviation from environmental wavefunction collapse as the primary collapse and decoherence mechanism.

42. The reader is reminded that this quantum mechanical picture is not attempting to explain miracles scientifically, but rather to explain them religiously in way that does not contradict science.

43. *Tahanun*, daily morning prayers. See, for example, *Sidur Rinat Yisrael* p. 84.

44. According to Maimonides, *tsadik verah lo* represents a case where the righteous man has temporarily lapsed in his closeness to God (*Guide* III:51). When this occurs the man's odds of having random misfortune

occur are increased. This explanation is consistent with a quantum mechanical picture. Alternatively, Maimonides and others reconcile *tsadik verah lo* by explaining that reward and punishment promised in the Bible refer to the world to come.

45. The reader may be wondering about the implications of quantum mechanics with regard to the conflict of free will and divine omniscience. In Pirkei Avot 3:15, R. Akiva states, "*hakol tsafoy veharshut netunah*," (everything is expected – but permission is given), reflecting the Rabbinic struggle with the ramifications of God's omniscience. Quantum mechanics, however, can be applied to this philosophical paradox as well. Using R. Akiva's language to analyze the conflict, the first clause can be taken to describe the concept that God has perfect knowledge of the initial superposition state. "*Veharshut netunah*," conveys that the wavefunction still has not collapsed, and thus multiple outcomes are still possible. Further direct analysis of free will and quantum mechanics will be explored in a subsequent essay.

46. Recent studies in pediatric endocrinology have shown that although the genotype determining gender may be determined early on, the phenotype occasionally can develop aberrantly, thus providing justification for gender related prayer during the second and third trimester of pregnancy. (see B. Ergun-Longmire et. al., *J. Ped. End. Met.*, "Clinical, Hormonal and Cytogenetic Evaluation of 46, xx Males and Review of the Literature," 18 (2005): 739–748). This reality does not contradict the essence of the Talmud's discussion in Berakhot, but merely emphasizes that the point of irreversible collapse is ambiguous and our perception of it will change with continued scientific knowledge; nevertheless, such a point does invariably exist.

Similarly, this reasoning can be used to explain the case given in Bava Metziah 42a, in the example of prayer before, during and after counting one's crop. Permission is given for praying for bounty before and during the counting but not after, since that would be a futile prayer. We may logically disagree with any allowance for prayer even before counting, since it is rational to assume that the crop was determined, albeit with unknown value, even immediately preceding the counting. From our vantage point, as well as from the perspective of the *mishnah* in Berakhot discussed earlier, determination of an event is the salient distinction, not knowledge of its determination. However, the anonymous author of this Talmudic statement in Bava Metziah may have felt otherwise about the timing of the onset of the crop's irreversible status. Thus, while we can disagree with where the

Talmud chooses to draw the temporal line designating the boundary for prayer, it is nevertheless, once again, most clearly drawing one based on its perception of irreversibility.

Furthermore, the gemara in Bava Metziah continues with a statement in the name of R. Yitzhak, that blessings can only be manifested in things that are "*samuy min ha'ayin*," (hidden from sight). Conceptually and even in choice of language, this philosophy is reminiscent of our quantum mechanical interpretation that Divine intervention can only occur in things that are hidden from sight, i.e. those that have not yet been observed.

47.   This recognition also can be used to provide additional reasoning behind the Talmudic discussion concerning up until which point a divine decree can be changed through *teshuvah*, repentance. One opinion in the Talmud states that once Yom Kippur has passed and the decree sealed, no amount of sacrifice and repentance can alter the decree (Rosh Hashanah 17b). The example is given that in the event that little rain has been decreed due to Israel's sins, God will not change the decree to one of plentiful rain even if the Jews repent. However, God could alter the effective outcome, albeit not the literal decree, by causing all the decreed rain to fall at a beneficial time. The Talmud struggles to define the parameters within which God alters His decrees, but clearly is of the opinion that certain limitations to divine intervention exist. Our quantum treatment, however, can perhaps, provide the missing rationale for why God would circumvent a decree rather than negate it. In this example of rainfall, collapse and decoherence governing the amount of rainfall could have already occurred; however, the particular details of its timing might still be undetermined defined by a superposition state.

48.   *Shulhan Arukh*, O.C. 230:2.

49.   This distinction can be used as an alternative reconciliation for several apparent contradictions in the Bible. For example, the verse in Deut. 15:4, "For there will never be a poor person among you," is immediately opposed by verse 15:7, "When you shall have a poor person among you." This conflict can be resolved by recognizing that the blessing describing the abolishment of poverty refers to a people governed by divine measurement. On the other hand, the verse describing the practical reality of prevalent poverty follows environmental wavefunction collapse.

50.   On Shabbat 156a, Rashi comments that prayer and meritorious actions can change one's fate for the better. See also Rosh Hashanah 17b–18a.

51.   *keri*, happenstance, derives from the same root, k – r – h, as *karkha* and *nikro nikreit*. See note 12 and accompanying text.

What's the Matter with Women?

GENDER IN THE THOUGHT OF MAHARAL OF PRAGUE[1]

Aryeh Bernstein

R abbi Yehudah ben Bezalel Loewe of Prague (1525–1609), known popularly by the acronym of his Hebrew name, Maharal, was one of the most prolific European Jewish thinkers of the Early Modern period, producing substantial works of legal rulings, comments on the Bible and Talmud, and themes in Jewish thought. Much scholarship has been devoted especially to his thought, locating him in his European cultural context as well as the development of Jewish intellectual history. One area which has received attention is his ideas about gender, with some scholars depicting Maharal as espousing an egalitarian conception of gender. It is our view that these scholarly discussions have not proceeded as systematically as they should, and have therefore yielded errors in understanding. In this article, we will attempt to explain how gender works for Maharal, not only in terms of statements about men and women, but as a theme which interacts with other themes of hierarchy, nature, and eschatology and often even guides those themes. After presenting the theory of complementarity of men and women which some scholars have proffered, we will problematize it by examining the ways the neo-Platonic categories of "form" and "matter", which Maharal applies to men and women respectively, operate throughout his thought. From there we will specifically explore the theme of dominance in Maharal's thinking about men and women and demonstrate how it plays out in socio-economic and sexual planes. Against this backdrop, we will investigate Maharal's ideas about the way the image of God is manifest in human beings and especially in men, revisit the theory of complementarity, and tease out the implications for Maharal's eschatological vision.

I. *The Theory of Complementarity of Man and Woman*

Certain statements of Maharal have led some scholars to imagine him to have an egalitarian conception of gender. For example:

> "Everything that God made in this world, He created in male and female pairs. For the male is form and the female is matter.... God couples them and binds them together" (GH, cap. 56, p. 249).

> "There is no reality more whole than the coupling of groom and bride, for man, even as he is the most whole of the lower creatures, does not have whole reality until he marries a woman.... Therefore, they said that when one rejoices for the groom and bride, it is as if he has offered a thanksgiving offering, for the groom and bride are a divided reality, for this is a man and that is a woman; therefore, they are completely divided, and their coupling is from God, who couples them and settles individuals together" (TY, cap. 30, p. 90).

Most prominently, Byron Sherwin describes male and female for Maharal as "complementary opposites":

> "The male is form; the female is matter. One cannot exist without the other...Man needs woman and woman needs

man…Apart, they are incomplete, bereft of all opportunity for perfection. Together, they are of a single essence. Together, they provide each other with an opportunity to realize the purpose of their individual essences. Pulling in separate directions, their existence can never truly be actualized. Only tension, disharmony, and imperfection would prevail. But pulling together toward their common goal they can achieve perfection."[2]

Sherwin distinguishes this category of complementary opposites in Maharal's thought from "contradictory opposites", which are "mutually exclusive", logically implying each other's existence, as form and matter, but requiring each other's obliteration. While he lists a number of examples of "contradictory opposites"[3] man and woman are his only example of "complementary opposites".

Even a cursory perusal at scattered statements of Maharal about men and women will suffice to make one raise an eyebrow at Sherwin's optimistic claim.[4] For example, we find that man has the high level – every high level having the qualities of fewness, smallness, and hiddenness – whereas woman has the quality of being revealed (TY, cap. 49, p. 153). The fact that women give birth indicates that they are physically weak, since giving birth involves a change for the woman – change being weak, soft, and malleable, as matter – while unchanging things are hard and strong, as form, exemplified by men (TY, cap. 49, p. 153). Women are whole inasmuch as they are human beings, but they are not as whole as the level of maleness (NY, cap. 48, p. 168–9). Women are physically uglier than men, since light pertains to the image of God (DH, pp. 143–44, on Avot 3:14)[5] and to the nonphysical, which is gendered male, while the more material something is, that is, female, the uglier it is (HA 3:35).[6] Women are intellectually inferior to men. Women have small mental capacity (TY, cap. 56, p. 167),[7] while men are spiritual-intellectual – "*sikhli*" (HA 2:38).

A mere listing of negative statements about women and femaleness and corresponding positive statements about men and maleness will not suffice, however, to illuminate the dynamics of gender in Maharal's thinking. Once we locate these dynamics within the larger context of Maharal's thought system, we will understand that the very same texts that scholars read to indicate equality actually testify to the intractably hierarchical relationship between maleness and femaleness. We will further find that gender maps out the other major dynamics in Maharal's conceptual tectonic and suggests his entire eschatology, which we will discover to be thoroughly androcentric.[8]

II. *Form (Tzurah) and Matter (Ḥomer)*

A. OVERVIEW

Maharal's dominant paradigm for the relationship between man and woman is that of form (*tzurah*) to matter (*ḥomer*). The philosophical centrality of this dyad goes back to Plato and Aristotle, but while this dyad is the dominant organizing principle of Maharal's thought, it functions differently there than in Aristotelian and medieval philosophy. For Maharal and other sixteenth century thinkers, these terms functioned not scientifically, as they did in medieval philosophy, but metaphysically: form is anything that perfects or brings about something else, while that which is perfected or brought about is matter. In this way, the terms always signify hierarchy in a binary relationship.[9] Yoram Jacobson well summarized the meanings of form and matter in Maharal's thought[10]:

> [Form and matter] no longer appear in his writings as objects of philosophical analysis in reality as it is, but as *conflicting, valued principles within a theological context*.... Matter, or the material, lacks actualized reality and, therefore, is a reduced and deficient reality.... Contrary to matter, form is whole and lacks nothing (NY, cap. 14, p. 83). The Maharal describes it as "an established thing"...and in it the principle of the order that rules the universe is revealed (GH, cap. 14, p. 70). In a certain sense, one may say that the form expresses the active divine principle, while matter represents the passive, receptive principle (NO NGH, cap. 4, p. 159), that changes and is acted upon.... God is the supreme formative principle of reality, the form of the world, the source of its order.... [F]orm is the "actor and king", while matter is subjugated under it and submissive to it. Therefore, "subservience is the domain of matter, and form is free" (GH, cap. 43, p. 162).... As opposed to matter, which is bad, since it is imprinted with lack and deficiency,

form embodies good, which "indicates that which is separated from the material"...(TY, cap. 12, p. 42).... Matter is the reality of subjugation, slavery, and exile, while form is a state of redemption.

B. FORM AND MATTER IN OTHER AREAS OF MAHARAL'S THOUGHT: A COMPARATIVE CASE-STUDY

The form-matter paradigm is not limited to describing the relationship of the sexes and, indeed, is a dominant axis in the Maharal's entire ontic taxonomy. Every binary pair is arranged hierarchically along this axis, including man-animals, Rabbi-community, father-children, Israel-the nations. Maharal asserts that "It is known that form is analogized to man and that to which it is form is analogized to female" (HA 1:135), suggesting that every form-matter binary pair should be understood in gendered terms, such that God-form is the "man" and Israel-matter is the "woman" in that relationship, Israel-form is the "man" and the nations-matter are the "woman" in that relationship, etc. Gender is a frame, then, perhaps even the frame *par excellence*, for understanding all hierarchical relationships of form-matter. Therefore, understanding what these concepts signify elsewhere in his world order should prove instructive toward our comprehension of his conceptions of gender.

As an example of the dynamics of form-matter elsewhere in Maharal's thought, we will examine Maharal's descriptions of Torah, a most central piece in his taxonomy. "The Torah, inasmuch as it is God's decree, does not relate to the material...; it has no material aspect whatsoever" (TY, cap. 12, p. 42). Regarding the use of the word "good" to describe Torah, in Proverbs 4:2, Maharal says, "The language of 'good' connotes that which is separated from the material and this is known, since that which cleave to the material are absence and lack, which are bad, and there is no doubt in this matter whatsoever" (*ibid.*). As the opposite of material, then, Torah is the paragon of form. An essential element of form is that it completes matter. Thus, Torah is form and completion to man[11], who is considered form and completion to the world (*ibid.*). Similarly, Israel is form to the whole world, for Israel completes everything (*ibid.*). Within the Jewish people, the ignoramus ('*am ha-'aretz*) is not spiritual-intellectual (*sikhli*), but only natural and material (NY, cap. 34, p. 156).

In these examples, we have seen man represent both form and matter; this highlights a crucial element of Maharal's thought structure: these identities are not absolute, but relational. The whole world is constructed of hierarchical layers in which one item may be matter relative to what is above it and form relative to what is below it.[12] Similarly, woman is not essentially form or matter: she is form as she relates to animals and matter as she relates to man, and so with all things in the physical world. For Maharal, and, indeed, for Neo-Platonists in general, this reality in relationships is neither psychological nor epistemological, but metaphysical (*ibid.*, 93).[13]

As we saw regarding Torah, form is good relative to matter. That women are matter (or "the receiver of form", BHG, Be'er 5, p. 95) and men are form and separate from the material, then, encodes a value hierarchy that regarding each other, men are good and women are bad. In these relationships, not only is the item that is form relative to its binary partner considered better than the one that is matter, but it is more *real*, as well, as masculine and form represent actuality while feminine and matter represent only potentiality (HA 3:107).[14] For example, God, the ultimate, eternal reality, is total, perfect form. For our theme, man=form=good is *more real* than woman=matter=bad. At the end of this article, we will return to consider what this means for Maharal's eschatological vision.

We have seen how Maharal imagines male and female to be thematized in the world and how that connects to other identities in the world and in the cosmos. We will now explore more fully how this plays out in the relationship between real men and women.

III. *The Relationship of Dominance between Man and Woman*

The identity of man toward woman is one of dominance. It is complementary only in the sense that since man needs to manifest that domination in order to be fully actualized, therefore, he needs to be in relationship to woman in order to be whole. It is entirely a mode of power assertion, through which form becomes fully realized as form by dominating, influencing and perfecting its corresponding matter. We will see that it is this exercise of dominating that actualizes the man's maleness as form and it is the fact of being dominated by the man-form that actualizes the women's femaleness as matter.

This power dynamic is actualized both on socio-economic and sexual planes of relation.

A. THE SOCIO-ECONOMIC PLANE: OWNER-PROPERTY

Maharal frames his discussions on the relationship between man and woman in the context of marriage.[15] In that context we will see that he understands the wife to be the property of her husband – less significant than his house and livelihood, but more significant than his other possessions. Maharal's basic perspective on the marital relationship is clear enough: "In the order of the world[16], woman is beneath her husband" (OH 107, on Esther 1:22).[17] The specific form for this hierarchy is that the wife is the property of her husband.[18] This is exemplified for Maharal in the Talmudic opinion on BT Nedarim 41a that lack of a wife is a comparable lack for a man as lacking sustenance for body and soul (HA 2:19), these paradigmatic of possessions in his interpretation. A man has many possessions, though, so the question remains where woman stands in the hierarchy of her husband's property. Maharal argues that, man, in his earthly life, is drawn more to woman than to other acquisitions, but from the perspective of his lofty potential (*ma'alat ha-adam*), according to *sekhel*, it more befits his dignity that his house take precedence. Maharal comments on the Ten Commandments' prohibition against coveting another man's wife or house, "Do not covet your neighbor's house; do not covet your neighbor's wife or his male slave or his female slave, or his ox, or his donkey, or anything of your neighbor's" (Exodus 20:14):

> "Scripture divided [the text], to specify 'Do not covet' [in reference both to house and woman][19], because it mentioned here all of the possessions. There is a separation between the possessions, because one possession can be the cause of the next, such as the house, which is the cause of all of the others, for if he has no house, he won't marry a woman, for where will he put the woman? He needs a house for her, in the way of the modest women, and all his possessions he puts in the house...Therefore, Scripture [elsewhere] first says, 'When you build a new house...' (Deuteronomy 22:8) and only afterward, 'When a man acquires a wife...' (*ibid.*, 13)" (TY 42, p. 130).

In the proper state of man's affairs, his house takes precedence over his wife. The house is his essential possession, the cause for all others, and the line of demarcation between public and private. His wife is an example of or even a paradigm for all of his other possessions, which are to be kept inside his house. His emphasis of the modesty of women recognizes and normatively undermines the possibility of a wife rebelling against her prescription in the house and identity with other movable property.

Maharal's point about the priority of house over wife is reflected by the language of the verse, which enumerates house before wife. However, when the Ten Commandments are repeated, in Deuteronomy 5, the order is reversed, listing wife before house. Maharal rallies this apparent countertext to bolster his point: this and all other differences between the two sets of the Ten Commandments are explained by a simple genre difference between Deuteronomy and the first four books of the Torah. Whereas the first four books of the Bible reflect the perspective of the Giver of Torah, God, Deuteronomy embodies the perspective of the receiver of Torah, man. Therefore, in Deuteronomy, "From the side of the receiver, material man, obviously the woman takes precedence for man" (TY, cap. 45, p. 138), whereas the opposite order presides in Exodus: "from the side of the loftiness and honor that are in spiritual-intellectual man, who is no longer material, house precedes woman" (*ibid.*). Base, material man values his wife more than his house, but truly actualized, spiritual man of form invests greater value in his house.

Maharal's exegesis of a Talmudic passage will illustrate this point. "R. Yose asked Elijah the Prophet, 'It is written, 'I will make him a helpmate' (Gen. 2:18), but in what way is woman a helpmate to man?' He replied, 'When a man brings wheat, does he eat wheat? Flax, does he wear flax? Doesn't she brighten his eyes and stand him up on his feet?'" (BT Yev. 63a). The simplest understanding of this passage would be that woman is the helpmate for man, *par excellence*, because only she enables man to function in his world and to utilize its raw materials. Maharal, however, flips this meaning on its head: "With his livelihood she is man's helpmate, for a person is lacking in his livelihood, since livelihood is above everything" (HA 1:135). Since woman is helpmate to man only in that she enables him to use the world's materials, therefore, it is those materials that are the ultimate helpmates of man and woman is secondary to them, as a vessel is of subsidiary importance to the goods it contains.

Wife occupies a lower rung on the ladder of property than a house does, but this is only to the extent that a wife is property. Maharal affirms that woman is not entirely property and has a non-material element that other property lacks. "There is a great difference and separation between them, because woman fully attaches to man and she is his completion, whereas the other things are merely acquisitions" (TY, cap. 45, p. 138). Therefore, the Deuteronomic Decalogue uses a different term for the prohibition of "coveting" one's neighbor's wife (*taḥmod*) than it does with other possessions (*tit'avveh*). Maharal asserts that the former – which is the word used in Exodus for everything – is a less materially-oriented word than the latter, signifying woman's less material essence than that of other property (*ibid.*).

Is one's wife, then, lower or higher than his other property? The resolution of this problem lies in the difference between livelihood and proliferation of property. For Maharal, the former is of deep, spiritual significance, while the latter is lowly and material. Regarding the "*ta'avah*" (lust) for possessions in the Deuteronomy Decalogue, he specifies that "lust for a thing, which is *proliferation* of possessions, is a material lusting" (*ibid.*, my emphasis). The Exodus Decalogue, by contrast, uses the term *taḥmod* for both wife and other property, because the commandments assume the perspective of the sublime, where wife, indeed, is beneath house and that which it represents. For Maharal, a man's wife is secondary to his livelihood, but not as lowly as proliferation of property. In order to understand what separates material woman from other material things for Maharal, we will now turn our attention to her status in relation to her husband in sex.

B. THE SEXUAL PLANE:
MALE DOMINANCE AS NATIONAL DESTINY

For Maharal, we will see that the sexual relationship between man and woman fundamentally gives expression to man's domination and subjugation of woman, a dynamic that is for her benefit as it fulfills her essential place in the natural order. How this plays out in an individual couple's sexual relationship takes on cosmic significance since for Maharal, this sexual dynamic of domination is a microcosm for the divinely-charged geopolitical destiny of Israel and the nations.

Maharal takes for granted that the man is essentially active and the woman passive in coitus (GA 3:118). This much is a Rabbinic commonplace. Maharal extends this point to explain that legal reasoning would indicate that women should, in principle, be exempt from liability for sexual transgressions, "since she is *qarqa' 'olam* (Sanhedrin 74b)[20] and does no action." This, he explains, is why the Torah had to mention explicitly that women are liable for such sins (GA 3:118). She is passive in the encounter, but responsible for it. It is instructive to look to another context to flesh out the meaning of the active/passive binary for the Maharal. Regarding charity, Maharal writes the following:

> "One who gives charity, in that he influences others, cleaves to God in his influencing the other. God is called 'Source of life', who constantly influences existing things and does not cease this influence.... [One should give charity] at every time that he can influence, for in that he resembles his Creator, who constantly influences" (NO NHTz cap. 2, p. 171).

If active influence = Godly, then man's active relationship on passive woman is thematized as *imitatio Dei*. This Godly role is one of dominance and power wherein the one influenced is degraded by being influenced: "There is a degree of disgrace to one who receives charity, because he has lacking/*ḥisaron* (*ibid.*).

Maharal goes well beyond the familiar assumption of male activity and female passivity in that he encases the ideal dynamic of marriage in one forged by rape. The Torah teaches that a man who rapes an unbetrothed woman is obligated to marry her and is prohibited from ever divorcing her (Deut. 22:28–29). In its own patriarchal context, the Torah's point is to troubleshoot: since the woman has been victimized and her value on the marriage market lowered, she is vulnerable to a life abandoned, without financial support or protection, so the Torah makes the rapist responsible for providing for her eternally. Maharal, however, reads this not as *post facto* protection, but as the strongest form of marriage. Marriage is meant to be eternal and this is the only example of marriage that by law must be eternal. Therefore, marriage out of necessity – the rape marriage – is marriage *par excellence.* In justifying the compulsion through which the Torah was given at Sinai,[21] he comments that "Any necessary coupling and union has no undoing or turning back, such as regards one who rapes a woman" (TY, cap. 32, p. 94). Further,

> "When one rapes a woman, such that the union is from the side of the form, that is, the man…then this union will have eternal existence…because this union is from the side of the form, and not like a union that is from the side of the woman, for the woman, too, is a receiver, and a receiver has changeability, for every receiver is from the side of the material, which has changeability" (TY, cap. 51, p. 158).

Maharal encodes rape as the forger of the ideal marriage, one which is absolutely eternal and contingent on nothing, such that the eternality of rape-created marriage serves as the emblem for Sinai, the ultimate strong covenant: God raped Israel so that Israel could not get out of the relationship.[22] Read against the backdrop of his comment that "the essence of why the Torah gave woman to man is for the good of the woman" (HA 4:164), a sexual ideal emerges in which a husband rapes his wife for her sake, to do her the service of binding her to him eternally, with no out. This is a relationship of subjugation through dependence: just as Israel is subjugated to and dependent on God, just as the receiver of charity is subjugated to and dependent on the giver, so, too, the wife is subjugated to and dependent on her husband. It is true both that the dependent position in this relationship is degraded and that it benefits from the degradation. This is not an internal contradiction for Maharal: the lower position of the material, subjugated party is a given fact, intrinsically true in its place in the order of the world; the point made on top of that is that the lofty party of form helps her (this lower party is gendered as female) by influencing her.[23]

Maharal is aware that a given woman might not enjoy or choose this kind of relationship. "Beneficial" does not necessary equal "desired" for the subjugated party. He makes his comment that "the essence of why the Torah gave woman to man is for the good of the woman" on the statement in BT Niddah 31b explaining that the reason the Torah requires a woman to bring a sin-offering after giving birth is that in the pains of birthing she swore not to return to sexual relations with her husband. That is, the Talmud posits the personal undesirability of the sexual relationship from the woman's perspective. When Maharal says there that a marriage of dominance is good for the woman, he does not mean to make an empirical observation that women in the world prefer it. He means that it is good for her *in spite of the fact that she may well not prefer it*, just as the Torah is good for Israel even though Jews often find it burdensome and choose not to follow it. Indeed, he opines that "one who influences enjoys influencing more than the receiver enjoys receiving" (HA 4:24).[24] His comment that only doing good for another can be called pleasure/benefit (HA 3:35) suggests an assumption that even regarding the physical act itself, only men and not women find it pleasurable, since, through the act, the husband acts on and, therefore, does good to, his wife.[25] Since she is not influencing him at all, she can derive no pleasure. According to Maharal, in sex men subjugate women and that subjugation is good for women.

For Maharal, the husband-wife relationship is not merely a dynamic between two persons localized in their familial unit, but emblematizes the state of the world in relation to its ultimate redemption. Just as he describes the relationship between God and Israel in terms of a husband-wife dynamic, he similarly maps Israel and the nations onto the axis of husband/wife. There is an important difference, though. Unlike the God-Israel relationship, in which God is firmly encoded as the husband and Israel as the wife, the battles between Israel and the nations are specifically struggles over who will be the husband and who the wife. In their unredeemed, exilic relationship, the nations are the husband and Israel the wife, such that when she no longer pleases him, he divorces her (NY, cap. 18, p. 93). He refers here to the Jews' hostile treatment at the hands of the fickle nations, who expel them from their lands whenever they tire of them. However, this portrait describes only the contemporary, exilic state of affairs, but not the true order of the world. According to the latter, Israel is the man and the nations are the woman. If a man is meritorious, he rules over his wife and so shall it be for Israel in its natural, redeemed state.

> "Israel with the nations is like the level of man with woman, regarding which is written, 'and he shall rule over you'

(Gen. 3:16). However, if the man is not meritorious, then the woman rules over her husband and so it is, God forbid, if Israel is not meritorious, then the nations rule over them…. The nations become the males and Israel's strength weakens like a female" (GA 5:118).

C. SAVING SEX BY SPIRITUALIZING IT

Maharal's neo-Platonism presents him with two problems when it comes to sex. Since men are form, which is spiritual-intellectual, and women are matter, which is physical, then shouldn't women, and not men, control sex, which is physical? This highlights a more fundamental problem: since spiritual/intellectual form is good and physical matter is bad, shouldn't sex, as the most physical of acts, be understood as bad? This, indeed, is the dominant perspective of the earlier and contemporary philosophers and theologians whose traditions he shared and against whom he polemicizes.[26] Maharal treats these problems in his comments on a series of 'aggadot thematically organized around sexuality and the construction of the male body on BT Bava Metzia 84a. His comments are found in almost identical form in HA 3:32–5 and BHG, *Be'er* 5, p. 92 and following. We will see that Maharal maintains both the positive, Rabbinic attitude toward sex and his neo-Platonic values by making a single assertion that solves both of the aforementioned problems and erects a frame for a number of other dyads that order the hierarchy of the world. Sex, when performed correctly – with proper, male dominance – is, in fact, not really physical, but spiritual and driven by God.

Maharal polemicizes against the popular view that sex in general is base and degrading, mainly on account of the necessity of sex for procreation. He emphasizes that in its essence, there is nothing "bad"[27] in the union between a man and his wife, but because man often engages in it to feed material lust, the sacred act is sullied (HA 3:32). In essence, he agrees with his interlocutors, who devalue things carnal; Maharal saves sex by spiritualizing it. ("*They* are talking about the 'bad' sex; *I* am talking about the 'good' sex!") Sex to feed lust is bad; sex to procreate is good. As we will see below, even better than that is sex to exercise influence and domination of the man over the woman. Moreover, by describing "bad" sex as "material", of which female is emblematic in his thinking, women become implicated in all that is base in sex, while a redemptive future should be imagined in which actualized man can redeem spiritual sex by fully dominating it. It bears recalling here that the best and truest form of marriage for Maharal is one forged through rape.

Maharal develops his idea of spiritual sex in his comment on a Talmudic story in which a matron challenges the ability of two obese rabbis to have sexual relations with their wives.[28] One retort, "love pushes the flesh", seems to mean in context that their sexual prowess can overcome the physical barriers that flesh erects before these obese would-be lovers.[29] By contrast, Maharal spiritualizes this carnal statement, decoding "love" as referring to the Divine characteristic in heterosexual coupling, which, by virtue of being from God, can overcome the physical obstacles. The alternate retort offered by the gemara, "like the man is his 'might'" reads contextually as male bravado, the rabbi bragging that his penis is enormous in proportions to his obesity, so that his fat doesn't get in the way of his sexual performance. Maharal inverts and even undermines this by adding one element, namely, that the penis's strength is spiritual. Since its power is from the soul, it spiritually overcomes the physicality of the flesh to enable intercourse:

> "For this limb is, itself, the difference between man and woman [and] is given a special strength that it is not physical, like other limbs, and it rules and pushes with the power of the might given to it, until it finishes its task" (*ibid.*).

Instead of meaning that his penis is super-large, such that it overcomes the obesity, the statement means that his penis is supercharged spiritually. The penis always has to overcome the latent physicality in sex in order to spiritualize it. The flip side of the assertion, of course, is that the woman's role in sex is entirely physical, since she lacks the spiritualizing tool, which, the reader recalls, is "*the* difference between man and woman". Maharal has his cake and eats it, too. Sex may be physical, but since the penis is spiritual, the more it exerts its control, the more it spiritualizes sex. The man earns sexual superiority while not being sullied as "physical" or "material" and becomes more and more Godly the more he dominates sex.

Maharal's cosmology of male, physical domination comes into sharper relief in his discussion of anal sex (BHG, cap. 2, p. 36), which the Talmud (BT Sanhedrin 58b) permits, but which he claims that Gentiles deride as base, leading them to attack Judaism. Maharal justifies it by explaining that there are two dimensions to sexual relations between man and woman. In the first, sex for reproduction, human beings are like the rest of the animal kingdom, and this aspect is achieved only through vaginal intercourse. The second dimension is manifesting the completion of man. Just as man is the completion for the rest of creation, man, form, needs to be completed by material woman. He achieves this completion, apparently, through his sexual use of his material wife. "Since man is considered as form to woman, everything is from him, and any way he uses her is permitted to him", as evidenced by the gemara he cites in which Rabbi analogizes marital sex to a man buying meat from the butcher: it is his and he may consume it any way he likes (BT Nedarim 20b). Maharal goes on to explain that there are two ways for form to relate to matter. Sometimes it connects by imprinting itself into the matter and sometimes it remains separate from it. Emblematic of the first – the lower of the two – is vaginal intercourse, while anal intercourse is emblematic of the second. The latter mode is higher, because the form becomes complete through molding its matter without actually being affected by it. Since the sacred state of affairs is for form to dominate matter – that is, for the husband to dominate his wife – anal sex is not base, but exalted and spiritual.

This is not a mere expression of preference for how the world should function. At stake is the enterprise of world-making, that is, allowing the universe to exist as fully as possible. It is the way of the world for that which is separate to act on the matter (GH, cap. 40, p. 150). Recall our discussion above that *imitatio Dei* is accomplished through manifesting dominance over others in influencing them. Here, since anal sex influences without being influenced at all in return, it is higher and more Godly than vaginal influence, through which the man does influence the woman, but is somewhat influenced by her in return. Furthermore, "Matter has no reality and even form that is imprinted in reality does not have complete reality" (NO NHT, cap. 12, p. 51). When a husband has anal sex with his wife, because he fully expresses dominance and control over her without being influenced by her in turn, he more fully manifests his own reality – his unique man-ness, which is his form-identity.

The consequence of this dynamic is the disappearance of the female/material from the world, such that since the whole purpose of sex as dominating matter has been transcended, the world to come is a sexless, homosocial reality. In this light, Maharal explains that David and Jonathan's love is greater than the love of man for woman:

> "The love of man for woman is because they are 'one flesh'
> (Bereishit 2:24)…and the love and connection in being
> one flesh is not as great as love of friends whose souls are
> bound to each other…because unity/oneness is not as per-
> tinent to flesh as it is to souls, which connect completely"
> (DH 5:17, pp. 261–62).

Woman being subsumed into man is equivalent to mankind being subsumed into God: God is total form;[30] earthly, masculine form subsuming all matter means that the entire world is form, that is, Godly. A hint at this in the earthly world was Moses, who, in his essence, was separated from the material. Therefore, "only he separated from woman and was called 'man of God'" (TY, cap. 12, p. 42).

IV. The Image of God in the Maleness of Man

We have seen that for Maharal, in dominating women sexually, men become more real, which is to say, more realized in their true essence as form. We also suggested the ways in which this dynamic emblemizes or prefigures man's identity with God, who, as the Form of all forms, is to dominate and subsume the entire world. We will now directly address this theme of the theological implications of Maharal's gender tectonic, specifically noting that for Maharal, dominating women sexually manifests the "image of God" in men.

We saw above that Maharal understands the penis to be spiritually charged. This notion is pregnant with implications for his cosmology. He states that the penis is the completion of the man, and, as the physical end of the body, which the whole body faces (HA 3:34), its *piece de resistance*, since "the completion is more essential than anything" (*ibid.*)[31]. Through the penis a man is considered on the way to being actualized (*be-fo'al*)[32], since through it man is recognizable as man, and not woman, making him form, which is the epitome of full actualization (*ibid.*).[33] The BHG version pushes the envelope further. After explaining how the penis actualizes man, Maharal adds enigmatically, "And when you understand this, you will understand the level of the image of God in man" (BHG, *Be'er* 5, p. 95).

Yoram Jacobson has provided us the key to deciphering this enigmatic statement in his superb, thorough treatment of the image of God in Maharal's thought.[34] First of all for Maharal is that the image of God is not a physical image of God – there can be no such thing – nor is it, as Maimonides claimed, man's intellectual capacity. Rather, the physical world is like clothing for the separate, Divine world and, accordingly, the "image of God" is a physical reflection, appropriate to the physical world, of the separate, non-physical, Divine reality.[35]

The essential Divine quality manifest in man's physical being is God's domination over all, reflected in man's upright stature. When man comes to depict God,

> "Who is king of over all, and has no [physical] presence, he will depict an upright picture, even though, one cannot, God forbid, give any image depiction of Praised God.... Nevertheless, what is found in the Holy One is depicted in physical man, whose creation is in uprightness, and not like the rest of the living creatures, which walk bent over, for one who walks bent over shows that he has a master over him...but Praised God has none over Him. Therefore, it is said about man, who is upright, that he is in the image of God" (DH, p. 142).[36]

The image of God is the quality of domination and mastery: as God is over the whole universe, so is man over the world, as emblematized through his physical uprightness.[37] This, in turn, clarifies what Maharal means when he says that the penis's actualization of man demonstrates his embodiment of the divine image. We saw above that the Maharal understands any active influencing of a passive other to be *imitatio Dei*. The penis is a man's tool of active influence on his wife, especially when it is empowered to act sexually, that is, erect. The erection is an extra manifestation of mankind's erect posture that, accordingly, represents power and domination. This is precisely the implication of saying that the penis defines man as man and form, as opposed to woman and matter, and explains why it exemplifies the image of God that is in man and not woman.[38]

v. *Complementarity Revisited*

The next step should be to consider the place of gender in Maharal's eschatology, that is, where this all leads. Lest we fall into myopic oversight or vertiginous acontextuality in making that jump, let us briefly review our beginnings and take stock of where we are. I opened this article with the following passage from Maharal: "Everything that God made in this world, He created in male and female pairs. For the male is form and the female is matter.... God couples them and binds them together" (GH, cap. 56, p. 249). This is how Byron Sherwin quoted the passage in presenting his concept of man and woman as complementary opposites. Unfortunately, this excerpt is too fragmentary to provide a proper sense of Maharal's point. A fuller citation of the same passage will demonstrate that the sole text that Sherwin brought to demonstrate his idea of complementarity much more supports the hierarchical model I have proffered:

> "'Everything that God made in this world, He created in male and female' (BT Bava Batra 74b). For the male is form and the female is matter and this thing is known, and matter is nothing but beginning, for form is wholeness of existence and there is no existing thing in the world that is not from matter and form, and The Praised One couples them and binds them together. And their binding is an issue all its own.... Behold, there are three facets: one is matter, the second is form, the third from the side of the binding of matter and form...[and] matter is called beginning and form is called end-goal and completeness, and the binding of matter and form is something other than the two parts...." (GH, cap. 56, p. 249).

Man and woman are complementary inasmuch as unity is achieved only through their coupling, which is divine. Nevertheless, man's encoding as form, end-goal, and completeness and woman's encoding as matter and beginning locks them in an intractable hierarchy. Sherwin errs in failing to grasp Maharal's identification of man (i.e., humankind) as man (i.e., male), which precludes complementarity of the egalitarian sort that Sherwin seems to promote. This equation makes the following sentence of Maharal's difficult to translate, but revelatory for the gendered nature of humankind: "*Ha-'adam...lo niqra' 'adam 'ela' kesheyesh lo zug 'imo, she-ne'emar, 'zakhar u-neqevah bara' 'otam'* [Genesis 1:27] *va-yiqra shemam 'adam*" (GA 1:15). I render it as follows: "Man is called man only when he has a partner with him, as it is said, 'male and female He created them' and He called their name man." This Adam is not an androgyne, although he does encompass both sexes. Rather, man reaches fullness – man becomes fully man – when he attaches woman to himself, subsuming her in his identity. Man is not fully fit to perform his purpose in the world without a woman to complement him, while woman has no purpose in the world, other than to enhance man's (to be understood both as "the male" and as "humanity") achievement of his purpose by existing under and submitting to his domination.[39]

Haggai Ben-Artzi argues that Maharal posits a three-staged chronological process running through form-matter relationships, beginning with a stage of ascetic withdrawal from things material, elevating to a level of harmonic balance between them, and culminating with the accomplishment of purifying and sanctifying matter.[40] Ben-Artzi proposes a more nuanced and correct read than Sherwin, but repeats Sherwin's error in perceiving there to be a stage of harmonic balance. Ben-Artzi correctly understands Maharal to view ascetic separation from matter as a necessary, but immature stage, while placing highest value in sanctifying the material and subsuming it into the spiritual. However, he missteps in his construction of the middle stage, which should not exist at all and should, instead, be understood as part of the third stage, of purifying and sanctifying matter. In chapter three of *Netiv Ha-Torah*, Maharal writes that "*Sekhel* is called man to the body". Ben-Artzi correctly explains that "if so, relations between man and woman are the model" for the relationship between *sekhel* and body:

"'For *sekhel* is the father to all of man's abilities and guides them as a father raises his children' [NO NHT, cap. 3,

p. 15] – relations between a father and his children are the second image. What is the meaning of these images? *It is clear* that the removal or annulment of matter is not intended, if matter is like woman vis-à-vis her husband or like children vis-à-vis their father. The task of a good husband or the ideal father is to 'rule over his family and to give each one of his family members the portion fit for him' [*ibid.*].…. What is reflected here, *without a doubt*, is the ideal of harmony and balance as the purpose of man's moral service."[41]

According to his own framework, he should read this text as a "stage 3" text, not "stage 2". For Maharal, lining up *sekhel* with husband/father and body with wife/children hardly reflects harmony, at least not if we define "harmony" as distinct from the "sanctification" of Ben-Artzi's stage three. Maharal's man functions schematically the same way whether as husband or as father and completes himself through exercising dominion over his wife and children, who are schematically identical to each other.[42] In these and other contexts, a figure of form "purifies the material" by subsuming and subjugating it.

VI. *The Eschatology of Gender*
The role of men, then, is to dominate and subjugate women, which expresses the ultimate cosmic purpose of all form to dominate and subjugate matter, which, in so doing, manifests the image of God, who is entirely form. We will now explore where this central theme of Maharal's thought is meant to lead and what it means with regard to the trajectory and endpoint of the cosmos. We will see that for Maharal, the eschatological purpose of the universe is for the world to return to the state of total form, to be achieved via form's total subjugation of matter such that matter becomes entirely subsumed until all that is left is form. Gender will be a dominant axis along which to understand this process.

"Even though opposites (*haphahim*) oppose (*mitnaggedim*) each other from their own perspectives, nevertheless, when the opposites are together, they complete the whole and

96

for this, they connect together in order to complete the whole…Don't argue that this applies only to opposites like fire and water, each of which is considered reality, but that it does not apply to opposites of which one is considered good and the other bad. This is not the case, for, of course, even if it is evil and not reality, nevertheless, the two of them complete the whole, for it, too, is a necessity of creation…Opposites have one source, for reality is not divided; that is why opposites come from each other, for they have deep oneness/unity, for they complete each other to be without lack, for when there is a thing and its opposite, nothing further lacks. That is what oneness/unity is all about: nothing lacks. The process of reuniting is to return to God, the Actor, who is One and has all" (GH cap. 5, pp. 35–36).

For Maharal, it is man's nature that "he cannot reach wholeness in this world, and he always has to be given to a process of becoming whole, of departing from potential to actualization."[43] The mechanism for this process is that God creates a thing and its opposite and brings them together in unity wherein they return to God, who is their singular, unified source. The obvious question is: Why did God do it this way? If God manifests perfect unity, which is ultimately good and is the final eschatological destiny of the created world, why did God create the world fractured? Maharal's answer is that to do it otherwise would have been philosophically impossible. The created, by virtue of being a receiver, cannot be a complete creation.[44] One created thing must be accompanied by its opposite in order to be a complete creation, for they connect to each other. The Actor of all connects His created to its opposite, from which it would otherwise be separate. This plays out on the dimension of gender as follows: God creates man. "Man", here, signifies "male human" in the initial phase of creation and "mankind, embodied as male human elevated" in the end of days. For man to be able to achieve his eschatological destiny, to become more fully form and more Godly, he must have an opposite to dominate and subsume. This is woman. At the earliest, rawest stage of nature, woman dominates the relationship, as evidenced by her bringing life into being and providing it sustenance through nursing. Man's origin as child parallels this development, since children are, schematically speaking, women.[45] In a more mature stage of development, man conquers and controls woman. This is the state of affairs in our adult world. Eventually, man subsumes woman to the point of her phenomenological evaporation from the world; thereby man and woman, the opposites, are "united" – inseparable within his triumphant and exalted identity. So has the created being fulfilled its mission to be whole and Godly.[46] This basic theme of moving from a fractured, sullied state to a unified, divine state frames all other eschatological trajectories, including the journey from lack of understanding to understanding, from sin to repentance, and from exile to redemption.[47] As Rivka Schatz summarized it, "[t]he undoing of the corporeality of matter is the eschatological vision which underlies the entire 'order of existence' and opens the door to an eschatology of being."[48]

This eschatological vision fulfills a return to the beginning, before divine unity was ruptured through creation. As such, the process of the eschatology is already imprinted in Maharal's conception of the creation of the world, which is for him also a process of unification of the divine will with the created beings, striving toward completion.[49] The seed must rot in order to grow.

He develops this scheme in his comments on a Talmudic passage on how God spent the first day of creation, which tells that God culminated the primordial day playing with the Leviathan. (HA 4:22–26). Maharal specifically emphasizes that

> "It is not the way of the land to play with the female, because God, Praised be He, has no connection to the female, who is considered on the level of material, because He, may He be praised, is holy and separate from the issue of matter, so playing, which is connection, is not fitting between God, Praised be He, and the female" (HA 3:107).[50]

Why can't God play with the female? That is, why can't the holy connect to matter? This would be impossible; such a union would destroy the world (HA 3:106).[51] Creation, foreshadowing the eschaton, is a process of unification whose end demands disengagement with the material, arriving to a state of pure form. The goal of creation is to transcend the female; so should the physical, material female be transcended at the end of days. In differentiating the "fourth kingship" from the future, messianic, Davidic kingship, Maharal writes that the fourth kingship relates only to the physical world, whereas the future kingship will not relate to physical matters whatsoever (NY, cap. 18, p. 93). Similarly, in the world to come, there will be a total removal of the physical and souls will no longer be cast in bodies (*ibid.*, cap. 32, pp. 148–49).[52]

VII. *Conclusion*

We have seen throughout this study essentially one theme, repeated along many different particular channels, all gendered. God is unified form and seeks to manifest that in the world. Therefore, God chooses earthly beings who, on their respective planes, embody the most form they can, and connects them with their material opposites whom they should dominate into subsumed oblivion, a process through which form reunites them within God and actualizes them as fully real/fully male. The sexual connection God makes vis-à-vis man and woman is phenomenologically the same as God having Israel conquer its enemies and ultimately live free of them. This, for example, explains Maharal's hierarchy within methods of sexual intercourse and why he maps that onto the fault line of Israel and the nations.

Scholarship of the past generation has demonstrated that the Renaissance did not herald the equality of the sexes that earlier scholars had claimed. Maharal of Prague's intellectual legacy should be viewed as largely of a kind with his European context and his place in Jewish gender studies should be viewed as significant and problematic. For Maharal, there is a Promised Land of gender and that Promised Land is male.

WORKS CITED

All citations from the writings of Maharal are from the edition published by "Yahadut" in Jerusalem, 1970–72. I have cited page numbers from that edition and have included chapter numbers in order to enable looking up citations in other editions, as well. Following is the guide to abbreviations I have used in citing Maharal's works.

BHG	*Be'er Ha-Golah*
DH	*Derekh HaḤayyim*
GA	*Gur Aryeh*
GH	*Gevurot Hashem*
HA	*Ḥiddushei 'Aggadot*
NGH	*Netiv Gemilut Ḥasadim*
NHT	*Netiv Ha-Torah*
NHTz	*Netiv Ha-Tzedaqqah*
NKY	*Netiv Koah Ha-Yetzer*
NO	*Netivot 'Olam*
NY	*Netzah Yisra'el*
OH	*'Or Ḥadash*
TY	*Tif'eret Yisra'el*

NOTES

1. A draft of this paper was originally written for Prof. Alan Brill's course "The thought of Rabbi Yehudah Loew" at Yeshiva University's Bernard Revel Graduate School, spring 2002. I thank Prof. Bill for his helpful comments and for sharing with me a draft of his paper, "Maharal as an Early Modern Thinker," subsequently published in *Kabbalah* 17 (2008).

2. Byron L. Sherwin, *Mystical Theology and Social Dissent: The Life and Works of Judah Loew of Prague* (Rutherford, Madison, Teaneck: Farleigh Dickinson University Press, 1982), 71.

3. *Ibid.*, 72 and 209, footnote 9.

4. Sherwin's view should be understood in the context of scholarship on the Renaissance. Most (in)famously, Jacob Burckhardt wrote in *The Civilization of the Renaissance in Italy* (1860), 292, that "we must keep before our minds the fact that women stood on a footing of perfect equality with men." For more examples of this regnant view nearly a century later, see Joan Kelly, "Did Women Have a Renaissance?", *Women, History, and Theory* (Chicago: The University of Chicago Press, 1984), 47, footnote 1. Mid-20th century historians of the Jewish Renaissance viewed the period accordingly. Cecil Roth, while backing off from Burckhardt's "too sweeping" summation, did describe the Italian Renaissance as "from certain points of view an age of feminine

emancipation, in life if not in law.... and it was inevitable that this structure of society should be reflected in Jewish life as well." He, thus, described the Jewish Italian Renaissance as something of an "anticipation of the movement for the emancipation of women, at least in the social sense" (quoted in the Adelman passage below).

This view has fallen out of favor with contemporary historians of the early modern period. Howard Adelman refers to this view as a "mistaken notion that there was a liberating quality to the Renaissance", "Rabbis and Reality: Public Activities of Jewish Women in Italy during the Renaissance and Catholic Restoration," *Jewish History* (5:1, Spring 1991), 28. Joan Kelly has perhaps the most sweeping formulation of the dominant contemporary position among historians of the early Modern period: "there was no renaissance for women – at least, not during the Renaissance", 19.

Both Adelman and Kelly studied Italy, and not Bohemia. Nevertheless, the considerable cultural traffic across European national boundaries during the early Modern period indicates the relevance to our topic of their observations, both of the period and of earlier scholarship on it. Throughout *Be'er Ha-Golah*, Maharal refers to claims of European Gentile thinkers, though he does not quote them by name. He does quote and take issue with dominant Jewish, Italian thinkers who were explicitly involved with Gentile counterparts, such as Yehudah Messer Leon, who was a teacher of Pico della Mirandola. As for our topic, it seems that gender roles and identity in different locales in early Modern Europe were of a kind regarding major themes and trends.

5.   For a full treatment of the significance of light as the image of God and the implications thereof, see Yoram Jacobson, "Tzelem Elohim u-ma'amado ke-maqor ra'ato shel adam lephi ha-Maharal mi-Prague," *Da'at* 19 (1987), especially 108 and 122–24.

6.   Since woman is, by definition, material, for Maharal, how is it that a woman can be beautiful? He explains this as occurring solely on the spiritual merits of her father (NY, cap. 7, p. 50).

7.   Furthermore, when Maharal introduces the problem of Talmudic passages that seem silly and irrelevant, he says that they appear to uninformed readers as "like the words that old women speak", (BHG, *Be'er* 5, p. 88).

8.   Before delving into the body of the article, I will place one important caveat on Maharal's negative portrayal of woman and womanhood. We seem to find in his writings no castigation of women as seductresses or

whores – the dominant misogynist theme in early Modern, European culture, as well as a common theme in medieval Jewish thought. Regarding this theme in early Modern, European culture, see Merry E. Wiesner's (1993) discussion of the cultural encoding of honor as associated with sexual propriety for women, regardless of their class, and the evidence to support this from records of legal suits for defamation, Merry E. Wiesner, *Women and Gender in Early Modern Europe* (Cambridge, England: Cambridge University Press, 1993), 34. See also her comments on the cultural association of women's public expression with sexual dishonor (*ibid.*, 160). Accordingly, Lyndal Roper notes that participants in the Protestant Reformation vilified Catholic priests as whores of the devil, "women of the most lustful kind," Lyndal Roper, *Oedipus and the Devil: Witchcraft, Sexuality, and Religion in Early Modern Europe* (London and New York: Routledge, 1994), 43.

Though Maharal's thinking, including on gender, in many respects reflects Early Modern European ideas, as far as I can tell he does not denigrate women or womanhood as being defined by harlotry or seduction. Even in a passage in which the opportunity is golden to make such a claim, he specifically does not do so. In HA 2:37–38, discussing the snake of Eden, he comments that the snake is "the lack and absence of man...for every creature of lust is a creature of lacking". The gemara on which he is commenting compares an adulteress to the snake and in this context, Maharal describes wanting that which is not one's own as lack, because one who is whole need not seek other things. In many places, Maharal describes lacking as an existential quality that is emblematic of women. He also describes lust and want as chipping away at man's inherent separateness and wholeness. "Man is created lacking and every lacking is bad and therefore, he constantly yearns after evil, but the evil inclination cannot rule over one who is whole and not lacking". (NO NKY, cap. 2, p. 124 and Binyamin Ish-Shalom, "Tanin, Leviathan, ve-Nahash – Liphsharo shel Motiv Aggadi," *Da'at* 19 (1987), 99–101.) In light of all this, one would expect Maharal to describe all women as adulteresses who all want that which is not theirs – form.

Nevertheless, not only does Maharal not identify the snake with woman, but he explicitly contrasts the snake to woman. Man and the snake are completely opposite of each other in that they are two poles of form (*sekhel* and *ratzon*) that have the same matter – woman (HA 2:38). I have no explanation for this enigma, which merits further research. Of particular interest would be whether European Jewish thinkers roughly contemporary with Maharal emphasize the trope of women as seductresses or whores. I do note further in this paper that Maharal incriminates women more than men with that which is base in sex.

9. Alan Brill, "Maharal as an Early Modern Thinker," *Kabbalah* 17 (2007, pp. 49–73).

10. Jacobson, 112–13. I have incorporated Jacobson's citations of Maharal's writings into the body of the quotation, consistent with the format of this paper.

11. I intentionally use the word "man" here to refer to humanity. Because Maharal maintains the androcentric assumption humankind is normatively gendered male, this language will most precisely capture and, therefore, allow us to critique, the dynamics of Maharal's thought.

12. See Brill on this. It seems to me that this feature of hierarchical relativity can be best understood within the context of Maharal's general view of the relativity of human perspective. Tamar Ross, "Ha-nes ke-mei-mad nosaph ba-haguto shel ha-Maharal mi-Prague", *Da'at* 17 (1986), 81–96, argues that Maharal's conception of the relationship between miracles – which are literally experienced – and nature – whose laws are immutable – is that nature and miracles co-exist simultaneously from different vantage points. "The Maharal's innovation in this matter is in his seeing nature as no more than a function of partial consciousness or recognition, indeed legitimate, but limited to one perspective of a more complex truth".... Even ontic reality...is defined via the areas of relation of those who make distinctions in it, and from here is the difference between truth from God's side and [truth] recorded by [human beings]" (91–93) (my translation of the Hebrew). Following Ben-Zion Bokser's identification of Maharal with Pico della Mirandola's perspective on truth – "Syncretism" – as opposed to other Neo-Platonic perspectives, Ross explains that for this view, "truth includes a great number of true claims, and therefore, each position or school expresses a different, specific aspect of that same, universal truth" (*ibid.*, 95).

13. For more on this general point, see Brian Vickers, "On the Function of Analogy in the Occult", in *Hermeticism and the Renaissance: Intellectual History and the Occult in Early Modern Europe*, ed. Ingrid Merkel and Allen G. Debus (Washington: Folger Shakespeare Library, 1988), especially 276.

14. Avie Walfish, "Maharal's Symbolic System: *Netiv Gemilut Ḥasadim*," *Gesher* (1981), 199–216, especially 208.

15. In this respect, Maharal is consistent with early Modern thinking. Roper observes that marriage was a major emphasis of the German,

Protestant Reformation, wherein "marriage was conceived in bilateral terms: the governance of the husband was counterposed to the subordination of the wife, who ought to 'obey him as her head'. This paradigm of the relations between the sexes so saturated Reformation thinking that the discourse of wifehood began to displace that of womanhood altogether. There is almost no rhetoric of motherhood in the early years of the Reformation," (40). My impression is that references to motherhood are virtually nonexistent in Maharal's writings.

16. "Order of the world" ("*seder ha-olam*") is an omnipresent term in Maharal's writings, representing the hierarchized organization of emblematic, metaphysical truths that both describe and guide the universe. Walfish explains that "for Maharal, the centrality of symbolism lies in the fact that the rational Creator fashioned the world according to patterns that are repeated on various levels of reality: Torah, the cosmos, society, and the individual, all share certain structural features," (201). Vickers describes an "identical 'principle of order' running through creation" in microcosm theories, Neo-Platonism, and Ficino, (268).

17. Wiesner's discussion of early Modern, European marital politics can help us to contextualize Maharal's views on marriage historically. For example, one may register the words of the French jurist and political theorist Jean Bodin, from his *The Six Books of the Republic* (1576): "the husband's power over the wife…is the source and origin of every human society". Wiesner explains that statements of this sort were expressions of ideological warfare in the turbulently changing sixteenth century European body politic. A region for the playing out of the tension between gender and class in these highly hierarchical cultures was the question of female political rule in the case of women born into ruling families ascending to the throne. Male rule was often defended on grounds of comparing the state to a household, as James I said to Parliament: "I am the Husband, and the Whole Isle in my lawfull [sic.] Wife." The argument worked in the opposite direction as well, enhancing the authority of male heads of household by comparing them to monarchs. Both domains informed each other and both were derived from God. The spread of the Protestant Reformation accelerated the spiritualizing of this political ideology, as now religious leaders were themselves patriarchal heads of households (243).

18. This view seems to have been popular throughout early Modern Europe. For example, in England during this period, women who

killed their husbands were guilty not only of murder, but also of petty treason (*ibid.*, 34).

19. His discussion here refers only to the Exodus version of the commandments. The language is different in Deuteronomy 5:18 and Maharal treats these differences in TY, cap. 45. I will return to this below.

20. The phrase "*qarqaʿ ʿolam*" is exceedingly difficult to translate but fairly simple to understand. Literally, it could be rendered as something like "eternal land" or "mere land" and conveys the sense that woman in coitus is like earth – a passive recipient of intercourse, not unlike the role of the earth vis-à-vis rain.

21. The Talmud speaks in multiple voices about the nature of the revelation at Sinai. Some sources recall Israel's acceptance of Torah as coming out of exceptional and laudatory volunteerism: the people agreed to fulfill the Torah even before knowing its contents. These traditions have little place, if any, in Maharal's writings. The dominant tradition for him is the one brought on BT Shabbat 88a that God held the mountain over the heads of the people, threatening to drop it onto them if they refused to accept the Torah. Although that Talmudic pericope itself seems to view this tradition ambivalently, ultimately emphasizing the voluntary re-acceptance, Maharal exalts this compulsion as the highest form of relationship. Rather than defending Sinaitic authority against the charge of compulsion, Maharal defends Sinaitic authority *on the basis* that it was forged in compulsion.

22. Binyamin Gross, *Netzaḥ Yisrael: Hashkaphato ha-Meshihit shel ha-Maharal mi-Prague ʿal ha-Galut veha-Geulah* (Tel Aviv: Devir, 1974), 85, astutely points out that even the language with which Maharal describes the relationship between God and Israel evidences a distancing from any notions of mutuality or contingency. Instead of the word "*berit*" (covenant), which is the common term throughout Jewish literature, Maharal uses the terms "*ḥibbur*" (connection) or "*tzeruph*" (joining), which, unlike *berit*, do not necessarily imply mutuality of consent.

23. Elsewhere, Maharal explains language referring to Israel as God's sons in terms of the same absolute relationship that he describes here regarding a marriage forged in rape. The father-son relationship between God and Israel is absolute. It is impossible for Israel to depart from being God's sons; the relationship is compulsory. Even when Jews sin, and even when they cleave to idolatry, they are still God's sons. "This is because…the name 'sons' is on account of God being their Cause, like a father, who is the cause to the son, and this comes from the father's essence. This does not change with any sin…which is from the

side of the caused." Sin is a lack on the part of Israel, a diminishing of self from the whole (NY, cap. 11, p. 66).

24.   His context here is relationships between rabbi and disciple and between nursing mother and child.

25.   This view is not necessarily latent in the Talmudic text itself. The gemara, indeed, recognizes that a woman might swear off sexual relations because she finds them not worth the pain of childbirth (at least in the moment of those pains). It further classifies such a choice as sinful. However, it never denies women's pleasure in the physical act of sex, does not depict the woman as subjugated in sex, and, most significantly, makes no claim that those relations are good for the woman. Maharal, relative to the Talmudic passage on which he comments, innovates the notion that subjugation *per se* is good for her.

26.   In the middle of his treatment of BT Bava Metzia 84a, he makes his polemical intentions clear: "Indeed, know that [the Sages] came to teach us a wondrous matter, for many wise people, who, in their spiritual intellect study the world, say that the union of man and wife is man's shame, embarrassment, and disgrace, to the point of saying with absolute agreement that the sense of touch is a shame to us. This is what the Sages came to distance..." (HA 3:32).

27.   The BHG version has "minimizing" in place of "bad".

28.   Daniel Boyarin has offered illuminating analyses of these gemarot in their own literary contexts in *Carnal Israel: Reading Sex in Talmudic Culture*. Berkeley: University of California Press, 1993 (197–225), and, with slight changes, *Unheroic Conduct: The Rise of Heterosexuality and the Invention of the Jewish Man*. Berkeley: University of California Press, 1997, 87–150.

29.   E.g., Rashi's comment there, BT Bava Metzia 84a, s.v. "*Ahavah doheqet...*"

30.   NY, cap. 19, p. 101 and other places.

31.   This notion is familiar from other contexts, as well (see Jacobson, 115 and footnote 79 there), but regarding gender, Maharal plays somewhat fast and loose with its application in that he refers to woman as completion to man, but certainly does not describe woman *per se* as "more essential than anything". Regarding man's dominion over the other creatures, Maharal considers it significant that man was created last. By that logic, one would think that since woman was created after man, according to Genesis 2, she should rule over him! The same terms that present themselves as being firm, descriptive truths, emerge, on closer scrutiny, as slippery. Man is completion to woman by dominating her;

woman is completion to man by giving him that which he needs to dominate. The arbitrariness that so upsets Vickers is apparent here. If one steps out of Maharal's metaphysical matrix long enough to look at it from a different angle, one can easily imagine his principles yielding quite a different sexual topography. For example, since it is better to be hidden than revealed, it would follow that it is the vagina that runs on soul-power, while the penis is lower in its revealed crudity. Alternatively, since man is better than woman and male genitalia are revealed while female are hidden, then being revealed should be a sublime, spiritual state, just as the Torah was revealed at Sinai, while hiddenness is a lesser level. For another example of his arbitrary application of categories, see TY, cap. 49, p. 153 and GH, cap. 56, p. 249.

32. It could be instructive to compare Maharal's views on the penis to other sixteenth-century phenomena of the phallus in Christian, European culture. The simple fact that the codpiece was a most popular and controversial article of clothing for young men throughout that milieu should arouse our interest. While this fad met with rigorous censure from religious and civic leaders, Roper has provocatively argued that much of the literature "betrays not so much a cultural conflict as a shared vision", 119, inasmuch as it often engages in "linguistic exhibitionism, exuberantly paralleling the clothing it purports to condemn.... So the prefatory poem to the *Hosenteufel* apostrophizes those who wear such fine codpieces that one would guess there was the sweetest honey inside!" (*ibid.*) Maharal's voice was, apparently, one with his culture in encoding great centrality to the penis as the majestic center of the king's crown.

33. He does assert that bigger does not necessarily equal better; since the penis's qualities are emblematic, one would be mistaken to seek out gradational evidence of their manifestation in the flesh (HA 3:34).

34. Jacobson 104–07.

35. *Ibid.*, 105, based on DH, p. 142, on Avot 3:14. Since the image of God is only a physical representation of God, it is not, then, the loftiest level to inhabit, but only the loftiest level one can *embody*. Maharal asserts that Moses was *beyond* the image of God, because he reached the separate, non-physical state (*ibid.*, 105). To put this in gendered terms, Moses was more manly than other men, that is, less physical/material.

36. *Ibid.*, 106.

37. Although many of the details may be unique to him, Maharal did not innovate the notion that the image of God is manifest through domination. This core association was already prominent in the leading Italian thinkers on Maharal's philosophical radar screen. Charles Trinkaus

quotes Marsilio Ficino from the latter's *Theologia platonica*, II:225–26): "…man who universally provides for all things living and not living is a certain god. He is the god without doubt of the animals since he uses all of them, rules them, and teaches some of them…. He is, finally, the god of all materials since he handles all, and turns and changes them. Anyone who dominates the body in so many and such great things and acts as the vicar of immortal God is without doubt immortal…. Single animals scarcely suffice for the care of themselves or briefly of their offspring. But man alone so abounds in perfection that he rules himself first, which no beasts do, then governs his family, administers the state, rules peoples and commands the entire world. And as though born for ruling he is entirely impatient of servitude," Charles Trinkaus, *In Our Image and Likeness: Humanity and Divinity in Italian Humanist Thought* (London: Constable, 1970), 484. Trinkaus further quotes Pico della Mirandola: "we first know in [man] that image of God through which the rule and command of the beasts is given to him…. But having destroyed the image of God by the blemish of sin…we begin to be slaves of our own beasts…," 517.

38. Avraham Grossman brings examples of medieval rabbis, such as the Spanish Don Isaac Abravanel and the Provencal Ya'aqov Anatoli, who posited that only men, and not women, were created in the image of God. Avraham Grossman, *Ḥasidot u-Moredot: Nashim Yehudiot be-Europa Bimei-haBeinayim* (Jerusalem: Merkaz Zalman Shazar, 2001), 29–30. Maharal needed not go to that extreme in order to assert man's existential superiority to women, because for him, the image of God is not an absolute, but a relational category. The world is not divided cleanly between those who have it and those who don't; everything and everyone has a place on the hierarchy of image manifestation. Women occupy a relatively high rung, but a subordinate one to men.

39. Maharal reinforces this conception that woman's sole identity is as passive, subjugated completion of man in his comment that because it is the nature of form to seek completion, man will seek some other, lesser form of matter if he fails to find a woman (GA 1:32). It is unclear precisely what he means, since he rejects the notion that Adam had conjugal relations with all the other animals before Eve was created. Nevertheless, the main point remains that woman may be the most appropriate subject to man, but is replaceable, the essential task being, simply, that man-form be complete by subjugating someone or something.

40. Haggai Ben-Artzi, "Ha-Yaḥas bein Ḥomer ve-Ruaḥ be-'Netivot 'Olam' shel ha-Maharal," *Da'at* 18 (1987), 45–53.

41. *Ibid.*, 48–49; emphasis mine.
42. See above, note 23.
43. Ish-Shalom, 94.
44. For a fuller view of Maharal's philosophy of creation, see NY, caps. 2–3 and Alan Sinyor, "The Maharal on Creation," *L'Eylah* 28 (1989), 33–37. In short, Maharal posits that the singular God created one beginning, after which further additions and expansions accreted to that singular beginning, from the side of the receiver. This model repeats itself on every plane of creation, so that one beginning, by virtue of being caused (*'allul*), and not the Cause (*'illah*), necessarily needs addition and completion. Man is the beginning for the lower world, which is the world of complete mixing and integration. Woman is his completion.
45. See above, where I refer to the passage in *Netiv Ha-Torah* in which Maharal identifies child and wife as occupying the same material role in relation to their father/husband.
46. This process of ascent to unification echoes the eschatology of Ficino's theory of the immortality of the soul. Trinkaus describes "that it strives to become God…. Here the conception of man as living in the image of God is made completely explicit through the notion that the characteristic directions of human *conatus* are all towards deification," 487. Quoting from Ficino's *Theologia platonica* ii, 247, he writes: "The entire striving of our soul is that it become God. Such striving is no less natural to men than the effort to flight is to birds…. Therefore the human effort to become God can some day be fulfilled" (*ibid.*).
47. Martin Buber, *On Zion* (Schocken: New York, 1973), 84, and Rivka Schatz, "Existence and Eschatology in the Teachings of the Maharal (Part i), *Immanuel* 14 (Fall, 1982), 88.
48. Rivka Schatz, "Existence and Eschatology in the Teachings of the Maharal (Part ii)", *Immanuel* 15, (Winter, 1982/83), 64.
49. Ish-Shalom, 93–97, especially 96.
50. *Ibid.*, 97. Ish-Shalom cites an additional passage, from HA 2:24, in which Maharal adds that playing is inherently good in that it reflects wholeness.
51. *Ibid.*
52. For a good summary of this dynamic with regard to Jewish peoplehood, see Gross, 62: "Indeed, the development of the People of Israel is the gradual strengthening of a people, whose entire being is a striving to a complete separation between itself and nature and matter and a striving to a complete and continuous identity with the world of the spirit and metaphysics."

Equality or Equivalence:

A VERY BRIEF SURVEY OF *LEX TALIONIS* AS A CONCEPT OF JUSTICE IN THE BIBLE

Alan Tzvika Nissel*

I. *Introduction: Justice and Biblical Law*

In law school, the attentive student quickly learns to delete the word "justice" from her legal lexicon. Law professors frequently refer to the word cynically to distinguish it from "law," the more concrete concept that ought to preoccupy law students. Similarly, contemporary rabbis rarely rely on the axiom "an eye for an eye" to justify *halakhic* opinions, since it is not likely to resonate well with their congregants. While taking "an eye for an eye" is one of the most famous articulations of justice, the formula has long been perceived to mean revenge[1]. This view is expressly rejected in the Torah: "Thou shalt not avenge, nor bear any grudge against the children of thy people, but thou shalt love thy neighbour as thyself…".[2] Similarly, when an inquiring gentile once asked Hillel to be taught all of the Torah while standing on one foot, the sage famously responded "That which you hate, do not do to your fellow. That is the whole Torah; the rest is the explanation. Go and learn."[3]

This biblical concept of justice, *lex talionis* ("LT"), will be the basis of our brief discussion below.[4] Before proceeding, however, a few caveats are in order. The scope of our topic is *lex talionis* as a biblical concept of justice relating to non-capital offences in the Torah.[5] Additionally, this paper aims to contribute nothing or very little to the intellectual literature on the concepts of justice and LT; instead it is a very short survey of an ancient and nuanced topic that still resonates today. Finally, although the article employs a methodology geared to lay readers,[6] those interested in further study are encouraged to make recourse of the endnotes.[7]

In the rest of this introduction, we will set out a taxonomy of the concept of justice and will locate the LT within that framework. The *lex talionis* is not an idea that can be categorized as either criminal or civil, retributive or distributive, corrective or utilitarian, deontic or consequentialist.[8] Accordingly, the structure of this section is an oversimplification of the topic that is offered primarily for didactical purposes. This conceptual background will add texture to the ensuing analysis of *lex talionis*.

In Part II, we will partially trace the historical development of LT as it weaves through many Mesopotamian societies; in doing so, we will read the legal texts of ancient societies in order to glimpse at a few primary sources of ancient criminal law.[9] Then, as a backdrop to the subsequent discussion of LT in the Bible, we will introduce the relationship between the Mesopotamian and biblical laws of criminal punishment. In Part III, we will take a brief survey of biblical conceptions of justice. We employ hermeneutical tools to assess the competing interpretations of the three iterations of the LT in the Torah (*i.e.*, Exodus 21, Leviticus 24 and Deuteronomy 19). We will end this section by reviewing various attempts to reconcile these iterations. In the final part of this paper, we recapitulate our observations and revisit the relationship between law and society. We end our discussion with an assessment of the unique characteristics of *lex talionis* as a general principle of law in biblical society.

WHAT IS JUSTICE?

Intuitively, justice is about the right order of things in society. A famous international arbitrator once opined, "The essence of law is order; and of human law, order founded in justice."[10] But what is justice? The word itself is emotive and "sometimes seems to paralyse reflection."[11] Not every legal system or legal philosopher has a complete answer to the question "what is justice?" Plato, for example, did.[12] Aristotle did not.[13] Rawls did.[14] Nozick did not.[15] In order to begin to appreciate why and how the law punishes criminals, we must consider justice on two levels. First we will ask, "What is justice?" and broadly locate the etymological roots of the concept. We will then survey some philosophical views of justice (criminal justice in particular) since, to administer punishments justly, the law must provide justification for the act of inflicting pain on criminals.[16]

Etymologically, the Latin root of justice indicates the ideas of fittingness, exactness and uprightness.[17] In Old Norse too, justice is about evenness (*jafn* means "even").[18] The same root gives us the word "justification" – that is, the underlying reasons for one's beliefs and actions. A "just" or "justified" action or decision is one that can be defended as upright. Conceptually, Aristotle considered "justice" to be about taking measured actions and "injustice" to be about taking more than one's fair share.[19] The pioneer of the legal lexicon, John Bouvier, defines "justice" as "the constant and perpetual disposition to render to every man his due."[20] Semantically, then, a "just" action is a measured action, one that should be circumscribed by the law. The normative yardstick against which one's actions are measured is the principle of proportionality.[21]

While there are many philosophical approaches to justice, for didactical purposes, one can conceptualize them as falling into one of two categories: distributive and retributive justice. Distributive justice is concerned with the proper distribution of things (wealth, honor, power, *et cetera*). Distributive theories are forward-looking and con-sequentialist – *i.e.*, the consequences of any given law on society at large will determine its justness. An example of such a theory is utilitarianism, which asserts that an action should be assessed according to its contribution to overall utility – *i.e.*, whatever brings the greatest happiness to the greatest number of people.[22] An example of a utilitarian justification for punishment is deterrence; such theorists seek to deter both past and future offenders from committing crimes. The extent of each individual punishment is determined by balancing the maximization of a punishment's deterrent effect with the minimization of pain to be imposed on offenders.[23]

Retributive (or "corrective") justice is concerned with the proper responses to wrongs done. Retributive theories are retrospective in nature and usually deontic – *i.e.*, concerned with the fact of violation itself as opposed to its consequences for society. Such theories of punishment center on principles that specify reciprocal relationships and apply concepts like fittingness of punishment to wrongs done.[24] The subject of our discussion, *lex talionis* ("law of retaliation" in Latin), is often seen as an example of retributive justice,[25] since it requires that punishments be the same as the wrong. But why, according to such theorists, is it right to punish criminals? On what basis are punishments justified? Since it is a tenet of retributive justice that laws be obeyed (*pacta sunt servanda*), the fact of an offence triggers the justification for punishment. Offenders deserve to be punished according to their moral responsibility.[26] Thus, talionic punishments correspond to the wrongs done. This is the idea of proportionality, the valuation of the wrong committed and the corresponding penalty that should be meted out. The punishment shall fit the crime, "eye for eye, tooth for tooth" *et cetera*.

It is important to stress that these generalizations are offered for instructional purposes. *Lex talionis* is not necessarily incompatible with distributive theories of justice. The overlap between distributive and retributive justice runs deep and "'getting even' in its various senses is at the core of both."[27] Indeed, the LT can even serve as a basis for rejecting capital punishment ("life for life" notwithstanding).[28] Below, we will see that, far from outdated concepts that justify revenge, biblical iterations of the LT represent nuanced ideas about equal and equivalent punishment.[29]

JUSTICE, MORALITY AND THE LAW

How does morality[30] stand in relation to the law[31] and vice versa? To begin with, suppose we would like to accomplish certain moral objectives in our society – specifically, to attain a just society. We could take various measures to that end (*e.g.*, public education and economic incentives); one of the critical instruments that we would use is the law. Moral objectives, thus understood, constitute the *raison d'être* of the law in our society.[33]

By extension, a second aspect of the relationship between law and morality concerns the conditions of the validity of law – *i.e.*, what is it that gives a directive the status of a valid law? One of the most contested questions in this regard is whether or not given directives must comply with morality in order to be valid law. Some legal theorists argue that morality does play such a validating role in the sense that directives that fail to meet the minimum standard of moral appropriateness are not laws properly so-called.[34] Others argue that the criteria of legal validity include only social facts – *e.g.*, the legislator approved a specific document in compliance with certain procedural requirements – rather than moral valuations.[35] For these theorists, directives can count as laws whether or not they meet moral standards; however, they acknowledge that a gravely immoral law should be disobeyed on moral, extra-legal, grounds.[36]

A third way in which morality relates to law is by serving as a standard of adjudication – *i.e.*, a standard that, to some extent, guides and determines the adjudication of cases. Judges may make recourse to such standards insofar as (without such standards) the law does not present a straightforward determination for the outcome of specific cases. This happens, for example, with the application of open-ended provisions, such as the constitutional prohibition on cruel and unusual punishment, as well as the determination of penal sentencing. To be sure, it is a matter of controversy whether, when judges make recourse to such moral standards, they are applying something that is a part of the law or some extra-legal material. There are three main approaches to this relationship. One camp of legal theorists claims that the (implications of) moral standards is necessarily not part of the law; accordingly, when invoking such standards, judges are using extra-legal materials to create new law, rather than to apply pre-existing law.[37] In contrast, others argue that moral principles (whether or not the legislator articulated them explicitly in any directive) are an inseparable part of the sources that judges have recourse in order to identify the law.[38] A third, intermediate approach insists that the law consists only of the legislator's directives but acknowledges that the legislator may incorporate various doctrines that serve as a vehicle for moral principles (*e.g.*, the constitutional prohibition on cruel and unusual punishment); on this view, moral principles may or may not be a part of the law – depending on whether or not the legislator adopted them.[39]

Although the ways in which morality stands in relation to the law are somewhat contentious, there is at least a plausible basis for thinking that some crucial threads connect the two. Above, we only mentioned a few contexts that are particularly relevant to our brief survey – *i.e.*, the purpose of the law, validation of the law and determination of legal outcomes.

JUSTICE AND BIBLICAL LAW

The Bible does not expound a full theory of justice. It does, however, both invoke justice as an idea and iterate principles of justice (without so labeling them). Since the Bible dogmatizes God's authorship of biblical law (and thereby secures its binding nature), justice serves as an ideal to be employed in man's relationship to God as well as in man's interaction with his fellow men.[40]

Tsedek (the Hebrew word for justice) has a strong social component. Deuteronomy 16:21 famously states "Justice, justice shalt thou follow, that thou mayest live, and inherit the land which the LORD thy God giveth thee."[41] The Hebrew root of *tsedek*, like the Roman root of justice, means upright, straight.[42] In Jewish literature, the word is used as righteousness and social justice; the Bible employs the term to espouse peace, repudiate slavery, champion freedom, *et cetera*. While justice, as a value, is much discussed in the Bible, our primary focus is on the ways in which the Bible makes reference to general principles of criminal justice.

Conceptually, justice in the Bible is an ideal upon which citizens and judges should base their actions and decisions. The best-known example of a biblical conception of justice, and the one most relevant to our discussion, is the *lex talionis*. This concept is given its most complete articulation in the Bible in Exodus 21, which states (in part), "thou shalt give life for life. Eye for eye, tooth for tooth, hand for hand, foot for foot. Burning for burning, wound for wound, stripe for stripe." From a criminal law perspective, the principle serves as a legalistic restriction on a court's power, requiring that the punishment shall fit the crime (no more and no less);[43] the standard for this fittingness concept is proportionality – measuring the punishment according to the crime. However, while conceptually, the LT seems to have evolved into the general principle that punishments must fit crimes, it also retains a (paradoxically) widespread association with notions of revenge. To obtain an overview of the biblical concept of justice, both of these aspects must be addressed. The next section, accordingly, considers *lex talionis* as a cliché of justice.

JUSTICE AS CLICHÉ

The *lex talionis*, frequently referred to as "an eye for an eye," has become a popular idea about law that seems to have lost its original ingenuity.[44] The adage has been misunderstood by many as a primitive basis for punishment[45] or simply as a justification for revenge.[46] Any index of the usage of the LT in theaters and libraries depicts it as vengeance.[47] No doubt, this misinterpretation has contributed to the taboo-ization of "justice" in law school lecture rooms.

Far from a cynical labeling of justice, thinking about *lex talionis* as a cliché is a reminder that the concept is not just ambiguous, it is also especially accessible. Indeed, Robert Nozick once asked whether it was necessary "to offer any explanation at all of retributive punishment? Perhaps its appropriateness is just a fundamental fact, with nothing further underlying it. People who commit wrongs simply deserve to be punished."[48] This dramatic but also intuitive sense of justice portrays the LT as a human law meant to direct human passions – "an aesthetic principle of poetic justice…"[49] Some historians have even gone so far as to say that the accessibility of the concept added to the popularity of ancient Judaism.[50] We should, however, note a clear distinction between the two: "retribution is done for a wrong, while revenge may be done for an injury or harm or slight and need not be a wrong."[51]

The biblical iterations of LT convey nuanced ideas of justice. The Bible requires that a punishment be the same as the act that constituted the offense (*e.g.*, "eye for eye"). It is less clear what "the same" means. Some commentators insist that the Bible puts forth the idea of "mirror justice," where the punishment is identical to the crime. This understanding, however, is not necessarily the easiest way to read the LT in the Bible. According to one legal philosopher, the above purported reading is a simple but not a literal understanding of the text; it is merely incorrect. Jeremy Waldron argues that it is impossible "for the same act to be performed twice, at different times and with different *dramatis personae*."[52] Indeed, this view is reflected throughout Jewish sources. For example, Saadia Gaon (*ca*. 892–842 CE) famously relied on this argument against the ancient Karaites, the ancient sect who understood all biblical law as emanating from a literal interpretation of the Bible. Saadia argued that the biblical concept of "eye for eye" was evidence that the Bible should not be read literally since it is impossible to measure the punishment for an injury with absolute precision.[53] In this sense, the "same act" is a necessarily ambiguous criterion of justice such that the principle can only be interpreted as requiring that punishments be of the "same type" as the offense.[54] *Lex talionis*, in sum, is an indeterminate principle that can be interpreted strictly as requiring punishments to be identical or, more subtly, as requiring them to be similar to the offence committed.

With this in mind, in the next parts of this paper, we will survey three biblical iterations of the LT and the ways that they can be interpreted as principles of justice. Before doing so, however, we will familiarize ourselves with some ancient Mesopotamian criminal sources in order to later compare them to the LT in the Torah.

II. *History and Ancient Mesopotamian Law*
INTRODUCTION

The principle of "eye for eye" has been a fundamental of criminal law for at least three millennia. Articulated for the first time in the Laws of Hammurabi (ca. 19th century BCE), by the mid-fifth century B.C.E., the Romans had already codified it as the Roman law of retaliation (*lex talionis*).[55] Today, the idea that the punishment must fit the crime is ubiquitous; it has attained the status of a "general principle of law common to all civilized nations."[56] In this section, we will glimpse the history of the LT from its earliest mention in ancient Mesopotamian laws, through its iterations in the Bible. Contrary to popular accounts of legal history, we will not conclude that the principle of "eye for eye" was first interpreted literally as bodily mutilation and was later understood figuratively as equivalent compensation for harm caused.[57] Rather, we will see that both conceptions of justice – mirror and equivalent punishment – may have been used contemporaneously and developed in subtly different ways in each legal culture.[58]

SOME ANCIENT MESOPOTAMIAN CRIMINAL LAWS

The earliest written laws were written in the style of codes. While these early compilations were not codes of law (understood *stricto sensu*), they did cover many important legal issues, such as criminal punishment.[59]

The Laws of Eshnunna were written (ca. 1770 BCE) in a formal and accessible style without much in the way of elaborate principles. Provisions appear as though they were to be read literally. §42 casuistically prescribes that "If a man bites the nose of another man and thus cuts it off, he shall weigh and deliver 60 shekels of silver; an eye – 60 shekels; a foot – 30 shekels; an ear – 30 shekels; a slap to the cheek – he shall weigh and deliver 10 shekels of silver."[60] In this commercial context, we find a more glaring example of corrective justice:[61] §5 prescribes that "If the boatman is negligent and causes the boat to sink, he shall restore as much as he caused to sink."[62] These examples from the Eshnunna give an impression that the text was concerned more with commercial and social convenience than with substantive notions of justice.

Hammurabi, the Babylonian ruler who established one of the world's first metropolises, is credited as being the first to articulate the law of retaliation. It is well known that the Laws of Hammurabi is the longest and best organized of the law collections from Mesopotamia. What is less known is how "It draws on the traditions of earlier law collections and doubtless influenced those that came later."[63] Indeed, we will notice many rhetorical similarities as well as subtle (but significant) differences between Mesopotamian legal cultures. Below, we have listed some provisions from the Laws of Hammurabi that resemble those of the LT in the Bible:

> §127 "If a man causes a finger to be pointed in accusation against an *ugbabtu*[64] or against a man's wife but cannot bring proof, they shall flog that man before judges and they shall shave off half of his hair."[65]
>
> §195: "If a child should strike his father, they shall cut off his hand."[66]
>
> §196: "If an *awilu*[67] should blind the eye of another *awilu*, they shall blind his eye."[68]
>
> §197: "If he should break the bone of another *awilu*, they shall break his bone."[69]
>
> §198: "If he should blind the eye of a commoner or break the bone of a commoner, he shall weigh and deliver 60 shekels of silver."[70]

§199: "If he should blind the eye of an *awilu*'s slave or break the bone of an *awilu*'s slave, he shall weigh and deliver one-half of his value (in silver)."[71]

Hammurabi's Laws seems to have articulated criminal punishment as a legal response in kind (mirror punishment), whereas the Eshnunna's Law punished criminal injury formalistically (according to tables of compensation). Interestingly, the appearance of the same body parts in multiple sets of ancient laws (*e.g.*, eyes and hands) seems to indicate that they have been built on preexisting idiom rather than codified legal reforms.[72]

RELATIONSHIP BETWEEN
MESOPOTAMIAN AND BIBLICAL LAW

The publication of the "Code of Hammurabi" in 1902[73] convinced many legal historians of the heavy Babylonian influence upon biblical law.[74] These scholars viewed rabbinic commentaries on the Torah that interpreted "eye for eye" figuratively (*e.g.*, monetary worth of an eye) as apologetic attempts to reconcile biblical conceptions of justice with their own more modern sensibilities.[75]

The two texts are similar indeed. On one count, there are 24 instances of resemblances and analogies between Hammurabi and the Bible.[76] Stylistically, the iterations of the LT in both sources are set in the context of casuistically worded laws.[77] While neither set of written laws are codes in the strict sense of the term, they both seem to have been written to complement local oral traditions of law.[78] Such a claim is supported by recent scholarship claiming that the *lex talionis* was written like a restricted code whose meaning is embedded in a particular social context, where certain laws need not be explicit since basic understandings were shared.[79] In other words, in biblical times already, "an eye for an eye" was likely a popular idiom of justice and may have been used in the Bible to reinforce abstract formulations of criminal justice "by reference to an ancient concrete wording sounding the pathos of an emotional world."[80]

Other commentators, however, responded that LT in the Bible is fundamentally different from the retributive Laws of Hammurabi. Semantically, the Bible articulates the LT with significantly more texture than does Hammurabi's Laws.[81] For example, although both sets of laws use the casuistic style, only the Bible articulates the LT apodictically.[82] Also, the difference between cuneiform law (a set of laws, such as that of Hammurabi, written in this ancient script) and biblical law is borne out in their contrasting punishments for murder and in their application of the death penalty.[83] Teleologically, the purported purposes of the two sets of laws are also distinguishable.[84] According to one historian, even though it is probable that Abraham[85] was well acquainted with Hammurabi's Laws,[86] "There is not a scintilla of positive proof that the Pentateuch owes anything to Babylon."[87]

Thus, even a cursory comparison between the two sets of laws indicates both similarities and differences. The truth, of course, may lie somewhere in between these two camps. For example, both biblical and Babylonian society had developed a money economy that was able to measure harms in a more sophisticated way than other ancient societies.[88] Far from indicating that the Bible borrowed corporeal punishment from Hammurabi's Laws, the two sets of laws seem to reflect the possibility that both societies were able to assign monetary punishments for assaults committed. Indeed, from a theological perspective, a reason why the biblical conception was worded so similarly to that of Hammurabi is that the Bible embedded clichés within its text.[89] As Sarna explains, God prefers to speak in the everyday language of human beings to communicate His will.[90] This view is also supported by historical findings that the LT prevails in nearly every ancient legal code.[91]

III. *Brief Survey of Biblical Conceptions of Justice*
INTRODUCTION

Should crimes be avenged or should offenders be permitted to buy back their innocence? Based on the above discussion, it should not be surprising that it is a matter of debate whether "eye for eye" in the Bible was meant to be understood figuratively or literally. Even during the time of the Talmud, Jewish commentators were still reading the biblical iterations of the LT literally. Philo, Josephus and the Talmud record opinions supporting a literal interpretation – though by their time this was the minority opinion.[92] In the next section, we will look at the three iterations of the *lex talionis* in the Torah – Exodus 21, Leviticus 24 and Deuteronomy 19 – in order to assess the extent to which they were to be read literally and/or figuratively.

EXODUS 21

The LT appears in Exodus 21 as a provision of law regarding non-fatal assaults. Immediately following the Decalogue, the Bible articulates a series of provisions on social order (possibly hierarchically) beginning with slavery and then continuing with capital crimes, non-capital assaults and, finally, property laws. Specifically, the text reads as follows:

> v. 12: He that smiteth a man, so that he die, shall be surely put to death.
>
> *   *   *
>
> v. 22: If men strive, and hurt a woman with child, so that her fruit depart from her, and yet no mischief follow: he shall be surely punished, according as the woman's husband will lay upon him; and he shall pay as the judges determine.
> v. 23: And if any mischief follow, then thou shalt give life for life,
> v. 24: Eye for eye, tooth for tooth, hand for hand, foot for foot, v. 25: Burning for burning, wound for wound, stripe for stripe.

Numerous exegetes have commented on the specific wording of this passage.[93] Two important questions for the purpose of our brief discussion of justice are: what is the difference between he "shall surely be put to death" and "thou shalt give life for life?" and why are the two principles separated from each other in the text? The separation seems to indicate that the punishment for unlawful killing with a guilty mind is death and the punishment for unlawful killing without a guilty mind is compensation in exchange for the taken life;[94] the two terms, then, signify distinct punishments that correspond to different levels of moral responsibility.[95] Moreover, Numbers 35:31 specifically prohibits judges from commuting punishments for murder;[96] a murderer may neither escape capital punishment by paying off the victim's family the "value" of the life he took nor may he be pardoned – a unique feature of biblical as opposed to cuneiform law.[97]

But if the Bible did not intend to mean "life for life" literally, then why did it not just say so? Indeed, the use of the word "mischief" seems to indicate a justification for retribution in kind (death, maiming, *et cetera*). The LT, we see, can be read both as prescribing equal body mutilation and as equivalent compensation. A comparative analysis of the biblical iterations of the LT will serve to support this observation.[98]

LEVITICUS 24

Sequentially, the next usage of the LT in the Bible comes in Leviticus 24, where the context is ritualistic laws – as opposed to social order laws in Exodus 21.[99] After laying out the laws of religious holidays, the Sabbath and those against cursing God, the Bible invokes the principle of *lex talionis*. After mentioning the LT, the Bible returns to its discussion about cursing God. As will be seen, the iteration of the LT in Leviticus corresponds to this context and differs significantly from that in Exodus. Specifically, the text reads as follows:

> v. 17: And he that killeth any man shall surely be put to death.
>
> v. 18: And he that killeth a beast shall make it good; life for life.[100]
>
> v. 19: And if a man cause a blemish in his neighbour; as he hath done, so shall it be done to him;
>
> v. 20: Breach for breach, eye for eye, tooth for tooth: as he hath caused a blemish in a man, so shall it be done to him again.
>
> v. 21: And he that killeth a beast, he shall restore it: and he that killeth a man, he shall be put to death.
>
> v. 22: Ye shall have one manner of law, as well for the stranger, as for one of your own country: for I am the LORD your God.

A few textual differences are immediately apparent. First, "breach for breach" is added in Leviticus. Second, life, burning, wound and stripe are left out. Third, and most significantly, Leviticus clearly includes general principles of law[101] in its iteration of the LT – *e.g.*, "as he hath caused a blemish in a man, so shall it be done to him again."

This iteration categorically supports neither the figurative nor the literal readings of the LT in the Bible. On a structural interpretation, this text (as in Exodus 21), seems hierarchical: unlawful killing of a human with a guilty mind is punishable by death, unlawful killing of an animal is punishable by compensation and, by extrapolation, physical injuries are punishable by commensurate compensation.[102] If this list is hierarchical, the same way that property damage warrants compensation so too does non-fatal injury to humans require restitution rather than physical wounding. We should note that (unlike in Exodus 21), there is no mention in this passage of the accidental killing of a human here. This omission can either imply that the law remains unchanged (*i.e.*, "life for life" is to be understood as commensurate compensation);[103] it can also be used to confirm a literal reading (*i.e.*, it confirms that unlawful killing – whatever the mental state of the perpetrator – warrants the death penalty). Similarly, the repetition of v. 21 may imply that in distinction to unlawful killings, *only* property damage can be compensated rather than avenged.

However, the use of "life for life" in v. 17 supports a figurative interpretation of the passage. The verse seems to employ the idea of reciprocity to mean equivalent as opposed to equal (or mirror) justice in non-capital offences. Indeed, the provision about capital offences, v. 17, does not invoke the LT principle; the usage is that of "shall surely be put to death" rather than the talionic "life for life." However, v. 18, about equivalent compensation for property damage, does invoke the LT. This would indicate that the subsequent vs. 20–21 should also be understood to mean equivalent rather than mirror justice.[104] Applying this observation to the iteration of Ex. 21:23 ("And if any mischief follow, then thou shalt give life for life") supports the interpretation of the LT as a general principle of law about equivalent reciprocity and not as a justification for body mutilation. The abstract principles of vs. 19 and 21, it should be noted, can be interpreted to support either a strict or a flexible understanding of the LT.

Thus, while this iteration can be read either to mean equal (*i.e.*, mirror) or equivalent (*e.g.*, compensatory) retribution, LT in Leviticus leans more in the direction of the latter than does Exodus.

DEUTERONOMY 19

As in Leviticus, the iteration of the LT in Deuteronomy is a principled one, a seeming application, rather than explication, of the LT. As in Exodus, but unlike in Leviticus, the passage in Deuteronomy is more concerned with social order[105] than religious majesty; namely, Deuteronomy 19 discusses judicial control over society.[106] As will be seen, v. 21 articulates the LT as the principle underlying the punishment for false witnesses. Specifically, the text reads as follows:

> v. 16: If a false witness rise up against any man to testify against him that which is wrong;
>
> v. 17: Then both the men, between whom the controversy is, shall stand before the LORD, before the priests and the judges, which shall be in those days;
>
> v. 18: And the judges shall make diligent inquisition: and, behold, if the witness be a false witness, and hath testified falsely against his brother;
>
> v. 19: Then shall ye do unto him, as he had thought to have done unto his brother: so shalt thou put the evil away from among you.
>
> v. 20: And those which remain shall hear, and fear, and shall henceforth commit no more any such evil among you.
>
> v. 21: And thine eye shall not pity; but life shall go for life, eye for eye, tooth for tooth, hand for hand, foot for foot.

The last verse quoted above lends strong support for a more literal interpretation since it appears to contrast the ideas of pity with the LT ("thine eye shall not pity; but life shall go for life..."); on this reading, LT is about mirror justice. Still, the context of Deuteronomy pulls in the opposite hermeneutical direction. Similar to the iteration in Leviticus, the LT is expressed more abstractly. This indicates that unlike its iteration in Exodus, which may be said to have had a technical aspect to it (*e.g.*, in cases of injury to the eye, an eye must be exchanged), the usages in Leviticus and Deuteronomy were applied by way of principle – *e.g.*, false witnesses are punished to the extent to which they intended to do harm to their brother *because* life shall go for life, eye for eye, *et cetera*.[107]

Furthermore, Deuteronomy articulates the LT as עין בעין rather than עין תחת עין – *i.e.*, the text drops the prepositional תחת and replaces it with ב. (Since both prepositions can be translated as "for," this nuance is often lost in translation.) David Daube sees in this subtle variation a new aspect of biblical justice. Whereas the iterations *lex talionis* in Exodus 21 and Leviticus 24 concerns restitution for injury, Deuteronomy applies the LT to false testimony, where no injury exists. False witnesses must be punished for the harm that they intended to cause even when no injury ensues. The fact of violation, therefore, implies sin. The prepositional ב in עין בעין allows for this broader interpretation of punishment as atonement in addition to restitution.[108]

Finally, though the ב in עין בעין, can be read to mean "for" (like תחת), it is also frequently used in the Bible to mean "with."[109] On this reading, Deuteronomy requires that false witnesses be punished *with* exactly the "eye" that they sought to be taken from the defendant. Thus, v. 21 employs the *lex talionis* at once both figuratively ("eye") and literally ("with"). The Bible is surely not restricting this passage to the singular case where a false witness seeks to have the defendant's eye gorged; the "eye" is used figuratively. Further, on this interpretation, the Bible couples v. 19 ("do unto him, as he had thought...") to v. 21 ("And thine eye shall not pity..."), so as to require that judges not exercise their judicial discretion mercifully: "but life shall go *with* life, eye *with* eye, tooth *with* tooth...." The prepositional "with" is thus read literally. One can speculate that perhaps it is only in this context of courtroom legalism – rather than self-help vigilantism – that the Bible employs the *lex talionis* to mean mirror justice.[110]

In sum, each biblical iteration of the LT can be read literally; however, when read together, the three passages emphasize more of an abstract principle than a narrow rule.

RELATING THE ITERATIONS

While some biblical iterations of the LT are more concerned with the concept of justice as reciprocity, none of them lend conclusive support to reading the LT as either vengeful or compensatory justice. Some commentators are certain that the LT was meant literally to require mirror justice. Others are as sure that it was written symbolically to guide compensatory justice. In unpacking the meanings of this cliché of justice such indeterminacy is hardly surprising. Indeed, it is possible that the LT was built-in to the Bible with constructive ambiguity.

Furthermore, extracting an essential meaning from the biblical iterations of the LT cannot avoid the well-known pitfalls of adjudication in general. Critical legal thinkers have effectively demonstrated how it is impossible to reapply the same legal provision identically in every case.[111] Each set of facts is unique and is it the duty of judges to determine the relevance, if any, of the particularities of each case. Thus understood, the talionic list of eyes, teeth, *et cetera* "is actually a general statement of legal policy that formulates the abstract principle of equivalence and restitution in concrete terms."[112] The difference between equal and equivalent justice, then, may be understood as one of emphasis, a matter of degree. As Philo writes, the judge must examine "the propriety of increasing or diminishing the punishment."[113]

IV. SOME THOUGHTS ON JUSTICE IN THE BIBLE

Thus far, this paper has presented its findings in more of a descriptive rather than an argumentative style. Before ending, however, we will suggest a more contentious claim: namely, while the Laws of Hammurabi is the first document to articulate "eye for eye" as a principle of mirror justice, the Bible is the first text that employs the LT as a general principle of law regarding the equivalent punishment. Before elaborating upon this possibility, it is worth recapitulating our observations.

We began our very brief survey by making three preliminary disclaimers. First, we restricted our scope of inquiry to justice as a general principle of law regarding non-capital offences in the Torah. Second, the purpose of the survey was didactic, with the goal of clarifying some important topics rather than of making original claims about the topic. Third, the style of the piece was to simplify as much as possible in the text and to problematize those generalizations for the interested reader in the endnotes. The introduction thus offered an overview of the concepts underlying our study – justice, morality, clichés and their relationship to biblical law. In the next part of the paper, we compared a few demonstrative ancient criminal systems of Mesopotamia in order to illuminate their similarities and differences.

We consciously refrained from historicizing, since understanding the LT as a product of historical development – *e.g.*, from self-help to institutionalization or a state of nature to social contract – is beyond the scope of this paper.[114] With these observations in mind, we are now better prepared to speculate on the meaning of justice in the Bible.

While *lex talion* does appear originally in the Laws of Hammurabi, there, it seems to have meant mirror justice. In contrast, the iterations of the LT in the Bible mark the first recorded articulation of justice as a general principle of equivalent punishment. Outside of the Bible, one does not find an ancient legal text that articulates the legal concept that the punishment shall fit the crime. We saw that ancient criminal legal systems included both forms of criminal punishment: body mutilation and compensation. The Laws of Eshnunna, for example, specify monetary amounts that may have served as the monetary substitute for retaliatory body mutilation; however, these amounts do not seem to have been meant to represent the fair value of each injury notwithstanding the similarities between the Laws of Hammurabi and the Bible, the former lacks the textual nuance of the latter for such a reading.[115] It is, thus, possible that the idea that the punishment shall fit the crime made its first written appearance in the Torah.[116] (The claim here is *not* that this idea of justice does not predate the Bible, only that we do not have a written articulation of its prior existence.)

Ultimately, however, it is one thing to assert that the meaning of LT in the Bible ranges between two ideas; our analysis, however, would remain incomplete if we did not then ask what the shared values are between those two poles of meaning.

SO WHAT IS LEX TALIONIS?

Lex talionis is the legal principle that requires just valuation of the punishment in question.[117] In a recently published book, William Miller argues that "the talion puts valuation at the core of justice; it is about measuring."[118] Indeed, historically, "pretty near everything… had a price, for even though you could not quite buy honor, you could surely buy honor *back*, or redeem it."[119] Valuation underlies the principle of justice as both equal as well as equivalent punishments. The former conception sets out the ideal of exacting mirror justice. When possible, this view may require corporal punishments (*e.g.*, a seeing eye in exchange for a seeing eye). When impossible, it may require compensation (*e.g.*, money from blind person in exchange for a seeing eye). The latter conception grants more discretion when determining punishments for wrongs committed. Injury is not the only object of valuation; moral responsibility for causing injury is also critical to the determination of punishments. Since the same injury can have been caused in more and less morally culpable ways, the latter conception emphasizes the open-endedness of the LT and fits punishments to the facts of each case.

Common to both approaches is that justice is served and satisfaction achieved "when one 'gets even' by repaying one's debts and getting repaid when owed."[120] If "eye for eye" is the ideal of biblical justice, measuring harm and punishment is its realization. Something seems real insofar as it is measurable.[121] Accordingly, the Bible instructs courts to determine the proportionality of punishments so that the guilty can repay their debts to and later rejoin society. "Letting justice be done" can thus be understood as the popular desire to have courts actualize the ideals of justice.[122]

LEX & SOCIETY

One final note on the principle of proportionality as the yardstick of justice: in the context of criminal justice, proportionality refers to the standard upon which the valuation of punishments is to be based.[123] It is commonly thought that in developed legal systems – as opposed to biblical societies – general propositions on proportionality were replaced with more specific rules that maximize the predictability of legal outcomes by minimizing judicial discretion.[124] Nevertheless, the rub of proportionality is that it must always have a normative component.[125] What one society may consider just punishment, another may deem cruel and unusual.[126] While some legal systems may emphasize the principle of legal equality (*e.g.*, through elaborate criminal codes),[127] others may prefer the value of legal equivalence (*e.g.*, by granting their courts more discretion to fit punishments to each crime).[128] The principle of proportionality, thus, is always open to abuse.

NOTES

* Doctoral candidate at the University of Helsinki.

I am deeply indebted to Aliza Kramer, B.A. candidate at Bar Ilan University, for her research assistance. I thank Noam Gur for comments and corrections on the section discussing the relationship between law and morality. I would also like to thank Judah Kraut and Barry Wimpfheimer for commenting on earlier drafts. Finally, a debt of gratitude goes to my wife, Sarah Morduchowitz Nissel, for our ongoing and invaluable discussion on justice. This essay was written in memory of a dear childhood friend, Beth Samuels, who was always keen to talk about, listen to and lecture on all things normative. *Tehe nishmatah tzerurah bitzror hachayim* – may her soul be bound in the bond of eternal life.

1. Jeremy Waldron, "Lex Talionis," *Arizona Law Review* 34 (1992): 25–52, at 25.

2. Leviticus 19:18; unless otherwise stated all biblical translations are those of the King James Bible.

3. Talmud (Babylonian), Shabbat 31a (author's translation); *see also* Philo, *The Works of Philo: Complete and Unabridged* (*trans.* C.D. Yonge, Hendrickson Publishers, 2006), The Special Laws, III, §XIII (76) at p. 601. Justice as reciprocity is a central theme in both the Torah and Talmud (that is, in both the "written" and "oral" bodies of Jewish law). An oft quoted source from the New Testament "All things therefore whatsoever ye would that men should do unto you, even so do ye also unto them" (Matt. VIII. 12). One interesting early Jewish source of justice that is often overlooked is the apocryphal Book of the Wisdom of Solomon. In the context of the Passover narrative, it states: "Wherewithal a man sinneth, by the same also shall he be punished" (xi. 16). These sources seem to be based on the idea that has since come to be known as the "Golden Rule." The positive inflection imposes a moral duty to love and the negative inflection, as articulated by Hillel, requires punishment for wrongs *to the extent* that they should not have been committed – measure for measure, the punishment should fit the crime. I first thought of this Hohfeldian relationship when reading an article by Kaufmann Kohler and Emil G. Hirsh in the Jewish Encyclopedia ("The Golden Rule," also available at JewishEncyclopedia.com, accessed 21 December 2007). This idea of punishment as the application of the principles of measure for measure can also be found in Sanh. 90a (divine punishment), Sot. 8b (adultery), Ned. 32b (priests). Tangentially, we should note that, not surprisingly,

"measure for measure" articulation adopted from Sotah (rather than "eye for eye") became the preferred articulation of this principle for rabbinical scholars from the time of the Mishna onwards.

4. Law of retaliation is a loose translation of *lex talionis*, which, in turn, is a loose representation of the biblical concept of "eye for eye." These terms are used interchangeably throughout this article.

5. For an analysis of the *lex talionis* as it appeared in the rest of the Bible (including the New Testament), *see*, *e.g.*, James F. Davis, *Lex Talionis in Early Judaism and the Exhortation of Jesus in Matthew*: 5:38–42 (New York: Continuum International Publishing Group, 2005).

6. On this distinction when talking about law, *see* James Bernard Murphy, "The Lawyer and the Layman: Two Perspectives on the Rule of Law," *The Review of Politics* 68 (2006): 101–103.

7. The methodology employed here is modeled on Oxford University Press' *Very Short Introductions*. Namely, the body of the paper includes numerous (sustainable) generalizations that are then problematized in the endnotes.

8. *Compare* Waldron *supra* note 1 to Joel Feinberg, "Noncomparative Justice," The Philosophical Review 83, No. 3 (Jul. 1974): 297–338; *see further, infra*, A Brief Survey of Biblical Conceptions of Justice.

9. We should note that the Bible, much like in other texts of ancient laws, does not use the term "crime" nor does it categorically distinguish between civil and criminal laws. According to Hyman E. Goldin, "The absence of the term *criminal law* is, doubtless, a reflection of the fundamental premise of Jewish jurisprudence, namely, that the revealed will of God is the sole source of all Jewish legislation, and that consequently every punishment act constitutes a *sin*, a violation of God's will" (*Hebrew Criminal Law and Procedure* (New York: Twayne Publishers, 1952), at p. 11). David Daube adds to this point: While there is clearly a penal element involved in the LT, "What does not seem to have been much noticed is the opposite phenomenon, the presence in ancient times of civil law notions in what to-day would be pure criminal law affairs" (*Studies in Biblical Law* (New York: Ktav, 1969, originally published Cambridge: Cambridge University Press, 1947), at p. 102). In other words, while it is widely appreciated is that the LT is a criminal law concept, what is under-appreciated is that texts as old as the Pentateuch, already allowed for compensation in lieu of corporeal punishment. In all likelihood, Daube argues cautiously, "criminal law notions and civil law notions are of equal age." That said, "The difference between the primitive stage and the present lies chiefly in this,

that the two, criminal law and civil law, were not always so strictly distinguished as they are nowadays" (at p. 103).

In this author's view, if the reader wishes to follow-up on any one source herein referred to, she should read Daube's article on "Lex Talionis" in *Studies in Biblical Law* (pp. 102–153).

10. William L. Penfield, "International Arbitration" *American Journal of International Law* 1, No. 2 (1907): 330–341, at 339.

11. Jan Paullson, *Denial of Justice in International Law* (Cambridge: Cambridge University Press, 2005), at p. 2.

12. *See, for example,* Plato, *Republic* (Book 1).

13. *See, for example,* Aristotle, *Nicomachean Ethics* (v).

14. *See generally* John Rawls, *A Theory of Justice* (Cambridge: Harvard University Press, 1971).

15. *See generally* Robert Nozick, *Anarchy, State, and Utopia* (New York: Basic Books Inc., 1974).

16. Criminal justice theories seek to answer questions such as why should we punish, how much should we punish, how we should punish, whom should we punish, *et cetera*. This very brief survey, however, only touches upon the first two of these questions. A good primer for these ideas is Antony Duff and David Garland's essay, "Introduction: Thinking about Punishment," in *A Reader on Punishment*, eds. A. Duff and D. Garland, (Oxford: Oxford University Press, 1994). There are other disciplines that focus on the latter two questions we asked above. The sociological approach, for example, asks why particular punishments are used in each society and why other forms of punishment were abandoned; an influential work in this regard is Michel Foucault, *Discipline and Punish: The Birth of Prison* (New York: Random House, 1977).

17. *The American Heritage Dictionary of the English Language*, Fourth Edition. Houghton Mifflin Company, 2004. http://dictionary.reference.com/browse/justice (accessed: December 20, 2007). As Milton Fisk puts it, "Justice joins or fits together the persons, groups, or principles that stand in opposition in a conflict situation," *The State and Justice: An Essay in Political Theory*, (Cambridge: Cambridge University Press, 1989), at p. 74.

18. William Ian Miller, *Eye for an Eye* (Cambridge: Cambridge University Press, 2006), at p. 8; this is also the case with *tsedek* (*see infra* note 42).

19. *See* Delba Winthrop, "Aristotle and Theories of Justice," *The American Political Science Review* 72, No. 4 (1978): 1201–1216, at p. 1202.

20. John Bouvier, *Law Dictionary*, 8th edition (Kansas City: Vernon Law Book Company, 1914) as cited in Moore, *infra* note 32, at p. xxiii.

21. John Stuart Mill, *Utilitarianism* (Oskar Piest ed., New York: Macmillan, 1957, originally published in 1861), at p. 70.

22. Mill, *supra* note 21.

23. *See generally* Kent Greenawalt, "Punishment," *Journal of Criminal Law and Criminology*, Vol. 74 (Summer, 1983) 343–362, at p. 351–2.

24. *See* Douglas N. Husak, "Why Punish the Deserving?" *Noûs*, 26, No. 4 (1992): 447–464, at p. 456.

25. Waldron *supra* note 1, at 1.

26. Some argue that retributivism and LT are two different things, that the former is a justification for punishment while the latter is a way of measuring that punishment (i.e., proportionately) – see, e.g., Leo Zaibert, *Punishment and Retribution* (Aldershot: Ashgate, 2006), at p. 105 (LT "encapsulates, simultaneously, a lower and an upper limit to what can be justifiable by way of punishment. Lex Talionis thus cuts both ways and to that extent it is not easy to assert that it is necessarily, always unduly harsh" (at p. 106)). This article takes a contrary approach. Namely, the LT is more than about measuring punishments; it is also about the justification for those punishments.

27. Miller, *supra* note 18, at p. 140.

28. Many legal philosophers point this out – *e.g.*, Waldron, *supra* note 1, at 25 and Zaibert, *supra* note 37, at 105; *see further*, *infra*, A Brief Survey of Biblical Conceptions of Justice.

29. According to Cohn, *lex talionis* turns up in the Bible as both identical (e.g., "eye for eye") and equivalent formats (e.g., "the hand that sinned shall be cut off" of Deut. 25:12). The former can be understood as a talionic punishment *stricto sensu* and the latter as talionic *lato sensu*. This paper only looks at the stricter understanding of the LT. *See further* Haim H. Cohn, "Talion," *Encyclopedia Judaica* (Jerusalem, Keter Publishing 1971), 15:742–743, at p. 742. NB: the term "equivalence" is not used here to mean "something to do with" (as Cohn uses it) but to mean "similar to."

30. In this subsection, the terms justice and moral philosophy (or ethics) are used interchangeably. However, more precisely, justice concerns the general arrangement of society, which can be ordered according to legislation, personal moral codes, and other sets of rules. Moral philosophy, *stricto sensu*, concerns the systematic study of rights and wrongs. In this subsection, we will provide an overview of the relationship between secular law (such as parliamentary legislation) and

moral philosophy (such as the biblical conception of *lex talionis*). In this sense, then, justice can be seen as a branch of applied morality (or ethics). For an interesting discussion on the relationship between these two concepts, but *see, e.g.,* Douglas W. Kmiec, "Judicial Selection and the Pursuit of Justice: The Unsettled Relationship Between Law and Morality," *Catholic University Law Review* 39 (1989): 1–27. Kmiec argues that the relationship remains unsettled even within specific political camps. The distinction between morality and justice is not significant for the purposes of this subsection. *See also* M. Katherine B. Darmer and Robert M. Baird, *eds., Morality, Justice and the Law: The Continuing Debate* (Amherst, NY: Prometheus Books, 2007), at p. 11; in the book's Introduction, the editors grapple with the many ways in which legal theorists treat the three concepts.

31. For an excellent and brief overview on the competing conceptions of Law over the past hundred years, *see* Robert P. George, "What is Law? A Century of Arguments," reprinted in M. Katherine B. Darmer and Robert M. Baird, *eds., Morality, Justice and the Law: The Continuing Debate* (Amherst, NY: Prometheus Books, 2007), 37–53.

32. A great international arbitrator, John Bassett Moore, once wrote that a primary justification for the existence of a system of enforceable rules is to make it possible for a society to run as it should. Law, thus seen, is the technique of justice; it is the formal means of carrying out a society's underlying political (or moral) values. Of course, this is a never-ending process such that on a macro scale, says Moore, justice is never done. But, on a micro level, it requires that everybody is credited and blamed as proportionate in each society (*International Adjudication – Ancient and Modern History and Documents: Together with Mediatorial Reports, Advisory Opinions and the Decisions of Domestic Commissions on International Claims, Modern Series Vol. I* (New York, Oxford University Press, 1929), at pp. XXII–XXIII).

33. However, see following paragraph regarding some controversial aspects of the relationship between law and morality.

34. For an influential contemporary natural law account, *see* Gustav Radbruch, *'Gesetzliches Unrecht und übergesetzliches Recht'*, first published in the *Süddeutsche Juristen-Zeitung* 1 (1946): 105–108, translated by Bonnie Litschewsky Paulson and Stanley L. Paulson, "Statutory Lawlessness and Supra-Statutory Law," *Oxford Journal of Legal Studies* 26, No. 1 (2006): 1–11; John Finnis, *Natural Law and Natural Rights* (New York: Oxford University Press Inc., 1980 , Ch. 12: Unjust Laws).

35. Hence, they are often referred to as positivists, but this label is not

entirely accurate; *compare* HLA Hart, *The Concept of Law* (New York: Oxford University Press Inc., 1961) to Joseph Raz, *see* Ch. 12: Unjust Laws. *The Authority of Law: Essays on Law and Morality* (Oxford: Clarendon Press, 1979), Ch. 3: Legal Positivism and the Sources of Law; Joseph Raz, *Ethics in the Public Domain: Essays in the Morality of Law and Politics* (New York: Oxford University Press, 1996) at pp. 230–235.

36. The role of morality as validator of the law is a controversial one. We have indicated one, perhaps the most direct, way in which morality can function as a validating factor of the law. While there are various other, more indirect, possibilities for morality to play that role, it is outside the scope of this brief survey to enumerate them.

37. For a representative view, *see* Joseph Raz, *supra* note 35, at pp. 233–234; Joseph Raz, "Postema on Law's Autonomy and Public Practical Reasons: A Critical Comment," *Legal Theory*, Vol. 4 (1998) 1–20, at pp. 4–6.

38. *See, e.g.,* Ronald Dworkin, *Law's Empire* (Cambridge: Harvard University Press, 1986).

39. *See, e.g.,* Jules Coleman, "Negative and Positive Positivism," *The Journal of Legal Studies*, Vol. 11, No. 1. (Jan., 1982), pp. 139–164.

40. For more on the blunt but perhaps helpful distinction between the ways in which morality relates to religious as opposed to non-religious (or secular) law: *see* Julius Kaftan, "Authority as a Principle of Theology," *The American Journal of Theology* 4, No. 4 (Oct., 1900): 673–733; Brian J. Shaw, "Habermas and Religious Inclusion: Lessons from Kant's Moral Theology," *Political Theory,* 27, No. 5 (Oct., 1999): 634–666; Patricia Springborg, "Leviathan and the Problem of Ecclesiastical Authority," *Political Theory* 3, No. 3 (Aug., 1975): 289–303; *see also infra* note 84.

41. This is the translation of the Jewish Publication Society.

42. Edmund Perry, "The Meaning of 'Emuna' in the Old Testament," *Journal of Bible and Religion* Vol. 21, No. 4 (Oct., 1953): 252–256, at p. 253.

43. It is in this sense that the word just (meaning: only or merely) comes to us.

44. By original ingenuity, we do not intend to convey the idea that justice once meant either equality and then became equivalence (or vice versa). Such oversimplifications about the "development" of criminal law are not relevant to such a brief survey; *see further infra*, note 57 and *supra* note 9, at p. 122 ("Quite often, though a phrase may be used ap-

parently expressing the idea in question, it is merely a phrase, emptied of most of its original content" – p. 122.)

45. Jeremy Waldron, *supra* note 1, at p. 46.

46. An example: recently "A Hamas leader said there would be quick retaliation: 'The Hamas response will be like an earthquake.' 'An eye for an eye…a politician for a politician,' he said." (Associated Press Report, June 10, 2003, as cited in James Davis, "Jesus and the Law of Retaliation (Lex Talionis) Matthew 5:38–42," Studies in the Gospel of Matthew, available on Bible.org at http://www.bible.org/page.php?page_id=1066 (last accessed: December 20, 2007).

47. *See, e.g.,* John G. Cawelti, "Myths of Violence in American Popular Culture," *Critical Inquiry* 1, No. 3. (Mar., 1975): 521–541, at 530.

48. Robert Nozick, *Philosophical Explanations* (Cambridge: Harvard University Press, 1981), at p. 366; *similarly,* Ellsworth Faris, "The Origin of Punishment," *International Journal of Ethics,* Vol. 25, No. 1. (Oct., 1914), pp. 54–67, at p. 54.

49. Miller, *supra* note 18, at pp. 64–65; tangential to the topic of Jewish law as responsive to human nature, *see* Hanina Ben-Menahem, "Maimonides on Equity: Reconsidering the 'Guide for the Perplexed' III:34," *Journal of Law and Religion,* Vol. 17, No. 1/2 (2002): 19–48, at pp. 23–24.

50. A.S. Diamond, "Any Eye for an Eye," IRAQ 19 (1957): 151–5 as cited in Bernard S. Jackson, "Evolution and Foreign Influence in Ancient Law," *American Journal of Comparative Law* 16 (1968): 372–390, at p. 386. Jackson disagrees with this finding of Diamond. Professor Miller claims that other, more historically particular factors were sure to also have played a role. For example, talionic cultures tended to be honor cultures where more than quantitative measuring of harm was at stake (Miller, *supra* note 18, at p. x). Indeed, according to some historians, early Israelite society was similar to the Bedouin vengeance-obsessed state of nature people, where people would regularly gouge each other's eyes out […seriously] (*see* Johann D. Michaelis, *Commentaries on the Laws of Moses* 192 (1814): 214–15 ("Of the Laws respecting the Goel or Blood-avenger") as cited in James Q. Whitman, "Ancient Rights and Wrongs: At the Origins of Law and the State: Supervision of Violence, Mutilation of Bodies, or Setting of Prices?" *Chicago-Kent Law Review.* 71 (1995): 41–84, at p. 55). *See further infra,* note 57.

51. Nozick, *supra* note 48, at 366.

52. Waldron, *supra* note 1 at p. 32. A concept that is shared by both distributive and retaliatory is the principle of equality before the law (a

related but distinct idea to the rule of law). In a society where no one acts in exactly the same way, how does the law account for the nuances of each factual matrix? This is the problem of legalism, or the task of balancing the general interest of equality with the specific interests of the accused. As we have seen, justice requires that individuals be treated in accordance with their rights and deserts, a judge is meant to consider the mental state of the accused (e.g., intent), any exculpating factors (e.g., self defense), *et cetera*.

53. Quoted by another medieval exegete, Ibn Ezra, in his Commentary on Ex. 21:24 and Lev. 24: 20.

54. *See also* Philip Berger Benny, *The Criminal Code of the Jews* (London: Smith, Elder, & Co., 1880): "The *lex talionis* was simply a law by which a person deliberately and purposely and maliciously inflicting upon another certain specified injuries, was liable to have similar injuries inflicted upon his own person" (at p. 22).

55. §8:2 (Torts or Delicts): If a person has maimed another's limb, let there be retaliation in kind, unless he makes agreement for composition with him – *see further* Boaz Cohen, "The Relationship of Jewish to Roman Law," *The Jewish Quarterly Review* (1944), 267–280 and Boaz Cohen, "The Relationship of Jewish to Roman Law (Continued)," *The Jewish Quarterly Review* (1944), 409–424.

56. *See further* William A. Schabas, "Perverse Effects of the *Nulla Poena* Principle: National Practice and the Ad Hoc Tribunals," 11 *European Journal of International Law* Vol. 11. (2000), at pp. 521, 522; Susan Lamb, "*Nullum Crimen, Nulla Poena Sine Lege* in International Criminal Law," in Antonio Cassese, Paola Gaeta and John R.W.D. Jones, *eds.*, *The Rome Statute and the International Criminal Court: A Commentary, Vol. 1* (Oxford: Oxford University Press, 2002), at pp. 733, 740; Gordon Ireland, "*Ex Post Facto* from Rome to Tokyo," *Temple Law Quarterly* Vol. 21 (Jul. 1947), at p. 27.

57. Briefly, proponents of the self-help model agreed with those of the social contract theorists in assuming that there had been some sort of "state of nature" in which violence was widely prevalent. The former, however, did not accept the proposition that the violence of this state of nature had been disorderly and chaotic – rather, it was ad hoc order that was founded in the systematic organization of vengeance. The self-help model had the early state arising out of the effort to supervise and institutionalize this spontaneous violence in the state of nature (a good synopsis can be found in Whitman, *supra* note 50, at 41–42; classic expositions include Maine, *infra* note 59, at pp. 320–1

and Weber, *infra* note 74, at p. 137, and generally, Weber, *Wirtschaft und Gesellschaft: Grundriss Der Verstehenden Soziologie* (5th ed., 1976), at p. 516.). According to classic social contract model, state institutions substitute orderly punishment for chaotic revenge (*see, e.g.,* Ze'ev W. Falk, *Hebrew Law in Biblical Times* (Provo: Brigham Young University Press, 2nd ed., 2001), at pp. 73–75). Nowadays, more post-structuralist approaches acknowledge that "Revenge always coexisted with a compensation option" (Miller, *supra* note 18, at p. 25). As will be discussed in the final part of this paper, rather than study legal history in search of the truths about human nature, researching the history of individual legal systems can reveal many values underlying specific societies.

58. Moshe Greenberg, "Some Postulates of Biblical Criminal Law," in *Yehezkel Kaufmann Jubilee Volume*, (Jerusalem: Magnes Press, 1960); Martha T. Roth, "Ancient Rights and Wrongs: Mesopotamian Legal Traditions and the Laws of Hammurabi," 71 *Chicago-Kent Law Review* (1995) 13–38, at p. 13; *see infra Deuteronomy 19*.

59. Martha T. Roth, *Law Collections from Mesopotamia and Asia Minor*, 2nd ed. (1997), at p. 215; Nachum Sarna, "Excursis 6 to Exodus," in Nachum Sarna (ed.), *The JPS Torah Commentary: Exodus* (Philadelphia: Jewish Publication Society, 1991) 273–276, at p. 275; Sir Henry Sumner Maine, *Ancient Law* (1861, reprinted by Dorset Press in 1986), at pp. 12, 305; *see also infra* note 78.

60. Roth, *supra* note 59, at p. 65.

61. See *supra What is Justice?*

62. Roth, *supra* note 59, at p. 60.

63. Roth, *supra* note 59, at p. 71.

64. "A member of a group or class of priestesses, with special privileges, sometimes of royal lineage…" (Roth, *supra* note 59, at p. 273).

65. Roth, *supra* note 59, at p. 105.

66. Roth, *supra* note 59, at p. 120.

67. "The term used for…the general, nonspecific, 'person' as subject of a law provision" (Roth, *supra* note 59, at p. 268).

68. Roth, *supra* note 59, at p. 121.

69. Roth, *supra* note 59, at p. 121.

70. Roth, *supra* note 59, at p. 121.

71. Roth, *supra* note 59, at p. 121; *see* §§200–1 for teeth, §§202–5 for cheeks, §§206–8 for fights, §§209–214 for women/fetuses.

72. See Miller, *supra* note 18, at p. 197.

73. Vincent Scheil (one of the discoverers of Hammurabi's Laws as excavated in Persia), "The Code of Hammurabi," *Editio princeps*, Tome IV,

Textes Elamites-Semitiques of the Memoires de la delegation en Perse (Paris, 1902). This discovery did not mark the beginning of the study of comparative (Mesopotamian) cultures, but it did catalyze the field. The first secular evaluation may have come from John Spencer, in *De Legibus Hebraeorum Ritualibus et Earum Rationibus* (1685); *see further, infra* note 90.

74. Compare R.F. Harper, *The Code of Hammurabi, King, of Babylon about 2250 B.C.* (Chicago: Chicago University Press, 1904) *and* Max Weber, *Ancient Judaism* (trans. and ed. Hans H. Gerth and Don Martindale; Glencoe: The Free Press, 1952, originally published in German in 1921), at pp. 62, 438–9 *to* S.A. Cook, who (in the minority at the time), in *The Laws of Moses and the Code of Hammurabi* (London: Adam and Charles Black, 1903), argues for the dissimilarity of the two texts.

75. For example, even as the law evolved to adapt to new circumstances, these changes were read in to the text of the Bible using traditional hermeneutical methods. According to one scholar: by the time of the Talmud, "a number of the Mosaic ordinances had become utter anachronisms. Some were perfectly impracticable; one or two were no longer even understood. The exigencies of the age and the circumstances of the people necessitated the adoption of several enactments unknown to the Pentateuch. Throughout, however, the whole of the penal code of the Talmud – as in its various stages of development – the Divine origin of the Hebrew legal system is never for a moment lost sight of" (Benny, *supra* note 54, at p. 18). In this way, new insights were read into the Bible since "the Lawgiver could not have intended the *lex talionis* to apply to cases of bodily injury" (Goldin, *supra* note 9, at p. 54).

76. J.H. Hertz, *The Pentateuch and Haftorahs*, 2nd ed. (London: Soncino Press, 1987), at p. 404.

77. Case-by-case legal reasoning, often written in the conditional style of "If X happens, apply the law Y." *See further* James G. Williams, "Concerning One of the Apodictic Formulas," *Vetus Testamentum*, 14, No. 4 (Oct., 1964): 484–9, critically questioning Albrecht Alt's famous claim that apodictic laws originated in legal form in the Bible.

78. On the specific oral tradition of ancient Israelite society, *see* Yung Suk Kim, "Lex Talionis in Exod 21:22 25: Its Origin and Context," *Journal of Hebrew Scriptures*, Vol. 6, Art. 3 (2006) 1–11, at pp. 3–5, available online at http://www.arts.ualberta.ca/JHS/Articles/article_53.pdf (last accessed 20 December 2007); Nachum Sarna argues that none of the "codes" of the time were codes in the strict sense of the term since, *inter alia*, they omit important spheres of legal practice that were governed

by oral traditions (*supra* note 59, at 275); Maimonides too ultimately relies on Oral Law to justify the LT (*Moses Maimonides, The Code of Maimonides: Book Eleven, The Book of Torts* (trans. Hyman Klein) (New Haven: Yale University Press, 1954), "Laws Concerning Wounding and Damaging," 1:2, at p. 160) – *see further* Irwin H. Haut, "Lex Talionis: Views, Ancient and Modern, Particularly, those of Maimonides," 14 *Dine Yisrael* 7 (1991–1992); *see also infra* notes 89 and 90.

79. Bernard S. Jackson, *Wisdom-Laws: A Study of the* Mishpatim *of* Exodus *21:1–22:16* (New York: Oxford University Press 2006), at p. 25.

80. Jackson, *supra* note 79, at pp. 200–1, footnotes omitted. *See further* David Weiss Halivni, *Midrash, Mishnah, and Gemara: The Jewish Predilection for Justified Law* (Cambridge: Harvard University Press, 1986) – according to Halivni, the Bible used a "justifying" or "vindicatory" legal style in an effort to signify that "it reckons with the will of the people to whom the laws are directed" (at pp. 13–14).

81. See *infra* Some Thoughts on Justice in the Bible.

82. The more doctrinal or general command style in which biblical law was formulated – *e.g.*, "Thou shalt not do X."

83. In cuneiform law, the death penalty for murder can be commuted or pardoned. Also in cuneiform and in contrast to biblical law, many non-fatal social crimes are punished by the death penalty. In contrast, as Greenberg has written, "in biblical law life and property are incommensurable..." (Greenberg,, *supra* note 58, at p. 27). Similarly, Nachum Sarna, while acknowledging the similarities between the Laws of Hammurabi and Moses, famously argues that the differences between the two sets of laws are revolutionary – the Bible grants human life a unique, non proprietary, status; it is fundamentally more egalitarian, *et cetera*...(*supra* note 59).

84. In cuneiform law such as Hammurabi's, "In accord with the royal origin of these laws is their purpose: to establish justice.... Whereas in biblical law, the idea of the transcendence of the law receives a more thoroughgoing expression. Here God is not merely the custodian of justice or the dispenser of 'truth' to man, he is the fountainhead of the law, the law is a statement of his will." As a matter of religious law, this makes violations of certain biblical laws not just crimes but sins (Greenberg, *supra* note 58, at p. 22). *See further, infra* note 108.

85. Academics remain divided over the actual existence of Abraham – *compare* William Foxwell Albright, "The Biblical Period," in *The Jews, Their History, Culture and Religion*, ed. L. Finkelstein (New York: Harper and Brothers, 1949) pp. 3–69 and David Rosenberg, *Abraham:*

The First Historical Biography (Cambridge: Basic Books, 2006) *to* Julius Wellhausen, *Prolegomena to the History of Ancient Israel* (New York: World Publishing Co., 1957) *and* William G. Dever, *Recent Archaeological Discoveries and Biblical Research* (Seattle: University of Washington Press, 1990).

86. W.W. Davies, *Codes of Hammurabi and Moses* (Berkeley: Apocryphile Press, 2006, first published in 1905), at p. 11.

87. Davies, *supra* note 86, at p. 9; *see also* Cook, *supra* note 74, at p. 39 and Hertz, *supra* note 76, at p. 405; *compare further, e.g.,* Haim H. Cohn: "True talionic punishments were undoubtedly practiced in biblical and post-biblical times" (*supra* note 47, at p. 742) *to* J.H. Hertz: "There is in Jewish history no instance of the law of retaliation ever having been carried out literally – eye for an eye, tooth for a tooth " (*supra* note 76, at p. 527).

88. Weber, *supra* note 74, at p. 62.

89. For example, it is possible that "eye for eye" was an early cliché that was later moderated in ancient legal text from requiring corporeal punishment to allowing for commensurate compensation instead. In other words, oral traditions may have developed vengeful notions of justice that were later moderated in the texts. According to Samuel Mendelsohn, "the earliest penal laws were enacted for emergencies, after the commission of the crime; and since they were framed with special reference to immediate occasions, they were dictated rather by blind popular impulse, than by the logical conclusions reached by the calm deliberations of legislative wisdom" (*The Criminal Jurisprudence of the Ancient Hebrews* (New York: Hermon Press, 2nd ed., 1968), at pp. 10–11). Why, was the text left intact however? Why not just modify it to more accurately reflect the new approach (e.g., "the worth of an eye for an eye" instead of leaving the rule as "eye for eye"). According to David Daube, in ancient texts "There is a code leading with various matters. Some day it is decided to add another rule on one of these matters. Now a strictly logical mind would insert the new rule, in accordance with its contents, between these or those two of the old provisions. As a matter of fact, however, it is not inserted in this manner. The existing code is left undisturbed, and the new rule simply tacked on at the end" (Daube, *supra* note 9, at p. 74).

90. "Dibrah torah kilshon bnei adam" (God spoke in the language of man). The idea is known in Latin as *scriptura humane loquitur – see further* Stephen D. Benin, "The 'Cunning of God' and Divine Accommodation," *Journal of the History of Ideas* (1984) 179–91, at p. 180. Sarna lists the

following citations for "Dibrah torah kilshon bnei adam:" Sifrei 112:11; Yev. 71a; Ket. 67b; Ned. 3a-b; Git. 41b; Kid. 17b; BM 31b, 94b; Sanh. 56a, 64b, 85b, 90b; Mak. 12a; Av. Zar. 27a; Zev. 108b; Bek. 31b; Arak. 31a; Ker. 11a; Nid. 32b, 44a (*supra* note 59, at p. 276); contrast Miller, *supra* note 18, at p. 22.

91. "The talio holds good in old Hebrew law, in the Koran, and is as characteristic of early Semitic legislation as of other ancient legal codes" (Cook, *supra* note 74, at p. 249, footnotes omitted).

92. Cohn, *supra* note 29, at p. 742. According to

93. For example, why does the Bible say "thou shalt give life for life?" According to Benno Jacob, the text dictates it is compensation. "Thou shalt *give*" (Ex. 21:23), according to Jacob, cannot refer to *taking* a limb, but only to *giving* its monetary equivalent (as cited in Nechama Leibowitz, *Studies in Shemot* (Jerusalem: The World Zionist Organization, 1976) at pp. 251–252); Davis *supra* note 5, at p. 39.

94. This reading is supported by the "life for life" iteration in Leviticus.

95. This reading is supported by the structural interpretation found in *Toldot Yitzchak* on Ex., Ch. 23; see also San. 24b; according to the Talmud victims get compensated for 5 things: damages, pain, medical expenses, loss of wages and embarrassment. The Talmud discusses this at length as well as how to evaluate and valuations themselves, all which are written in terms of principles rather than straight-up equations (Bava Kama 83b–84a).

96. "Moreover ye shall take no satisfaction for the life of a murderer, which is guilty of death: but he shall be surely put to death" (Num. 35:31).

97. See Greenberg, *supra* note 58 and Roth, *supra* note 58, at p. 25.

98. For a contemporary biblical criticism reading, *see* Jackson, *supra* note 79, at pp. 185–188, who asks why the LT formula in Exodus 21:24–5 is attached to that regarding the pregnant women victim (vv. 22–23)? Can a fetus lose a tooth? Jackson concludes that the passages are actually not organically connected, but were placed together because of the "life for life" in v. 23.

99. Bernard S. Jackson, "The Problem of Exod. XXI 22–5 (Ius talionis)," *Vetus Testamentum*, 23, No. 3. (Jul. 1973), 273–304, at p. 303.

100. The second half of this verse is a translation of Jewish Publication Society, rather than of the King James Bible (which translates it as "beast for beast"). Daube agrees with the former and disagrees with the latter (*supra* note 9, at p. 112).

101. *Contrast* the idealistic views regarding "general principles of law" of Bin Cheng, *General Principles Of Law as Applied by International Courts*

and Tribunals (London: Stevens & Sons, Ltd. 1953), especially at p. 24 *to* the more cynical views of Hanina Ben-Menahem, *Judicial Deviation in Talmudic Law: Governed by Men, not by Rules* (New York: Harwood Academic Publishers, 1991), at pp. 12–14.

102. See *Mekhilta of R. Ishmael, Mishpatim* §5. Since *kofer* applies to capital cases (Exod. 21:30), monetary compensation must than apply to a non-capital case – *see further* Bava Kama 83b–84a.

103. This approach is taken in the Midrash Tanaim on Deut., Ch. 19 as well as in the Talmud: Ket. 35a and Bava Kama 83b.

104. On this view, the taking of a human life is fundamentally different from all other offences: "taking of life cannot be made up for by any amount of property, nor can any property offense be considered as amounting to the value of a life" (Greenberg, *supra* note 58, at p. 27).

105. The laws of war are discussed before and after the iteration of the LT and directly afterwards, property law is discussed.

106. This point was recognized long ago by an early scholar of biblical studies, Enoch Cobb Wines: "In our exposition and defense of this law, it is, as already hinted, important to observe, that it did not authorize the retaliation of injuries by individuals, and so make each man a judge and avenger in his own cause. Such a principle as this never entered into the mind of the Hebrew lawgiver. It is abhorrent to the whole genius of his legislation, and would have been as earnestly repudiated by him, as it is by any one of his assailants. In every instance of the application of the principle of the lex talionis, it was the duty of a legal tribunal to adjudge, and of the public executive power to inflict, the punishment." (*Commentaries on the Laws of the Ancient Hebrews: With an Introductory Essay on Civil Society and Government* (New York: G.P. Putnam, 1855), at p. 272).

107. According to the Pharisees (Mak. 5b), the iteration of the LT in v. 21 is a conceptual one that is meant to clarify a specific legal rule – namely, false testimony is only punishable if failed (whereas the Sadducees argued based on v. 19 that false testimony is only punishable if successful) – David Daube, "Witnesses in Bible and Talmud," in David Daube and Calum Carmichael, *Witnesses in Bible and Talmud* and *Biblical Las of Talion* (Oxford, Oxford Centre for Postgraduate Hebrew Studies, 1986) 1–20, at p. 11.

108. Daube, *supra* note 9, at 129–130. This approach is supported by Mekhilta R. Simeon Ben Yohai §§19 (עין בעין is מידה במידה) as well as Mekhilta of R. Ishmael, Mishpatim §8. Indeed, the rabbinic approach to the LT was to modify the cliché from "body-part for body-part" to "measure

for measure" (מידה כנגד מידה); *see also* Tal. Bava Batra 88B; Rosh, Tal. Baba Batra, Chapter 5.

109. I owe this idea to Rabbi Aharon Halevi Epstein, *Aruch Hashulchan: Choshen Mishpat, Hilchot Chovel BeChavero* para. 6.

110. Indeed, biblical scholars often refer to a "Deuteronomy school" that represents God as the God of just compensation (*see* Weber, *supra* note 74, at p. 216).

111. *See* Waldron, *supra* note 1, at p. 32 *and generally*, Duncan Kennedy, *A Critique of Adjudication* (Cambridge: Harvard University Press, 1997).

112. Sarna, *supra* note 59, at p. 126.

113. Philo, The Special Laws, III, §xxxiii, *supra* note 3, at p. 183; on the related principle of "equity" in Jewish law, *see* Ben-Menahem, *supra* note 49, especially at pp. 32–34.

114. Greenberg,, *supra* note 58. In some Western societies, for example, the idea of punishment as public censure may play a significant social role – *see* Andrew von Hirsch, "Censure and Proportionality," in A. Duff and D. Garland *supra* note 16, at p. 112.

115. *See further*, Roth, *supra* note 58, at p. 25; *see* Jackson, *supra* note 99, at p. 298 (the old view erroneously regarded the LT as "primitive" or "natural," and as representing the earliest stage of legal advance).

116. Some would disagree. E.g., Leo Zaibert recently wrote: "While *lex talionis* can be seen in a charitable light, that is, as an incipient (albeit clumsy) attempt to say that there must be proportionality between the harm and the punishment (you cannot take an eye when the harm amounted merely to a tooth, and so on), it is obvious that such a view is different from retributivism" (*supra* note 26, at p. 106).

117. Waldron, *supra* note 1, at 46.

118. Miller, *supra* note 18, at p. *xii*.

119. Miller, *supra* note 18, at p. 130 (emphasis in original).

120. Miller, *supra* note 18, at p. 142; tangentially, the English word peace comes from the Latin pax (or pacare), which "derives from the idea of paying." Peace is about settling accounts, paying back what you owe – Miller, *supra* note 18, at p. 15; *compare* Daube, *supra* note 9, at pp. 133–144 *to* Jacob Milgrom, "The Legal Terms Šlm and Brḥšw in the Bible," *Journal of Near Eastern* Studies Vol. 35, No. 4 (1976) 271–273.

121. As the father of international law, Hugo Grotius has stated: "money is the common measure of valuable things" (*Opinion in the Lusitania Cases (United States v. Germany)*, 1 November 1923, Vol. VII *Reports of International Arbitral Awards (United Nations)* 32, at 33.

122. In contrast, some say, to divine justice in the Bible: "Well, God was never what we would call a proportionalist. God goes postal a lot, which is what human societies won't let their people do" (Laura Miller, "The fine art of revenge: A legal scholar says that "eye for an eye" justice is a lot more humane than you think," available online On Solon Media Group Inc, http://www.salon.com/books/int/2006/02/20/miller/print. html (last accessed: December 20, 2007).

123. Some Latin terms expressing the idea of proportionality include *pro rata, pari passu* and *pro tanto*.

124. *See* D.W. Greig, "Reciprocity, Proportionality, and the Law of Treaties," *Virginia Journal of International Law* 34 (1994): 295–403, at p. 298.

125. Sophie Boyron, "Proportionality in English Administrative Law: A Faulty Translation?" *Oxford Journal of Legal Studies*, 12 No. 2 (1992): 237–264, at p. 254 (a broad use of proportionality could prove to be another cloak hiding prejudices or policy considerations – at p. 255).

126. In a notorious example, the Medieval Church relied on the principle of proportionality to justify draconian punishments on religious dissidents – R.H. Helmholz, "Harold Berman's Accomplishment as a Legal Historian," *Emory Law Journal* 42 (1993): 475–496, at p. 491; Helmholz discusses this idea further in his later article, "Magna Carta and the ius commune," *University of Chicago Law Review* 66 (1999): 297–371, at p. 327–328. The Magna Carta (1225 CE) states: "Earls and barons shall be fined only by their equals, and in proportion to the gravity of their offence. A fine imposed upon the lay property of a clerk in holy orders shall be assessed upon the same principles, without reference to the value of his ecclesiastical benefice" (§§ 20, 21 respectively).

127. This is not to conflate "eye for eye" as equality with the principle of "equality before the law," but the two are related.

128. *See* Boyron, *supra* note 124, at pp. 254–5 for British and French legal systems; for an example of the problem of relating the European Legal concept of proportionality to that of German municipal law, *see* Margherita Poto, "The Principle of Proportionality in Comparative Perspective," *German Law Journal* 8, No. 9 (2007): 835–869, at p. 836.

Midwives and Moral Reasoning, Love and Law:

A GENDERED READING OF THE BOOK OF EXODUS

Andrew Rosenblatt

> *Upon the merit of righteous women*
> *Israel was redeemed from Egypt*
> Sotah 11b

The Talmud in Sotah 11b gives particular weight to the role of women in the story of the Exodus, "Rav Avira expounded that in the merit of righteous women in that generation were they redeemed from Egypt." Halachic literature teaches that the prominence of women in the Exodus forces an exception to the general rule that women are exempt from time generated commandments. Furthermore, an observant reader will notice striking gender issues within the first chapters of Exodus. As Pharaoh oppresses the Jews, one might look for a classical heroic figure that would stand up to the paranoid tyrant. However, when looking at these chapters it is only the Hebrew midwives, Miriam, and the Daughter of Pharaoh, who openly defy the decrees of the Egyptian king. Furthermore, even after a revelation is presented to Moshe at the bush, it is Tzipporah who saves him from the fate that should await a father who neglects the circumcision of his own son. One might argue that Moshe, and not any of these women, is the central male figure that rises as the savior or hero in this book. However, we should note that Moshe himself is raised in sequence by two women, without the hint of a male role model in the verses of the Torah. Furthermore, female actors in the books of Tanach are rare indeed, to see so many of them in such close proximity indicates that a new dynamic is at play.[1]

On the Midrashic level it is interesting to see the question of resistance debated with Aaron and Yocheved[2]. In the end, the one person who rises in defiance of the word of Pharaoh is Miriam. Again the one that defies the rules is female. These facts provide inspiration for a gender oriented reading of this book of the Bible[3]. We will look to see if we can find a new heroic, one that might bear particularly feminine characteristics and that will describe both the actions of the male heroes and inform the nature of the law that is presented.

In A Different Voice

To properly understand this gender orientation it would be wise to draw from classic research on gender psychology. Carol Gilligan, in her book *In A Different Voice: Psychological Theory and Women's Development* amalgamates her own research and that of others to present a comprehensive understanding of the differences in moral reasoning between genders. Her observations afford critical information and powerful methodologies in unlocking the meaning in the book of Exodus.

Based on responses to what is called Heinz dilemma, where children are given the following scenario, "a man named Heinz considers whether or not to steal a drug which he cannot afford to buy in order to save the life of his wife." Child subjects are asked not only what they would do, but also to articulate the reasoning that brought them to their conclusion. Gilligan concluded that boys mediated disputes based on rules and law, "they began to transpose a hierarchy of power into a hierarch of values, in this way he abstracts the moral from the interpersonal." On the other hand girls mediate the "Heinz dilemma with a network of connection, a web of relationships that is sustained by a process of communication"[4]. Thus as we probe the book of Shemot, actions that are motivated by rules and the abstraction of values into a set of protocols represent male action. On the other hand, decisions and actions which are motivated and animated by preservation or development of a relationship would thus represent the feminine modality.

Furthermore, Gilligan made the following observation while executing a TAT (Thematic Apperception Test)[5] analysis. Simple pictures, such as a man and a woman sitting on a park bench, two trapeze artists or a woman behind a desk in the background and a woman in a lab coat in the foreground were presented to individuals in the study who were then asked to compose a story based on the picture. Roughly 20% of the stories written by the men contained violent elements such as murder, stabbing, rape, or kidnapping, a smaller percentage of the women's stories contained violence of that nature. It was observed that as the individuals in a picture were more physically proximate, or could be perceived to more intimate, there was an increased incidence of violence in male stories. Conversely, there was an increased incidence of violence in females stories when the individuals were less physically proximate (with the single highest percentage of violent stories written by women in response to an image in which an individual was sitting alone). Making the assumption that the projection of violence into a story is a reflection of a fear and anxiety, Gilligan drew the conclusion that men project violence and perceive fear in situations that suggest intimacy, and that women do so in situations of isolation and competitive success.[6]

With Gilligan's findings in mind, we can investigate anew the exploration of the text of the book of Shemot. As we look not only for heroic action, but also a model for heroics within the context of the formation of *Am Yisrael*, the Israelite nation, we are well prepared to see if the Torah is embracing a masculine or feminine modality.

Heroics in Exodus

The first act of heroics is of course the refusal of the midwives to follow the instructions of Pharaoh (Exod. 1:17), "But the midwives feared God, and did not as the king of Egypt commanded them, but saved the men-children alive.[7]" The midwives here are motivated by a fear of God. Or differently described, it is their relationship with God that motivates them to defy the rules that the King of Egypt has devised for the long term preservation of his nation. They are not described as rejecting Pharaoh's wisdom because a different set of logical rules bring them to an alternate conclusion – even though such a thought process might have taken place, or might even be implied by the fear of God. It is the relationship with God that motivates defiance rather than a more logical analysis of the inequity or the ethical problems.[8]

We notice also that outside of the moments of marriage and conception Moshe's father does not present in the text of the narrative. It is his mother who realizes what needs to be done, his sister who watches from afar and then his mother who will return as midwife.

Interestingly, next to violate the laws of the Pharaoh is none other than his own daughter. As baby Moshe famously sits in his basket among the reeds in the Nile, it is daughter or Pharaoh who comes to greet him.

> **5** And the daughter of Pharaoh came down to bathe in the river; and her maidens walked along by the river-side; and she saw the ark among the flags, and sent her handmaid to fetch it.

> **6** And she opened it, and saw it, even the child; and behold a boy that wept. And she had compassion on him, and said: 'This is one of the Hebrews' children.'

Again we see a defiance of the rules of Pharaoh; the picture is quite startling as the Daughter of Pharaoh descends from the steps of the great house of the Egyptian king[9] to rescue this child – figuratively presenting us with a heroine leaving the structure of the laws of Egypt and motivated by a sense of connection and potential relationship with this child. It must be emphasized that her defiance is not motivated by the logical analysis that her father's rules are unjust she therefore engages herself in an act of calculated protest. Rather she is motivated by a sense of human connection with a particular child.[10]

The next moment of defiance is taken up by Moshe, who is without question male. Nevertheless, Moshe is raised by two women, his natural mother and the daughter of Pharaoh. Furthermore, the motivations for Moshe's act of defiance resembles more the sense of connection that Carol Gilligan finds characteristic of women, than the logical abstractions characteristic of men. As we see in the following (Exod. 2:11–12)

> **11** And it came to pass in those days, when Moses was grown up, that he went out unto his brethren, and looked on their burdens; and he saw an Egyptian smiting a Hebrew, one of his brethren.

> **12** And he looked this way and that way, and when he saw that there was no man, he smote the Egyptian, and hid him in the sand.

While this is no doubt an act of defiance, there is not really a sense that Moshe analyzed the inequity and therefore took defiant action. Rather, we are given the impression that Moshe established a connection with his brothers, he actually identified with their pain and stood to defend them out of that connection. Notice how the verse (11) emphasizes at the end that the victim was his brother, when this information is already assumed from the fact that the victim was a Hebrew. Similarly, Moshe does not see their suffering, but sees *in* their suffering – a point which nearly all commentators understand to communicate a heightened awareness of their true inner suffering.[11] This is a pivotal moment for Moshe as well, for he is clearly rejecting one social network, that of the "great house" of Pharaoh, for the social network of his Hebrew Brothers.[12] However, as we noted before the only persons to defy Pharaoh are the midwives and this young man Moshe who has been raised by two women. Thus a new kind of heroics emerges from these chapters in which *Am Yisrael*, the Israelite nation, begins to form. The Heroics are not those of men brandishing swords, or of great statesmen arguing for equality, but rather those who are inspired by their relationship with God, or with an infant or with their brothers to defy the evil decrees.

The Law of Relationship

The theme of relationships returns to a prominent place as the core of Torah law is revealed. The first statements of God atop Mount Sinai to his people define the nature of the law. One might expect the great principles of the Torah to serve as the first statement or prelude to the finer points. From an *a priori* point of view I would expect the statements of Rebbe Akiva or Ben Azzai That which is displeasureable for you do not do to your fellow, or this is the work of the *Toldot Ha'adam*, man was created in the image of God. However, the Torah does not open with a logically reasoned position of law, there are no truths that we hold self evident, no abstracted guiding philosophy, but rather the declaration of a relationship which marks the opening of the Ten Commandments. "I am the Lord your God who has taken you out of Egypt." Again the heroics, the pinnacle of achievement in the epic of liberation and revelation, is the establishment of a relationship. God chooses to open the revelation of the law with an exposition of the basis of God's relationship with his people. In Gilligan's analysis, it is characteristic of women's thinking to be motivated by relationships and the preservation thereof. The opening of the Ten Commandments and, in truth the next three commandments, emphasize of relationship creation and preservation with Hashem.[13]

Additionally should note the very language in which this law is presented. One of the most perplexing and challenging statements in the Ten Commandments is (Exod. 20:5) "Thou shalt not bow down unto them, nor serve them; for I the LORD thy God am a jealous God, visiting the iniquity of the fathers upon the children unto the third and fourth generation of them that hate Me;" The very description of God, the law giver and judge, as jealous is jarring and inconsistent with our assumptions about a dispassionate and logically based law system. However, as Hirsch[14] and others note, the use of the word jealous here is a type of anthropopathisim that communicates to the Jew the special and exclusive nature of his or her relationship to God. This is a word that accentuates relationship as no other word could. Jealousy is the lover's emotion; it is the emotion that speaks of betrayal, of a violent violation of the central component of the relationship. Surely, this descriptive language further highlights that this law operates in the feminine modality of relationship as opposed to the masculine or logical.

There are also those who have argued that it is these very anthropathisms, as well as the prominent descriptions of God as rahum, merciful, hanun indicate an "'ethic of care' and a jurisprudence of 'compassion,' or even 'maternal thinking'". The effect is certainly clear obedience to the law is born of the special relation; and the product of applying the law reflects the special relationship[15]. Both obedience and application reflect modalities that are distinctly feminine when we compare them to Giligan's conclusions.

Isolation and Intimacy

We noted that research reflected a difference in the perception of trauma between men and women, with men perceiving trauma at intimacy and women perceiving trauma at separation and competitive isolation. Comparison of the heroics in Exodus to Classical and Mesopotamian epics provides greater contrast and resolution to the feminine Take for example Homer's Odyssey where a traumatic hurdle for the returning Odysseus is to escape from the forced intimacy of Kalypso who holds him a captive guest on her Island. Contrast the Odysseus, "sitting on the beach, crying, as before now he had done, breaking his heart in tears, lamentation and sorrow as weeping tears he looked out over the barren water," with the will of Kalypso "So now you gods, resent it in me thatI keep beside me a man, the one I saved when he clung astride of the keel board all alone..." The hero in tears for the goddess holds him alone on her island.[16] Even the Sirens of the same work threaten to drive mad the sailors who are afflicted with the intimacy of the sirens voices. Similarly in the *Epic of Gilgamesh* we find the hero Gilgamesh unfazed when confronting the monstrous guardian of the cedar forest, Humamba, in mortal combat. However, when the goddess Ishtar proposes marriage, Gilgamesh assumes that such a relationship would be, "a palace that massacres warriors...a shoe that bites the foot of its owner...what bridegroom of yours ever endured forever?"[17] There is little doubt that the intimacy of marriage with the goddess represents an intense trauma. By contrast we will see that in the book of Shemot it is not intimacy, but rather separation, isolation and abandonment that generate the true trauma.

In *Sefer Shemot* there is one circumstance of violence that emerges from perceived intimacy. It is Pharaoh himself who perceives the threat posed by the Jew as a result of their closeness. (Exod. 1:7–10)

7 And the children of Israel were fruitful, and increased abundantly, and multiplied, and waxed exceeding mighty; and the land was filled with them. {P}

8 Now there arose a new king over Egypt, who knew not Joseph. 9 And he said unto his people: 'Behold, the people of the children of Israel are too many and too mighty for us; 10 come, let us deal wisely with them, lest they multiply, and it come to pass, that, when there befalleth us any war, they also join themselves unto our enemies, and fight against us, and get them up out of the land.'

It is specifically, Pharaoh's fear of a betrayal from within, from a group filling his quarters that motivates his violent action against the Children of Israel. The threat of the intimate fifth column presents only a *theoretical* threat in the distant future, yet the most extreme measure is taken against them.

Pharaoh's fear of intimacy is to be contrasted with the opposite in terms of the most significant trauma in the book of Shemot, the Golden Calf. Though, we are aware of the affliction at the hands of the Egyptians, our belief in God relieves us of panic when the Jews suffer under Pharaoh, or are trapped between his army and the sea. However, the true potential risk in this book is that the act of betrayal and violation – the worship of the Calf – will dissolve their relationship with God and bring about another flood like reduction of the people and a repopulation of the nation through Moshe. The narrative of the Calf story opens with the words (Exod. 32:1)

1 And when the people saw that Moses delayed to come down from the mount, the people gathered themselves together unto Aaron, and said unto him: 'Up, make us a god who shall go before us; for as for this Moses, the man that brought us up out of the land of Egypt, we know not what is become of him.'

It is precisely the fear of isolation that triggers the event of the Golden Calf. It is the fear that the man who connected them to God, perhaps even a man confused by the people for God himself, has left the people isolated and adrift, without connection. However, it is the aftermath of the sin that presents the true trauma – that God can no longer dwell among the Jewish people. (Exod. 33:1–11)

> 1 And the LORD spoke unto Moses: 'Depart, go up hence, thou and the people that thou hast brought up out of the land of Egypt, unto the land of which I swore unto Abraham, to Isaac, and to Jacob, saying: Unto thy seed will I give it – …. 3 unto a land flowing with milk and honey; for I will not go up in the midst of thee; for thou art a stiff-necked people; lest I consume thee in the way.' 4 And when the people heard these evil tidings, they mourned; and no man did put on him his ornaments. 5 And the LORD said unto Moses: 'Say unto the children of Israel: Ye are a stiff-necked people; if I go up into the midst of thee for one moment, I shall consume thee; therefore now put off thy ornaments from thee, that I may know what to do unto thee.' 6 And the children of Israel stripped themselves of their ornaments from mount Horeb onward. 7 Now Moses used to take the tent and to pitch it without the camp, afar off from the camp; and he called it The tent of meeting. And it came to pass, that every one that sought the LORD went out unto the tent of meeting, which was without the camp…. 9 And it came to pass, when Moses entered into the Tent, the pillar of cloud descended, and stood at the door of the Tent; and [the LORD] spoke with Moses…. 11 And the LORD spoke unto Moses face to face, as a man speaketh unto his friend. And he would return into the camp; but his minister Joshua, the son of Nun, a young man, departed not out of the Tent. {P}

The key point of this entire passage is that the intimacy between God and the Jewish people is now impossible, and untenable. The relationship has now been violated to force the worst of all possibilities – isolation from God's presence, the *Shechina*. The passage is virtually overflowing with separation and isolation. From God not being able to dwell among them to the removal of the tent of meeting, distance is the theme of the day, the consequence of sin to the point where it almost destroys the relationship altogether. Further, the comparative intimacy with Moshe draws a painful contrast to the lonely position of the *Bnai Yisrael*.[18] It is here that the Torah tells us that God spoke to Moshe as a man speaks to a friend, and it is only six verses later that Moshe feels close enough to ask God, show me your glory.[19]

Further proof that God's exodus from the camp of the Jews is the dramatic – though negative--climax of *Exodus*, is that Shemot closes with the resolution of the tension created by God's departure (*Shemot* 40:33–38).

> **33** And he reared up the court round about the tabernacle and the altar, and set up the screen of the gate of the court. So Moses finished the work. {**P**}
>
> **34** Then the cloud covered the tent of meeting, and the glory of the LORD filled the tabernacle.
>
> **35** And Moses was not able to enter into the tent of meeting, because the cloud abode thereon, and the glory of the LORD filled the tabernacle. – **36** And whenever the cloud was taken up from over the tabernacle, the children of Israel went onward, throughout all their journeys. **37** But if the cloud was not taken up, then they journeyed not till the day that it was taken up. **38** For the cloud of the LORD was upon the tabernacle by day, and there was fire therein by night, in the sight of all the house of Israel, throughout all their journeys.— {**P**}

The completion of the Tabernacle triggers God's return. Thus, the last verses proclaim not only the return of the Divine presence, "Then the cloud covered the tent of meeting, and the glory of the LORD filled the tabernacle", but also the enduring intimacy of God within the camp of the Jews throughout their journeys, "For the cloud of the LORD was upon the tabernacle by day, and there was fire therein by night, in the sight of all the house of Israel, throughout all their journeys."[20] I suggest that this closing act of return in *Sefer Shemot*, strongly reinforces the centrality of intimacy as a theme within this book.[21]

Interconnection over Hierarchy

There is one other strong difference between the moral reasoning of men and that of women that is emphasized by Carol Gilligan

> The reinterpretation of women's experience in terms of their own imagery or relationships thus clarifies that experience and also provides a nonhierarchical vision of human connection. Since relationships, when cast in the image of hierarchy, appear inherently unstable and morally problematic, their transposition into the image of web changes an order of inequality into a structure of interconnection... the ideals of human relationship – the vision that self and other will be treated as of equal worth, that despite differences in power, things will be fair, the vision that every one will be responded to and included, that no one will be left alone or hurt...[22]

More than anything Gilligan's conclusion is that for women the concept of interconnection triumphs over hierarchy and the logical outgrowth of the web of relationship is a structure of equality. Strikingly, the social structure introduced by the Torah over the Children of Israel embraces both equality and interconnection in sharp contrast to the social and authoritative hierarchy that is so characteristic of Egypt. There are many verses that communicate this concept such as the Ten Commandments: "You should not do any manner of work, thou, nor thy son, nor thy daughter, nor thy man-servant, nor thy maid-servant, nor thy cattle, nor thy stranger that is within thy gates"[23]. On the day of rest the Torah establishes complete parity between servant and master. Further examples include the Jews being described as a nation of priests [24], the wealthy shall not add nor the poor subtract from the half Shekel[25]. Even the concept of the release of the indentured Israelite in the seventh year is an expression of this social ideal. [26]

Conclusion

The research of Gilligan establishes that isolation is the fear, even a fear that triggers violent imagination in women. I suggest that the book of Shemot is teaching us a new heroism. It is not the heroism of the clever warrior statesman; it is not at all similar to the heroic Odysseus brandishing his sword. Rather, it is a different, feminine heroism, one in which relationship is valued over strength and in which connection is prized over logical abstraction. In the book of the Bible that tells the story of the birth of the Nation of Israel, the emergence of the Feminine heroic is both striking and instructive. It sets the field for the character of this people that will forever strive to maintain equality between themselves[27] and develop a network among themselves. But the feminine Heroic strives beyond human relationships to set the greatest prize as maintaining a close, intimate relationship with the Divine. The relationship with God is the rock upon which all of Torah morality is based; it is to be guarded beyond all else, its rupture being the greatest trauma.

Rabbi Andrew Rosenblatt is the Rabbi of Congregation Schara Tzedeck in Vancouver British Columbia.

NOTES

1. For further discussion of Female actors in Biblical literature see Adele Berlin, *Poetics and Interpretation of Biblical Narrative* (Sheffield: The Almond Press: 1993) 23–43.

2. Pesikta Rabati 47.

3. A very simple example of this concept is the distinction between the names of God, *Shem Havaya* (Tetragrammaton) and *Elohim*. The later is reflective of strict justice as in the Deut. 1:17, "Ye shall not respect persons in judgment; ye shall hear the small and the great alike; ye shall not be afraid of the face of any man; for the judgment is God's (Elohim); and the cause that is too hard for you ye shall bring unto me, and I will hear it.' On the other hand the Shem Havayah, (Tetragrammaton) often a contrasting modality, is understood to represent *Midat Harachamim*, or the attribute of mercy. The clearest connection between the Tetragrammaton (which in the following translation is "LORD") and the attribute of mercy is from Shemot 34:6: "And the LORD passed by before him, and proclaimed: 'The LORD, the LORD, God, merciful and gracious, long-suffering, and abundant in goodness and truth; The connection between the word *rachum*, mercy, and the word *rechem*, womb, and thus a more feminine perspective cannot be mistaken. Thus from a simple cursory analysis we can see that gender oriented descriptions have early place in Jewish Biblical analysis.

4.   Carol Gilligan, *In a Different Voice: Psychological Theory and Women's Development*, (Cambridge, Harvard University Press, 1982) 25–31.

5.   The Thematic Apperception Test is a standard psychological tool, similar to the Rorschach test. It differs from the Rorschach in that it uses actual pictures in place of ink splotches. Both tests are projective tests in they ask the subject to project information from the original image.

6.   Gilligan, p. 39–42.

7.   *The Holy Scriptures, according to the Masoretic Text: A New Translation*, (Philadelphia Jewish Publication Society of America, 1917), on line edition. All translations of the Bible are taken from the online edition of this source http://www.mechon-mamre.org.

8.   The Talmud in *Sotah* 11a points out that not only did the midwives defy Pharaoh, but the language implies that they caused the children to live. Coupled with Rashi's comment illuminating Shifra as one who would heal the women and Puah as one who would whisper in the ears of the children, the heroics of the this chapter speak to the connection of souls and the formation of relationships as opposed to the brandishing of swords and disobedience to the laws of an nefarious king.

9.   Nachmonides, Commentary on the Torah.

10. Nachmonides does present one reading in which the daughter of Pharaoh is attracted to the child purely for aesthetic reasons which would not support this thesis, however Nachmonides, Rashi and others seem to favor other interpretations.

11. The Targum Yonatan, translates *vayar* b'sivlotam as, "and Moshe saw into the suffering of their souls and into the magnitude of their labor," thus Moshe saw beyond their external condition and into the suffering of their souls.

12. The text tells us Moshe "turned this way and that and saw "*ki ein ish*", that there was no *man*. From a gender perspective it is tempting to look at such a phrase to be super-literal, meaning that there are no men. Of course as Hebrew has no neuter case it would be inaccurate to make such a statement. However, a similar interpretation is advanced by the Netziv who claims that there was no man present to stand up for this poor Hebrew slave. In terms relevant to our argument, we can say that there were none who would uphold the principles of moral logic and defend the Hebrew slave. Were there heroes willing to defy Pharaoh and defend the rights of the downtrodden, there would be an *ish*, a man.

13. This conclusion (irrespective of the modern methodology) is resonant with strong themes of Biblical and Rabbinic literature. Other texts that

articulate this point are the Binding of Issac, where allegiance to God in the relationship overrides the obvious moral objection. Less dramatically, Rashi Berachot 33b.

His attributes – He did not make them to inspire mercy, rather to place upon Israel the particulars of his laws, to inform them that they are His servants and the followers of his commandments, edicts and statutes, even those concepts that the Satan and the stranger may logically argue against to say for what purpose is this. Rashi's understanding is then that we follow the laws out of our sense of relationship with the Divine, and not out of a logical deduction. Furthermore, the story of the binding of Isaac is often interpreted along these lines. The story demonstrates faith over logic. Avraham trusts God, therefore he ignores the natural and logical impulse to reject the instructions. It is the patriarch's relationship with God the trumps his own sense of right and wrong.

14. Samson Raphael Hirsch, *Commentary on the Torah, Exodus*, Isaac Levy Trans. (London, The Judaica Press, 1966) 262.

15. Stone, Suzanne Last, "Justice Mercy and Gender in Rabbinic Thought" *Cordozo Studies in Law and* Literature, Vol 8, No. 1, A Commemorative Volume for Robert M. Cover (Spring-Summer, 1996) 139–177.

16. The Odyssey, Owen Lattiomore trans. (New York, harper And Row, 1967) 90, 91.

17. *Epic of Gilgamesh*. Andrew George, trans. (London, Peguin Books, 1999) 49.

18. There is one reading which presets what one might call the poster image of the feminine heroic. The reading, presented by the Chassidic master Rabbi Aryeh Leib of Gur, is perhaps outside a close literal reading; however his reading is very much in line with the overall dynamic of the narrative.

The Shemot Rabba 43 as well as Sefat Emet Shemot, Ki Tisah 5741 present the breaking of the tablets as an overt act by Moshe to avoid being separated from the Jewish people which was also in accord with the divine will. The literal breaking of the tablets of the law to maintain a relationship would seem to be the very image of the feminine Heroic.

19. Moreover, according to the Talmud in Berachot, Moshe is granted a personal perspective heretofore and since granted to no other, to see the knot of God's Tefilin I think it should also be noted that in addition to the intimacy of the 'gaze', there is an intimacy of symbol. The Tefilin themselves are more than a random icon, they are a symbol of love and connection. Maimonides places Tefilin in *Sefer Ahavah* (the Book of

Love) and the Talmud in *Berachot* also relates that God's Tefilin contain scrolls that articulate his love and connection to the Jewish people.

20. This theme of reconciliation is communicated very strongly in linguistic terms as the presence of Kvod Hashem and the cloud of glory that descends upon Sinai upon revelation and forgiveness are also mentioned here in exactly the same linguistic terms, where the word Kavod joined with the Tetragramaton is said to refer to God's presence. In this language there is a further link between the intimacy of Sinai and the reconciliation of the conclusion of Shemot see Shawn Zelig Aster, "The Phenomenon of Divine and Human Radiance in the Hebrew Bible and in Mesopotamian and Northwest Semitic Literature: A Philological and Comparative Analysis" (Ph.D. Dissertation, University of Pennsylvania 2006).

21. The theme of intimacy and estrangement in the human God relationship, though best established in the book of Shemot, finds resonance throughout Biblical and Rabbinic literature. Two examples of the many are Nachmonides commentary to Genesis 1:1, the Kina of Tisha b'av *Eicha Atzat apecha*, and an article on this subject "Yearning for Closeness to *Ha-Kadosh Baruch-Hu*" published in *The Lord is Righteous in all His Ways: Reflections on the Tisha b'Av Kinot, Rabbi Joseph Soloveitchik* Ed. Jacob J. Shachter (Newark Ketav Publishing, 2006).

22. Gilligan, p62–63.

23. Similar language is used in *Shemot* 23:12 and the conclusion that this equality is explicitly the result of the exodus from Egypt is articulated in the recount of the Ten Commandments in *Devarim* 5:13–15.

24. *Shemot 19:6.*

25. *Shemot 30:15.*

26. Rabbi Samson Raphael Hirsch, noticing the recurrence of animals in such verses goes even further including all God's creation under the umbrella equality.

27. Note as well the comment of Gershom Scholem indicating that Jews have never developed distinct social classes Scholem, Gershom *Sabbatai Sevi, The Mystical Messiah 1626–1676,*(Rutledge and Kegan Paul. London, 1973) 6.

Trigger Words and Simultexts:

THE EXPERIENCE
OF READING THE BAVLI

Zvi Septimus

I n his article, "The Further Adventures of Rav Kahana,"[1]
Shamma Friedman attempts to explain why it is that certain
stories in the Bavli share a large number of phrases and words
with other stories in the Bavli. Friedman argues that these
stories, linked by common language, also usually contain common
topics: "The plethora of rhetoric and phraseology in [one] story
which is similar to other passages in the Bavli is typical of late
aggadic compositions which draw upon existing Babylonian aggadot
for both language and content."[2] In other words, the final editors
of the Talmud reshape a shorter "early" story into a longer, more
complex "late" story. According to Friedman, the "late" story is
characterized by "exceptional length" and is "exceptionally creative
and innovative" in the reworking of its sources."[3]

Friedman points out that one of the "early" Bavli passages[4]
among the sample group that he provides is unique in relation
to the other "early" Bavli passages. This particular "early" passage

shares a larger number of words and phrases with the "late" passage.[5] Friedman therefore concludes that this "early" passage is the "main literary source" for the "late" passage.[6] The result of Friedman's source-critical examination of these texts is the creation of a linear, chronological narrative of Rabbinic and Stammaitic textual composition that extends backward from the Bavli to the Yerushalmi and beyond. Friedman traces the evolution of a particular Rabbinic formulation from its earliest fixed form through its various manifestations and manipulations into its final canonical materialization in the Bavli. He contrasts his approach with Jonah Fraenkel's notion of *segirut* (autonomy).[7] Fraenkel believes that each individual story found in Rabbinic literature must be analyzed without regard to any other piece of Rabbinic literature.[8]

Aryeh Cohen takes issue with Fraenkel's rigid analysis that ignores the literary function of its placement in a particular grouping of consecutive texts, the *sugya*.[9] Cohen argues that Fraenkel removes each story from its immediate context only to put "them into a new context – even if that context might be the collection of all 'Sage Stories.'"[10] Where Friedman attacks Fraenkel on the basis that Fraenkel ignores the obvious history of each individual text's transition from its earliest detectable state into its final form Cohen's critique of Fraenkel is somewhat stronger and goes to the heart of the intertextual relationship of all texts. Cohen posits that Fraenkel misunderstands his own re-contextualization as an a-contexualization. For Cohen, Fraenkel makes the mistake of ignoring the basic notion that all texts are necessarily read in some context and the removal of any text from its current context merely places it in another, perhaps artificial, context.

The analytical framework that I propose in response to Friedman and Fraenkel – what I call the "trigger word/simultext reading strategy" – attempts to explore the linguistic feature of the Bavli that Friedman has already pointed out in such a way that brackets the chronological narrative of the Bavli's evolution and focuses on the final product: "the Bavli." I also seek to expand Fraenkel's notion of *segirut* (autonomy) to the entire Bavli rather than any one story within it. In doing so, I demonstrate that if, as Friedman argues, there is creative "reworking" in the Bavli, then it is an activity that extends beyond the parameters of the story unit, or even the sugya. The Bavli as a whole is shaped and defined by this activity. This type of creative "reworking" is bidirectional with products becoming sources of each other, over and over. By reading the Bavli in this manner, a new type of thematic relationship between different stories in the Bavli emerges.

Friedman's method relies on the assumption that the source critic can trace the individual moves of a text's evolution, by both paying careful attention to the rough edges left behind in the editorial process and examining the relevant parallel texts. I assert that the editorial history of the Bavli is far more complex than the shifts and alterations that can be discerned by culling clues left behind by the editors in the form of rough edges and parallel texts. Analogously, the reader of this article might notice certain rough edges in my text, either in the form of an abrupt shift in language and style or in the form of an argument that does not seem to follow from its premise. This might lead the reader to conclude that a particular passage or group of words must have been the product of someone other than me. Alternatively, the seams found in my text might stem from the fact that I cut and pasted an entire paragraph from an essay that I had written on a similar subject at an earlier point in time. Both of these possibilities certainly could be true. In addition, if one were to view this article alongside its earlier versions one would certainly be able to make assertions about particular edits to my text. However, if one were to hit the "undo" key on my word processor, and watch the backward flow of actual edits that have occurred in the production of this article, then a far more complex story of the evolution of this text into its final form would unfold – one that is far beyond the scope of the tools of source criticism.

The Bavli Sugya at Kiddushin 70 is remarkable for its language. One of the interesting features of this Sugya is its transparent use of certain linguistic markers to point to specific texts found elsewhere in the Bavli. Source-critical techniques help illustrate the cause of this phenomenon – how such a Sugya was composed: originally, a mere skeleton of Kiddushin 70 existed and then, "later," due to some rupture or shift, the story was embellished with borrowings from these "earlier" Bavli passages.[11] The source critic uses this data to develop a theory about the source or nature of the rupture that led to this shift.

A non-critical reader, however, does not typically encounter the text through its historical layering. While the critic takes primary interest in the textual author and the process of authorship, a non-critical reader is interested in the book itself in its final state. The source critic sees the Bavli as linear in both pages and time. In contrast, the reader that I explore experiences the totality of the Bavli as a body of literature that is spherically shaped, self-referential, and self-contradictory, in no particular order. This Bavli reader encounters the linguistic markers of Kiddushin 70 as "trigger words" and is distracted – attracted momentarily toward other particular Bavli passages, "simultexts" – before returning to Kiddushin 70. An exploration of the reader's experience of the Bavli serves to highlight an aspect of the Bavli that has been underrepresented in modern Talmud scholarship: what the Bavli is rather than how it came to be.[12,13]

The Bavli's use of words and concepts in each individual passage assumes that its reader is fluent, on the level of orality, with the entire Bavli. The kind of reader that the Bavli assumes is akin to Wolfgang Iser's "implied reader."

> [The implied reader] embodies all those predispositions necessary for a literary work to exercise its effect – predispositions laid down, not by an empirical outside reality, but by the text itself. Consequently, the implied reader as a concept has his roots firmly planted in the structure of the text; he is a construct and in no way to be identified with any real reader.[14]

The reading strategy that I propose builds off of the work of Gerald Bruns and Daniel Boyarin. In *Intertexuality and the Reading of Midrash*, Boyarin suggests "that the intertextual reading practice of the midrash is a development...of the intratextual interpretive strategies which the Bible itself manifests."[15] Boyarin takes Bruns' claim that the Bible is a "self-glossing book"[16] and demonstrates how this self-glossing nature spawns the midrashic reading practices of the Rabbis. My claim is that the Bavli not only shares some of the self-glossing features of the Bible but that the Bavli presents itself to its reader in a manner that can only be understood when viewed as a whole. Where I go further than Boyarin is to look at the Bavli and its relationship to the Bible within the framework of the Bavli's own unique world.

For the reader of the Bavli the Bible is nothing other than the Bavli's Bible – an external book that only exists internal to the Bavli.

The purpose of this essay is to explore the experience and effects of reading the Bavli through its own internally marked linguistic system – the trigger word/simultext reading strategy. Although every reader of the Bavli brings a different set of external situations to the work, what unites each Bavli reader is the information, language, and methodologies internal to the Bavli. The Bavli reader therefore is not a reader situated at any particular point in history and therefore has little to say about history. The Bavli reader is only what all historical readers of the Bavli have in common. This reader excludes all other works and certainly does not approach the Bavli as a compilation of evolved components. In exploring the experience of this reader we can further define the nature of the book that is the Bavli. In this way the trigger word/simultext reading strategy resembles Jonah Fraenkel's notion of *segirut* (autonomy), only it applies not to one story but to the entire book.[17]

The Story:
Because of its length, I will present here a summary of the Sugya at Kiddushin 70:

SCENE I:

A man from Neharda'a walks into a butcher shop in Pumbedita and demands to be served. He must wait his turn, he is told; he will be served after the attendant (*shama*) of Pumbedita's leading Rabbinic authority, Rav Yehudah.

Defiantly, the visitor exclaims "Rav Yehudah is a glutton!"[18]

Rav Yehudah, upon hearing of this incident, promptly excommunicates the visitor. When further told of this man's tendency to call others (*inshi*) slaves, Rav Yehudah issues a public proclamation stating that the Nehardean is himself a member of the slave class. The Nehardean man storms home and petitions his own city's leading Rabbinic authority, Rav Naḥman, who issues a summons for Rav Yehudah to appear before his court. The Pumbeditan Rav Yehudah, unsure whether he should submit to the authority of the Nehardean Rav Naḥman, solicits Rav Huna's[19] political expertise on the matter. Rav Huna sees no reason, from a Rabbinic perspective, for Rav

Yehudah to appear before Rav Naḥman's court; nevertheless, Rav Huna advises Rav Yehudah to respect the office of the presidency (*bei nesiyah*)[20] and that he travel to Rav Naḥman in Neharda'a.

SCENE II:

Rav Yehudah arrives at the home of Rav Naḥman to find the latter working in his garden. Rav Yehudah pounces.

"A communal leader must never do manual labor in public… Thus said Shmuel (*hakhi amar*)!"

Rav Naḥman, unaware of the identity of his antagonist points out that it is only a *gundrita* (small fence) that he busies himself with.

Rav Yehudah jumps at the opportunity to correct Rav Naḥman's choice of words and demands to know why Rav Naḥman did not call the fence by its Biblical or Rabbinic designations (*ma'keh, meḥitzah*).

Ever the host, Rav Naḥman offers Rav Yehudah a seat (*safsal*), a fruit (*etrunga, etruga*), and an alcoholic beverage (*isparagos, anpak, anbaga*).

In each instance Rav Yehudah attacks Rav Naḥman on the basis of an elitist (*inshi*) non-Rabbinic word choice to describe each of these objects.

In one case Rav Naḥman's word choice is deemed arrogant (*ramat ruḥa*) by a statement quoted in the name of Shmuel.

When Rav Naḥman introduces his daughter and wife – Donag and *Yalta* – his ignorance of Shmuel's opinions about the usage of women is once again blasted by Rav Yehudah. Yalta intercedes between the Rabbis and demands that Rav Naḥman resolve the case (*shari lei tagrei*) before he is deemed an ignoramus (*k'sha'ar 'am ha'aretz*).

SCENE III:

Rav Naḥman asks Rav Yehudah to state the purpose of his visit.

"But you summoned (*shadar mar*) me here," says Rav Yehudah pulling the writ of summons from his pocket.

Rav Naḥman's initial reaction is to let him go but decides to formalize the court case in order to avoid reproof on the basis of Rabbinic nepotism (*miḥanfi*):

"So why did you excommunicate the man," Rav Naḥman asks Rav Yehudah?

"Because he annoyed my attendant!"

"So you should have whipped him – as Rav whipped people simply because they annoyed Rabbinic appointees!"

"I did better!"

"Okay, so then why did you proclaim him a slave?"

"Because he had called others slaves and Shmuel says that anyone who calls people slaves is himself a slave."

SCENE IV:

The man from Neharda'a now appears on the scene and addresses Rav Yehudah.

"You call me a slave! I am descended from the royal Hasmonean house!"

Rav Yehudah then quotes Shmuel and relates the fact that all claimants to Hasmonian pedigree are in fact slaves.

(*hahu yoma*) Rav Yehudah is supported by another Rabbi who remembers Shmuel's recounting that the last female Hasmonian girl shouted out, before jumping[21] from the roof to her death, that all future Hasmonian claim-bearers are slaves .

SCENE V:

The Nehardean man is proclaimed a slave.

That very day (*hahu yoma*) many marriage contracts are torn up in Neharda'a. Rav Yehudah returns to Pumbedita and makes proclamations altering the genealogical status of a number of people. One of these people, Bati the son of Tuvyah, on account of arrogance (*ramat ruḥa*) refused his manumission document upon being freed from slavery and therefore is still a slave.

THE TRIGGER WORD/SIMULTEXT READING STRATEGY:

It is appropriate to use a story in the Bavli that explicitly thematizes the importance of word selection, a story that contains an abundance of rare words and *hapax legomena*, to discuss the effect of the Bavli's own word selection on its reader. Kiddushin 70 contains certain rarely used trigger words that are also found, in combinations, in other Bavli simultexts.[22] These simultexts (*hatam*) have the effect of alerting the reader of our passage (*hakha*) to some theme or emphasis, previously unpronounced, and consequently serve the function of highlighting, complementing, and complicating ideas and subject matter found in our passage. In this instance, the simultexts all serve to alter the story's focus. Without the simultexts, Kiddushin 70 appears to be a story about the confrontation between Rav Yehudah and the Nehardean man. The simultexts all serve to shift the reader's focus to an unspoken, yet deeper, conflict between Rav Naḥman and the Nehardean man. The nature of this conflict will unfold as the simultexts are introduced.

Simultext:	*Kiddushin 70*	*Shavuot 30*
Trigger Words:	*Shari + Tagrei*	*Shari + Tagrei*
	ḤNF	ḤNF
	[*ʿam haʾaretz*]	[*ʿam haʾaretz*]
	[*shamʿei,*]	[*shamʿei,*]
	[*d'bithu*]	[*d'bithu*]

An example of how the trigger word/simultext reading strategy is employed is found in the expression *shari lei tagrei*. The combination of the verb *ShRA* and the noun *tigra*, meaning to resolve a dispute, is found only five other times in the Bavli. In addition, the verb ḤNF, is only used a handful of times in the Bavli to denote favoritism. Shavuot 30 has the verb ḤNF in close proximity to the combination of *ShRA* and *tigra* making it a simultext. The reader of Kiddushin 70 encounters the trigger words and is drawn momentarily toward Shavuot 30 which has Rav Naḥman debating ʿUlla regarding Rabbis showing favor to one another. This debate follows immediately after a discussion about whether the testimony of a woman is valid, introducing the idea that a woman should not have a public role.[23] The Shavuot passage also has several characters familiar to readers of the Kiddushin passage: the *ʿam haʾaretz*, *shamʿa*, and *d'bithu* which are all dealt with in situations regarding hierarchy and primacy in the dealings of a court.[24] The reader returns to Kiddushin 70 with added emphasis on these marginalized characters and their roles in court cases, especially the validity of the testimony of women which is the overt theme of Shavuot 30. The reader of Kiddushin 70 now has a heightened awareness of the irony of Rav Yehudah's initial objection to the use of women, as well as Rav Naḥman's eventual use of the testimony of a woman to establish the slave status of the Nehardean man.

From a higher critical perspective, the reader of Scene II is struck with two oddities in the construction of this part of the narrative. The first question that occurs to the reader is why are all four of these name-challenged objects necessary? Would the narrator have lost anything if it did not mention any particular one of the four props? What do the fence, chair, fruit, and drink add? The second question is what does the introduction of Rav Naḥman's wife and daughter add to the story? By working our way backward through the name-challenged objects following the trigger words to the simultexts and back again the answers to these questions are revealed and a new logic to the story emerges.

THE DRINK:

Simultext:	*Kiddushin 70*	*Berakhot 51*
Trigger Words:	*Isparagos*	*Isparagos*
	ShDR + *mar* (×3)	ShDR + *mar* (×2)
	Yalta	*Yalta*
	Anbaga	*Nebaga*
	[*Hakhi amar*]	[*Hakhi amar*]

The fourth name-challenged object that appears in Kiddushin 70, the alcoholic beverage, acts together with several trigger words to direct the reader to the Berakhot 51 simultext. The word *Isparagos* appears a mere four times in the Bavli, once in Kiddushin and twice in Berakhot 51. It is not the two paragraphs in Berakhot 51 containing the words *Isparagos* that are important for our purposes but rather the passage immediately following those two paragraphs. This point is quite significant and will be addressed later. The passage immediately following the two mentions of *Isparagos* contains several trigger words in combination which attract the attention of the reader of Kiddushin 70. These trigger words are: the rare combination of the verb *ShDR* together with the honorific *mar*; the character *Yalta*; the rare *Nebaga*[25]; and the formulaic interjection of *hakhi amar*[26] to rebut a practice in a similar manner to its use in Kiddushin 70.

Berakhot 51[27]:

'Ulla visited the house of Rav Naḥman. He broke bread; said grace; and gave the cup of benediction to Rav Naḥman. Rav Naḥman said to him: "Please send the cup of benediction to Yalta." 'Ulla replied: "Thus stated Rabbi Yoḥanan (hakhi amar): The fruit of a woman's body is blessed only from the fruit of a man's body, as it says, "He will also bless the fruit of your body." It does not say the fruit of her body, but the fruit of your body"…Meanwhile, Yalta hears and gets up in a passion and goes to the wine house and breaks four hundred containers of wine. Rav Naḥman said to 'Ulla: "Please send her another cup." 'Ulla sends a message to Yalta: "All this [spilled wine] is the wine (nebaga) of benediction." Yalta sends a message back to 'Ulla: "From wanderers, words; From rags, lice (kalmi)."

In addition to trigger words this passage has many features that are similar to Kiddushin 70. Both stories contain the following elements: (a) Yalta overhears a conversation about a guest sending her something (a greeting and some wine); (b) A controversy is set off by Rav Naḥman's insistence of an interaction between a guest and a female family member; (c) The guest justifies his sexist position quoting legal dicta preceded by *hakhi amar*; (d) Yalta sends her message through a messenger yet appears to hear what she heard directly. In fact, a source-critical approach to Kiddushin 70 would argue that the Yalta section of the Kiddushin text is actually an adaptation of Berakhot 51. In doing so, it would fail to explain how the two texts operate simultaneously on the reader to create meaning in the context of the Bavli, the book that this reader is actually reading.

The reading strategy that I propose brackets the genealogical relationship between these passages and reads them synchronically, demonstrating what the reader of the Kiddushin 70 gains when alerted to the themes and ideas contained within the Berakhot 51 simultext. This reading strategy seeks to explain how certain features of the Bavli operate on the reader in creating stronger meaning. To the reader, the aesthetic of the Bavli is more than the sum of its dia-chronically related parts.

Berakhot 51 highlights, for the reader of Kiddushin 70, that Yalta is the one to deliver the final word. The dialogue ends with Yalta's enigmatic and derogatory statement with no response from 'Ulla. As we will later see, this theme of the wife delivering the final word is at play in a number of Kiddushin 70's simultexts. What is obvious in the Berakhot simultext but not so in the Kiddushin passage is that Yalta also represents a threat of violence. By destroying the wine barrels, Yalta demonstrates that she has control over her own wealth and that it is actually her husband, Rav Naḥman, who is blessed through her. The final exchange in this story is a bit ambiguous and requires further explanation. There are several facts that lend insight to what she pos-sibly could have meant by saying "From wanderers, words; From rags, lice." What is the significance of *smartutei*, rags, and *kalmi*, lice?

Simultext:	*Berakhot 51*	*Niddah 20*	*Shavuot 30*
Trigger Words:	*smartutei*		*smartut*
	kalmi	*kalmi*	
	Yalta	*Yalta*	
	'Ulla ikl'a	*'Ulla ikl'a*	

Both of these words, *kalmi* and *smartutei*, are trigger words. *Smartutei* points back to the Shevuot 30 simultext.[28] *Kalmi* works together with *'Ulla ikl'a* and *Yalta*, all rare in the Bavli, to point to a new simultext, Niddah 20. The Niddah simultext thematizes the Rabbinic dominance over women and Yalta's exemption from this dominance. A number of women are reported to have brought their underwear to Rabbis who smell them to decide whether or not they are clean from men-strual blood. This is the prototypical image of Rabbinic dominance over women. Yalta, however, brings her blood to one Rabbi who, inci-dentally, does not smell it and deems it impure. Yalta then completely disregards this Rabbi's ruling and brings it to another Rabbi who de-clares it pure. Yalta, in a way, mocks the notion of her subservience to rabbinic authority.[29] This Niddah simultext works to highlight the position of Yalta in the rabbinic hierarchy, how she perceives herself in relation to those Rabbis, and consequently how they, as producers of this story, perceive her dominance over them. Her short appearance in the Kiddushin passage has her in a similar role. In addition, the power Rav Naḥman receives through his marriage to her underlies the entire drama.

What drives Niddah 20 as a simultext of Berakhot 51, and through Berakhot 51 a simultext of Kiddushin 70, is the trigger word *kalmi*. *Kalmi* makes a seemingly arbitrary appearance in the Niddah simultext in a section immediately following the Yalta story[30]. The *Kalmi* story deals with the mother of King Shapur who himself is a prominent figure in a number of simultexts which we will examine presently. These are the only two appearances of the word *kalmi* in the entire Bavli.

The fact that many of these trigger words appear in close proximity to, rather than within, a passage makes little difference to the Bavli reader – the reader is drawn in the direction of a simultext and absorbs all of its contents, context, and meaning. For the source critic, however, it highlights the risk involved in assuming that the longer or more verbose story is the later one. Such a supposition implies a finite and unidirectional movement from the main literary source to a later creatively reworked product. This theory is grounded in analysis of smaller extracted pieces of the Bavli rather than the composition as a whole. Once the notion of trigger words found in close proximity to, rather than within, simultexts is introduced, a source-critical approach should see the compositional work of the Bavli as bidirectional. If one passage receives language from another passage and its surroundings it is then just as likely to send its own language back to the initial passage and its surroundings, creating a more unified whole, as well as complex web of meaning for the reader. Although Friedman's method also allows for bidirectional influence, the type of bidirectional movement that Friedman conceives is the sum of two unidirectional moments of influence. The type of bidirectionality that I propose assumes a more dynamic relationship between a number of texts that influence each other, over and over, to the point that discerning which text is the original and which one is a creatively edited version of that original is no longer possible nor pertinent.

THE FRUIT:

Simultext:	*Kiddushin 70*	*Avodah Zara 76*	*Ketubot 60–61*
Trigger Words:	*Ramat Ruha*		
	Etru(n)ga	*Etruga*	*Etruga*
	Yalta		*Yalta*
		King Shapur	*King Shapur*
	Bati bar Tuvia	*Bati bar Tuvia*	
	Ramat Ruha		

The third name-challenged object in our Kiddushin 70 drama, the citron, *etruga*, works together with various other trigger words throughout the passage to point the reader to two separate simultexts: 'Avodah Zara 76 and Ketubot 60–61. *Etrunga* is a *hapax legomenon* in the Bavli.[31] The Aramaic *etruga* (without the "n") rather than the Hebrew *etrog* is itself quite rare in the Bavli. The majority of *etruga*'s appearances in the Bavli are in contexts relating to kingship. The arrogance (*ramat ruha*) of Rav Naḥman's use of the word *etrunga* steers the reader to the arrogance (*ramat ruha*) of Bati the son of Tuviah's refusal to accept his manumission document. Bati the son of Tuviah is only mentioned one other time in the entire Bavli and in that instance he appears together with the rare word *etruga*.

In a very short story at the close of tractate Avodah Zara, Bati Bar Tuvi(ah) and Mar Yehudah are sitting with King Shapur. King Shapur gives Bati Bar Tuvi(ah) a piece of *etruga* and then stabs his knife in the ground ten times before cutting a piece for Mar Yehudah. This physically violent image of King Shapur stabbing his knife ten times contrasts nicely with the meek Rav Naḥman of our story whose power stems from his relationship to the physical dominance of King Shapur over the Jews of Babylonia – and that, only through his wine-container-smashing wife.

The relationship of King Shapur to the word *etruga* as well as the role of Rav Naḥman as husband of Yalta and son-in-law to the exilarch is reinforced by trigger words pointing to the Bavli's discussion of the Mishnah at Ketubot 59b. The Mishnah discusses the work (*melakhot*) a woman is required to do for her husband and how those requirements are altered in a scenario where the woman is wealthy and brings maidservants with her into the marriage. One of the tasks (*melakhot*) a woman must do for her husband is to nurse her child. This leads the Bavli to a discussion of whether or not a woman may remarry while nursing a child. The Bavli cites a Beraita that allows a woman to remarry in a case where she turned the baby over to a wet nurse. The Bavli proceeds to recount how two Rabbis wanted to use this Beraita in deciding an actual case brought before them and a certain old woman curtailed their efforts by claiming that Rav Naḥman prohibited her to remarry in the same instance. (The use of a woman for testimony, especially when that testimony is brought in the form of a story from the past, is an important part of our Kiddushin passage and will be discussed later.) The Bavli objects to the possibility that Rav Naḥman prohibited this woman from remarrying by asking "But did not Rav Naḥman permit them (women who turned their babies over to wet nurses) to the house of the exilarch?" The Bavli then answers that the house of the exilarch is different because wet nurses do not back out of arrangements made with the house of the exilarch.[32]

According to one of the first readers of the Bavli, the Sheiltot of Rav Aḥai Gaon, the Bavli's question in response to the old woman's claim reads: "But did not Rav Naḥman permit Yalta?"[33] According to the Sheiltot, the Bavli answers similarly that the house of the exilarch is different because their children, once given to a wet nurse, are not returned. This text is important for our purposes because it clearly equates Yalta, in her own right, with the house of the exilarch. However, it somewhat confuses the reader as to the relationship between Rav Naḥman and Yalta. Some have suggested that Yalta was married three times:[34] She had a child with her first husband; then Rav Naḥman allowed her to marry again after turning her child over to a wet nurse owing to her affiliation with the house of the exilarch; she then subsequently married Rav Naḥman as her third husband. Although it is quite normal in the world of the Bavli for an important woman to marry an important Rabbi as a second or third marriage, as in the cases of Ḥoma and the daughter of Rav Ḥisda, it makes more sense to interpret this passage as referring to Rav Naḥman's marriage to Yalta. The Bavli asks: How can this old woman be correct? Did not Rav Naḥman marry Yalta even though she was still nursing a child from a previous marriage? Reading the Bavli's question in this way fits neatly into the Bavli's ambivalent representation of those Rabbis who were close to the government, quintessential among them Rav Naḥman, and, as we will see in another simultext, Rabban Gamliel. This reading also complements the theme of the Mishnah in whose context it appears in the Bavli, namely, how marriage laws are altered when one marries a wealthy woman.

As mentioned earlier, simultexts are significant when multiple trigger words direct the reader in their direction. The Ketubot simultext exemplifies the notion of proximity, also previously mentioned, that when multiple words operate as trigger words they sometimes can be found in the immediate proximity of a simultext rather than within it. Both the word *Yalta* and the word *etruga* appear fewer than ten times each in the Talmud. To put matters in perspective, the Bavli contains close to two million words. Just as *Yalta* is not necessarily a historical figure but rather a Bavli character of whom we can build a profile so too *etruga*, as linguistic marker, represents a character about which we can build a profile. *Etruga*, as a character, is further developed when it appears twice on Ketubot 61a in the context of King Shapur, the source of the exilarch's power, making use of a woman who in all probability was a minor.[35] The appearance of both of these words in a passage that comments on the Mishnah about marrying a wealthy woman highlights various aspects of the Kiddushin text, which itself follows in close proximity to a text warning against marrying a woman for money.[36]

THE SEAT:

Simultext:	*Kiddushin 70*	*Berakhot 27–28*
Trigger Words:	*Safsal*	*Safsal*
	Bei nesiya	*[Nasi]*
	Hahu Yoma (×2)	*Hahu Yoma* (×2)

The second object in our Kiddushin 70 drama, the chair, directs the reader to a very specific story found on Berakhot 27b–28a. The trigger words *safsal, hahu yoma*,[37] and the choice of the words *bei nesiya* to describe the exilarchy, normally designated *reish galuta*, work as a group to direct the reader's attention to a simultext regarding Rabban Gamliel's removal from the office of the presidency. In that story Rabban Gamliel insults Rabbi Yehoshua' which leads to his being voted out of office. He is replaced by Rabbi El'azar ben 'Azariah as president. After Rabban Gamliel apologizes to Rabbi Yehoshua' he is reinstated as president, albeit only to three fourths of his previous appointment. Reading Berakhot 27b–28a alongside our Kiddushin passage serves the purpose of highlighting several important aspects of the Kiddushin story.

Rabbi El'azar ben 'Azariah is, in Berakhot 27b–28a, a tenth generation descendant of Ezra and thus of the priestly caste. Rabban Gamliel, a descendant of the Davidic dynasty, is replaced by a priest. After Rabbi Yehoshua' accepts Rabban Gamliel's apology, the Rabbis initially lock the door to the study hall to prevent Rabban Gamliel from returning to power. It is only when Rabbi Yehoshua' is allowed to enter and present his argument that Rabban Gamliel is reinstated. Rabbi Yehoshua''s argument reads: "Let the sprinkler son of a sprinkler sprinkle; shall he who is neither a sprinkler nor the son of a sprinkler say to a sprinkler son of a sprinkler "Your water is cave water and your ashes are oven ashes?"" Rabbi Yehoshua''s argument is that Rabban Gamliel as a practicing political leader from a family of political leaders would be most fit for the office of presidency while Rabbi El'azar ben 'Azariah as an eighteen year old from a non-political family should not rule. What is of note is the fact that whereas Rabbi El'azar ben 'Azariah is the priest in this story, Rabbi Yehoshua' uses the priestly terminology "sprinkle" to describe Rabban Gamliel, the Davidic descendant. The trigger words used to direct the reader to the Berakhot simultext highlight the power struggle between the priestly heir to the Hasmonian dynasty and the Davidic exilarch, Rav Naḥman, in Kiddushin 70. When read alone, Kiddushin 70 pits Rav Yehudah against Rav Naḥman and Rav Yehudah against the Nehardean man. Berakhot 28b–29a reminds the reader of the unspoken conflict between Rav Naḥman and the Nehardean man. It is important to note that whereas the Hasmonian dynasty represents autonomous rule, the Davidic offices of the presidency and exilarch respectively receive their authority only through the custodial power of the Roman and Persian empires.[38]

Another aspect of Berakhot 28b–29a that enlightens Kiddushin 70 is the rhetorical role of the Rabbis. In Berkahot 27b–28a when it is decided that Rabbi El'azar ben 'Azariah will be made president after Rabban Gamliel is removed from office Rabbi El'azar ben 'Azariah seeks his wife's counsel before accepting the position. His wife tries to dissuade him. Although it is apparent from the story that Rabbi El'azar ben 'Azariah does indeed accept the position of president, the dialogue between his wife and him ends with her having the final word, "you have no white hair." It is only the miracle of his hair turning white, and not Rabbi El'azar ben 'Azariah's rhetorical expertise, that rebuts his wife's argument. This reminds the reader of the role of Yalta not only in our Kiddushin 70 story but more so in the Berakhot 51 simultext discussed earlier.

There are many fruitful ways to approach a rich literary text like Kiddushin 70. A formalist approach would focus on the internal integrity of the passage which might yield a heightened sense of the aesthetic makeup of the components of the text and the poetics of its narrative. A source critical approach to Kiddushin 70 would highlight how the various components of the text evolved and how those shifts in meaning reflect changes in the real-life conditions of its various authors. The approach I have advocated emphasizes what happens, from the reader's perspective, when the Bavli is seen as a highly fashioned and unified literary entity. My approach does not seek to harmonize various parts of the Bavli, merely to demonstrate how modes of interpretation shift emphases through the mechanism of the Bavli's internal linguistic markers. The trigger word/simultext reading strategy, I have proposed, expands Fraenkel's notion of *segirut* to the entire Bavli and builds on Friedman's notion of the creative reworking of the Stam, albeit in a bidirectional manner, in describing the spherical nature of the book as it is: the Bavli.

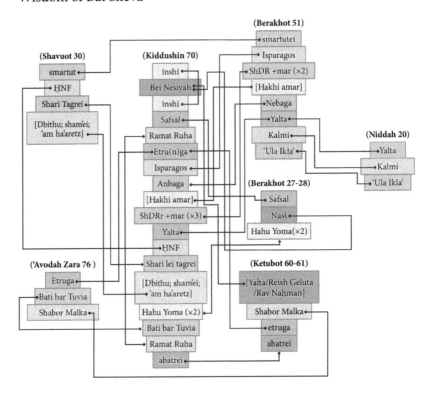

NOTES

1. Shamma Friedman, "The Further Adventures of Rav Kahana," in *The Talmud Yerushalmi and Graeco-Roman Culture*, ed. Peter Shafer (Mohr 2002), 3:247–71.
2. Ibid., p. 259.
3. Ibid., p. 259.
4. Bava Metzia 84.
5. Bava Kamma 117.
6. Friedman, p. 265.
7. In the words of Aryeh Cohen, "Fraenkel sees each story as "hermetic," having a strong "internal" and "external" closure. Aryeh Cohen, *Rereading Talmud: Gender, Law and the Poetics of Sugyot*, (Atlanta: Scholars Press, 1998), p. 72.

8.   Joanh Fraenkel, "She'elot hermeneutiyot beheker sippur ha-'aggadah", *Tarbiz*, 47 (1978), pp. 139–172.

9.   Cohen, p. 99. Cohen later defines his "working definition" of a *sugya*: [In block text] "a sugya is the primary context of all its parts – attributed and unattributed statements, aggadot, maasim, prooftexts, *et al*. Its parameters are established both structurally or intratextually, and thematically." Ibid, p. 148.

10. Ibid, p. 121.

11. Shamma Friedman writes "a secondary aggadic text often makes extended use of existing expressions and turns of phrase. Verbose use of stereotypic Talmudic vocabulary can be a marker of late narrative." Friedman, p. 248.

12. In addition, this exercise complements source criticism in that it describes an aspect of the nature of the art in the Stam's creative "reworking" of the sources – of the Bavli and into the Bavli.

13. A good example of a reading of Kiddushin 70 that focuses on the role of the author in the composition of the narrative, rather than the experience of the reader, can be found in Barry Wimpfheimer's forthcoming book on Bavli legal narrative. Since Wimpfheimer presents what I would deem "simultexts" as sources for the Stam's creation of Kiddushin 70a comparison of our readings would further explain the differences between an author-oriented and reader-oriented approach to the Bavli.

14. Wolfgang Iser, *The Act of Reading: A Theory of Aesthetic Response*, (The Johns Hopkins University Press, 1978), p. 34.

15. Daniel Boyarin, *Intertexuality and the Reading of Midrash*, (Indiana University Press, 1994), p. 15.

16. Bruns' term, as quoted in Boyarin. ibid. p. 39. [Gerald Bruns, "Midrash and Allegory" in *The Literary Guide to the Bible*, ed. Frank Kermode and Robert Alter, (Cambridge, Mass. 1986), pp. 626–627.]

17. The reader-oriented approach that I suggest can certainly be used to complement the work of Daniel Boyarin and Jeffrey Rubenstein. Both Boyarin and Rubenstein use various Rabbinic texts and their relationships to one another to try to map a Rabbinic "cultural poetics" (Boyarin's term). Boyarin's technique is to view all texts from the Rabbinic corpus as containing a certain "cultural problematic" that he then uses to ascertain information about the culture of those texts using a "hermeneutics of suspicion". Rubenstein focuses on the particular relationship between parallel stories found both in the Yerushalmi and Bavli and uses the differences between those stories to outline a culture

of the Babylonian Talmud. My main point of departure from these two scholars is my emphasis on the poetics of the Bavli as a book. Daniel Boyarin, *Carnal Israel: Reading Sex In Talmudic Culture*, (Berkeley and Los Angeles, California: University of California Press, 1993). Jeffrey L. Rubenstein, *Talmudic Stories: Narrative Art, Composition, and Culture*, (Baltimore and London: The Johns Hopkins UniversityPress, 1999).

18. The term for glutton, *Sheviskel*, is a play on Rav Yehudah's father's name, *Yeḥezkel* and introduces the notion of word play that dominates this passage.

19. Rav Huna was the leading rabbinic authority of a third city, Sura.

20. Rav Huna's advice only makes sense to the reader who is aware that Ran Naḥman's father in-law is the exilarch, a detail alluded to elsewhere in the Bavli. It is precisely this type of "gapping" that proves that the Bavli assumes that its reader knows the entire Bavli and that each individual passage in the Bavli must be read alongside all other passages in the Bavli. The trigger word/simultext reading strategy highlights certain passages that the reader is encouraged to read more prominently alongside other passages.

21. Literally: falling.

22. Trigger words may also be found in close proximity to the simultext rather than within it. The significance of this fact will be addressed later.

23. An interpretation of Psalms 45:14.

24. The idea that the wife of a *ḥaver* is just like a *ḥaver*, which comes up when Rav Huna's wife is called before the court of Rav Naḥman, contrasts nicely with the idea put forth in a simultext that I will discuss later. Berakhot 51b has 'Ulla telling Rav Naḥman that a woman is only blessed through her husband. In addition, the phrase "the wife of a *ḥaver* is just like a *ḥaver*" is introduced by "*hakhi amar* Shmuel" the only other time it is mentioned in the Bavli (Avodah Zarah 39a). The phrase "*hakhi amar* Shmuel" appears less than 30 times sprinkled throughout the Bavli yet 7 times in Kiddushin 70 alone.

25. *Anbaga* and *Nebaga* are the same word, the former represents the Babylonian pronunciation of the word while the latter represents the Palestinian pronunciation. Kiddushin 70 has the word being spoken by a Babylonian and therefore uses the Babylonian spelling of the word while Berakhot 51 has a Palestinian saying the word and therefore uses the Palestinian spelling. It is not uncommon for the Bavli to play with dialect in presenting dialogue and narrative. An example of this can be found in Kiddushin 70's use of the words *taska, daska,*

and *deyaska* in a part of the dialogue between Rav Nahman and Rav Yehudah which I did not include in my summary. The different meanings of these words, and the confusion they present to each participant in the dialogue highlights a lot of the themes found in Kiddushin 70 and its simultexts.

26. "*Hakhi amar* Shmuel" is a phrase that dominates Kiddushin 70, appearing 7 times, which is around 25% of its total appearances in the Bavli. 'Ulla, the Palestinian student of Rabbi Yohanan, employs the term *hakhi amar* for his own Rabbi in precisely the same way as Rav Yehudah in Kiddushin 70.

27. The following is my own translation of Berakhot 51.

28. A word that only appears four other times in the Bavli aside from these two simultexts.

29. Charlotte Fonrobert counters this type of reading of Niddah 20 with one that has the Bavli use Yalta as a way of expressing its own difficulties with having male rabbis control women's menstrual blood. Charlotte Elisheva Fonrobert, *Menstrual Purity: Rabbinic and Christian Reconstructions of Biblical Gender*, (Stanford University Press, 2000), pp. 118–127.

30. Once again, it is a trigger word found in close proximity to the simultext, rather than within it, that highlights the complex nature of the shaping of the Bavli into its final form, a form that elicits the reader to read simultextually, in the full and extended context of the simultexts.

31. The Ketubot simultext highlights a fascinating occurrence demonstrating how the Bavli's editorial process continues through the middle ages strengthening the relationship between simultexts through the use of new trigger words. On Ketubot 60a the word *eturnga* appears as a happax identical to the *etrunga* happax in Kiddushin save the inverted *v* and *r* and variant *t*. The word *eturnga* refers to the person who serves drinks to the Persian king. Kingship and serving drinks are both concepts that meaningfully refer back to our Kiddushin passage. Especially in relation to the use of a minor by King Shapur earlier on the page and the fact that it is the notion of Donag serving drinks that leads to a discussion of using women, even when a minor, in the first place. However, it is fairly clear that *eturnga* as it appears in the Vilna and Bomberg editions is merely a corruption of the word *akhvanger*, the *v* and *kh* being turned into a *t*. Is this merely a copyist error or part of a meaningful transitional phase in the aesthetics of the Bavli? If indeed merely a copyist error then is this evidence that

the copyist was unconsciously influenced by the other trigger word relationships between these simultexts in creating a new trigger word relationship? Whether intentional or not, this is certainly an example of the complexity of the bidirectional editorial process of the Bavli into its final form.

32. Rashi explains that they are in fear of the exilarchy.

33. *Sheiltot deRav Aḥai Gaon, Parshat Vayeira*, 13.

34. Reuven Margoliot. *leHeker Sheimot veKinuim beTalmud Meieit Reuven Margoliot*. Mosad Harav Kook, (Jerusalem,. 1960), pps 40–41.

35. This text reads: One who eats citron will have fragrant children. The daughter of King Shapur – her mother ate citron – and they would bring her out before her father as a primary fragrance [BT Ketubot 61a].

36. "Rabbah bar Rav Ada said that Rav said: Whoever marries a woman for the sake of money will have children who are not genetically fit." (Kiddushin 70a)

37. Although *hahu yoma* appears around eighty times in the Bavli an analysis of those appearances leads to understanding why it is a trigger word directing the reader particularly to Berakhot 28. Three factors lead the reader to the Berakhot simultext. First off, most of the time that *hahu yoma* appears in the Bavli it is in legal contexts regarding contract law (e.g. what if someone wrote a certain date in a contract and on that day [*hahu yoma*] etc.) Second, in the Berakhot 28 passage not only does *hahu yoma* appear twice it appears twice in the context of naming its Hebrew equivalent, *oto hayom*, as always referring to the story of Rabban Gamliel and the presidency. Third, Although 'on that very day' does not always refer to a political upheaval it is not a common enough expression to ignore its use when Rabban Gamliel is forced out of his Presidency (BT Berakhot 28a); Rabbi's death (BT Ketuboth 104a); Establishing laws for 'respect of the President' and Av Beit Din (BT Horayoth 13b); a story regarding the honor of the house of the Caesar (similar to honor of the house of the President) (BT Sotah 40a); Rabbi Ḥanin, the son-in-law of the House of the President (Moed Katan 25b).

38. I do not refer here to a historical reality but rather to the Bavli's own conception of the differences between these two dynasties. It is important to note that the Bavli differentiated between the periods of true Hasmonian autonomy and the period when the Hasmonians themselves became stewards of the Roman Empire. In this regard see BT 'Avoda Zarah 9a. When counting the days of the second temple the

Bavli divides the ruling parties into four groups: The Persians ruled for 34 years; the Greeks ruled for 180 years; the Hasmoneans ruled for 103 years; and the royal house of Herod ruled for 103 years. Rather than counting the rule of the Hasmonians as lasting for 206 years the Bavli divides the periods of autonomous Hasmonian rule and non-autonomous Herodian rule.

Women of the Exodus –

AN EXCERPT*

Shera Aranoff Tuchman and Sandra E. Rapoport

Serach, Asher's Daughter, Heralds the Redemption
EXODUS 3:16, 3:22, 4:31

Go and gather the Elders of Israel and say to them, 'The Lord, God of your fathers, Abraham, Isaac and Jacob, revealed Himself to me, saying, "Verily have I remembered you, and I have seen what is being done to you in Egypt."'

And every woman shall ask of her neighbor objects of silver and gold, as well as clothing, and shall give them to her sons and daughters, for you shall be victorious over the Egyptians.

And the people believed [Moses] when they heard that God remembered the Children of Israel...

God's conversation with Moses at the burning bush was significant on several levels. First, of course, is Moses' reluctant but eventual acceptance of his role as God's messenger to the people and to the Egyptian Pharaoh. But equally momentous is God's emphatic statement in chapter 3 verse 16 that the redemption is imminent. God's words, *verily have I remembered – PaKoD PaKaD'Ti* in Hebrew – have been awaited for hundreds of years. The people have labored and suffered, witnessed their newborn sons drowned before their eyes, and have despaired of redemption. Their lives, the lives of their parents, and the future lives of their children have become mired in slavery. They know no other way of life. Pharaoh is their master.

The Bible's double-use of the Hebrew word for "remember" as spoken by God to Moses is therefore highly significant. God knows that Moses will have a nearly impossible job convincing the Children of Israel that "God has truly remembered" them. Their entire existential being is that of slaves, and they will not leap to embrace this fugitive stranger's announcement of impending redemption. They will doubt him, will surely direct their anger against him, and will not rush to upset the status quo and anger the Egyptian king. The *midrashists* have therefore woven a rich tapestry explaining the Torah's use of this emphatic phrase, *verily have I remembered.*

The commentaries say that Bible's doubling of the word "remember" was an encrypted code that God transmitted to Moses at the burning bush in order to assist him on his mission to return to Egypt. Pirkei de Rabi Eliezer explains that such double words appear rarely in the Torah, and these in particular – because of their future momentous power – had been passed down in trusted whispers from father to son beginning with Abraham, then to Isaac, thence to Jacob, from Jacob to his favored son, Joseph, and from Joseph to his brothers. Throughout the years of the Children of Israel's unending bondage in Egypt, Jacob's sons died off one by one, and the future redemption's secret code – *PaKoD PaKaD'Ti* – was transmitted ultimately, according to the Talmud (Sotah 13a), to his eldest surviving issue, Asher's youngest daughter and Jacob's granddaughter, Serach. In this way, if someone calling himself "the redeemer" were to present himself to the Children of Israel, the elders would be able to judge whether or not he had in truth been appointed by God, by discerning if he possessed this secret code. It therefore fell to Serach, the daughter of Asher, (known in the *midrash* as Serach bat Asher) to confirm the veracity of any such putative redeemer. She alone possessed the knowledge of the code words. It is for this reason, according to the *midrash*, that the Torah says in verse 16 that God commands Moses to first *go to the elders.* The most revered of all the elders was Jacob's granddaughter, Serach. She would confirm Moses' authenticity, paving the way for his acceptance first by the other elders and then by the Children of Israel.

God's emphatic statement of remembering – *PaKoD PaKaD'Ti* – is that special quality of divine memory that will free one who has no hope. For this reason the elders will be aghast as well as hopeful when, later on in the Exodus story, Moses returns to Egypt with his brother Aaron at his side and announces that he has been sent by God to redeem them from slavery. Moses reveals to them, in that future meeting, God's three signs: the miracle of his staff that becomes a snake; the sign of his leprous hand; and the ability to transform the waters of the Nile into blood. Moses also speaks the encrypted phrase – *PaKoD PaKaD'Ti* – to disclose to the elders of Israel that redemption is imminent. The elders consult Serach bat Asher. They reveal all that Moses has shown to them, and she remains skeptical until they also reveal to her the code words that he had brought to them from God's mouth: *PaKoD PaKaD'Ti.* Immediately, recognizing the fabled code, Serach's ancient eyes become alight with excitement, her wrinkled visage is transformed in ecstasy as she points to Moses: "He is the man who will redeem Israel from Egypt!"

Ibn Ezra explains that this is the reason the Bible states, in chapter 4, verse 31, that *the people believed Moses when they heard that God remembered.* The momentous power of *PaKoD PaKaD'Ti* – *verily have I remembered* – first revealed by God to Abraham generations earlier, was destined to be confirmed by the daughter of Asher. It was Serach, granddaughter of Jacob and cousin of Moses, who confirmed Moses' bona fides to the elders of Israel and heralded the redemption. She was also a legendary wise woman who appears and reappears in *midrashic* lore over the course of eight centuries of Jewish history. The *midrash* credits Serach bat Asher with the knowledge that Joseph had not died a terrible death, but that his brothers had sold him to the caravan of Ishmaelites. She is also one of the seventy original souls who migrated into Egypt with Jacob, and the Talmud (Sotah 13a) has her pointing out to Moses the secret burial place of Joseph's bones on the eve of their exodus from Egypt. She is mythically present from the time of Abraham through the advent of Israel's servitude in Egypt, until the kingdom of David arises centuries hence, and according to Otzer Ishei

HaTanach is one of the fabled nine persons in Jewish history whose death is never recorded and who are said to have entered the Garden of Eden alive as a reward for their righteousness.

Beth Samuels likened Serach Bat Asher to "an Eliyahu figure who appears and reappears throughout the generations, a wise woman who, according to the *midrashim*, is immortal. In every generation where she appears Serach was the authority, the leader. Serach is a catalyst who transforms us – through her sensitivity, wisdom and teaching – from a state of darkness to a state of redemption."

Harking back to Moses' revelation at the burning bush, the reader will recall that in addition to the words *PaKoD PaKaD'Ti*, God also foretold a nearly unbelievable reversal of events. God predicted that as part of the redemption the Israelites would ultimately vanquish the Egyptians, and that *every woman shall ask of her neighbor objects of silver and gold, as well as clothing, and shall give them to her sons and daughters*. The commentaries ask pointedly why this prediction is restricted to the women? Why will the Egyptian women cede their wealth exclusively to their Israelite counterparts?

According to Nehama Liebowitz, the Egyptian women are returning to the erstwhile Hebrew slaves the valuable objects and jewelry that they had acquired from the Hebrew women over the years. In the wake of the Pharaoh's genocidal edict to murder the Hebrew male newborns, the desperate and ingenious slave women had bartered their valuables and clothing, begging the Egyptian women to overlook their hidden babies. Over the years, the Hebrews' homes became bereft of all valuables, while the Egyptians' homes swelled with the wealth they acquired from the Hebrew women as bribes to save their babies' lives. The commentary explains that God's prediction is a poetic reversal: when God redeems the Children of Israel, the slave women will have the upper hand, and the Egyptian women will give up their valuables and fine clothing to them. In reality, says the commentary, they are returning the valuables to their true owners.

It is not coincidental, says Nehama, that it is the *women* who are requesting the Egyptian wealth. It was the women who righteously enticed their husbands to continue to procreate, who bore their children against impossible odds, who stood up to the Pharaoh, and who, in the face of death, bartered for the life of each child one-at-a-time. For these reasons the women are spared attending their redemption in slave rags. God's prediction is that the Israelite women shall clothe their children in the fine raiment they requested of the Egyptian women once the redemption was upon them. Such was the hopeful message that Moses was to bear to his enslaved Israelite brethren.

*   *   *

Moses, Zipporah and their Sons Take Leave of Yitro
EXODUS 4:18–20

And Moses returned to Yeter his father-in-law, and he said to him, "Please give me leave to return to my brethren who are in Egypt, in order that I may see for myself whether they are still alive." And Yitro told Moses, "Go peacefully." For God had told Moses [while he was] in Midian, "Go, return to Egypt, for all the men who sought to kill you are already dead." So Moses took his wife and their sons and he set them upon a donkey, and he set out on the return path to the land of Egypt. And Moses had in his hand God's chosen staff.

The Bible meticulously narrates that after his revelation at the burning thorn-bush, Moses returned from his desert isolation to the tent of his father-in-law Yitro. According to Chizkuni Moses returned leading Yitro's flocks homeward for the last time. He was embarking on God's mission and truly did not know if he would ever return to Midian. Rashi explains Moses' return to his father-in-law in ethical terms. Moses was honor-bound to consult with Yitro before embarking on his return trip to Egypt because Moses had sworn to his father-in-law, in Exodus 2:21, that he would never depart from Midian without first seeking his blessing. The Talmud (Nedarim 65a) concurs, and narrates a *midrashic* conversation between Moses and God. Recalling Moses' oath to Yitro, God instructs him while he is still in the Sinai desert: "You swore an oath while in Midian; now return to Midian and seek absolution from your oath."

Upon his return to Yitro's tent Moses is greeted by his father-in-law, by his older son Gershom, and by his wife Zipporah, about to give birth to their second child. According to the Ramban, Zipporah had been pregnant when Moses left Yitro's tent months ago to lead the flocks to distant fertile pastures. Moses has returned in time to witness his second son's birth, beg leave of Yitro, bundle his wife and sons onto a donkey and make haste to return to Egypt as God commanded him in 4:20. Moses has no time to spare.

It is fascinating that God's instructions to Moses – both textual and *midrashic* – display God's understanding of Moses' most personal concerns. First, preempting Moses' fears, God reassures Moses that he is free to return to Egypt notwithstanding that he fled there years before and remained wanted for a capital crime. "You can return to Egypt. Those in Egypt who sought your death are themselves dead, and no longer pose a threat to your life." And second, God understands that Moses might think that God expects him to pick himself up immediately and head down to Egypt, without stopping first in Yitro's tent. But in the *midrash* God is instructing Moses that a man's oath freely given should be honored. After Moses is released from his oath to Yitro, God's expectation is that Moses "leave Midian behind and return to Egypt." After his revelation at the burning bush, Moses has been transformed from Yitro's shepherd into God's servant. It was past time to set out on the path to bring about the promised redemption.

Sha'arei Aharon presents a possibility that months before, Zipporah and Gershom had in fact accompanied Moses into the desert of Horeb when he shepherded Yitro's flocks, pitching their tent in the grazing lands in the foothills of Mount Horeb. Thus, Moses' return *to Yitro's tent* in 4:18 was in time to allow Zipporah to give birth to their second child in the comfort of her childhood home and with her sisters about her, to beg leave of Yitro, and to bid the old man goodbye.

Still, the predominant *p'shat* reading of verse 4:20 is that *Moses took his wife and their sons and he set them upon a donkey, and he set out on the return path to the land of Egypt.* Ramban recounts a fascinating *midrashic* conversation between Yitro and Moses when Moses and Zipporah were preparing to set out on the desert journey to Egypt. "So tell me, Moses. Where are you bound for now?" "For Egypt," he replied. "Egypt! In the name of Heaven why would you want to take my daughter and grandsons *into* Egypt? Egypt is the one place everyone is seeking to *escape!*" And Moses responds, "In the coming months there *will* be a great exodus from Egypt, and our people will journey from there to stand at the foot of Mt. Sinai, where they will hear the pronouncements of the One God. I will lead this exodus, and I will stand on God's mountain. Should not your daughter and grandsons witness this greatness?" And Yitro gave Moses his blessing. *Go peacefully.*

In fact, according to the 20th-century commentary of Meshech Chachma, it is Moses' faith in God's promise of redemption that allows him to take Zipporah, Gershom and their newborn son out of Yitro's comfortable oasis home and subject them to the rigors of desert travel and the certainty of hostilities once they arrive at their destination. And according to the *midrash*, when Moses finally arrives in Egypt leading the donkey that carried his wife and children, his credibility with the skeptical Children of Israel is enhanced. They appreciate how certain Moses must be of the veracity of God's promise of imminent redemption. For otherwise, they reason, it is inconceiveable that Moses would bring his wife and sons – one a newborn – to a place of bondage and constant danger. This putative redeemer, this man Moses, must place great store in God's promise. Perhaps, the lifelong slaves will think, just perhaps, the redemption really is at hand!

The power of God's word can be tangible and awesome, but it also can be mystical and incalculable, according to the biblical commentaries. The Midrash Tanchuma, Sh'mot Rabbah and Ba'al HaTurim refer to God's word to Moses in Midian (4:19): *Go, return to Egypt.* The implicit question is why the Bible states again in 4:19 that God told Moses to *Go, return to Egypt,* when God had already given Moses this command at the burning bush in chapter 3. Midrash Tanchuma explains that God's voice is the medium of miracles and wonders. Moses was introduced to God's voice at the burning bush, and there God outlined for Moses his mission to redeem the Israelites, and offered him reassurances and magical signs. But according to the *midrash* God's reiteration to Moses in Midian to *Go, return to Egypt* is meant to be understood as only *half* of God's message. Miraculously, God's voice simultanously spoke both to Moses in Midian *(Go, return to Egypt)*, and to his brother Aaron in Egypt! God's concomitant word to Aaron in Egypt (4:27) was: *Go forth and greet Moses who is on his way in the desert.* The *midrash* implies that while the great miracles are still to come – the plagues, the splitting of the Red Sea, the giving of the Torah – God's will is generous enough to encompass the relatively minor miracle of uniting brothers who have endured half a century of separation under fraught and daunting circumstances, and ensuring that mutuality and gladness fill their hearts as well as commonality of purpose.

This is the reason, says the *midrash*, that the Bible tells us in 4:19 what God instructs Moses, and in 4:27 in parallel language, what God instructs Aaron. God had assured Moses at the burning bush that he and Aaron would be partners in the forthcoming redemption. Thus, God's bifurcated voice in chapter 4 – simultaneously spoken but heard differently by Moses and Aaron worlds apart but to a single purpose – is the fulfillment of His promise to Moses. God knows that when Moses encounters Aaron in the desert on the way back to Egypt Moses will recall God's promise to him and he will be reassured. Moses' God is the God who keeps His promises, be they seemingly trivial or of enormous consequence.

These simultaneous iterations by God to Moses and Aaron appear in the Bible separated by three verses. The *midrash* explains that by this placement we learn that God's voice is bracketing a miraculous and momentous occurrence. It behooves us to pay close attention to what befalls Moses and Zipporah in the intervening verses that are strategically placed between the bookends of God's words.

* * *

The Incident at the Inn
EXODUS 4:24–26
And it happened on the way, at an inn, that God encountered him and sought to kill him. And Zipporah took a flint and cut the foreskin of her son, and she touched his legs; and she said, "For you are like a bridegroom of blood to me." Thence, it instantly withdrew from him; thus she said, "A bridegroom of blood for circumcisions!"

Moses and Zipporah have left Midian behind. Zipporah has taken leave of her father and her home and is venturing, for the first time in her sheltered life, into the vast desert terrain that separates Midian from Egypt. Her husband Moses, a courageous but solitary man, a shepherd and a thinker, has disclosed to her and her father that his God has spoken to him and instructed him to return to Egypt in order to redeem the Hebrews from their slavery. Moses is on foot, leading the donkey that is carrying his wife Zipporah and their sons Gershom and newborn Eliezer. They plod westward, the only humans as far as the eye can see as they cross the endless sunbleached dunes.

Finally, the desert night is upon them, and the tiny caravan stops at a tented settlement, at an inn that accepts desert wayfarers. It is while Moses, Zipporah and their sons are secluded at this inn that they experience one of the strangest incidents in the entire book of Exodus, a Biblical book that is rife with miracles as well as supernatural occurrences.

This incident is narrated in three verses between God's command to Moses to *Go to Egypt* and God's command to Aaron to *Go forth and greet Moses*. It has been called one of the most obscure or incomprehensible vignettes in the Bible. The 20th-century Torah commentator Yehuda Nachshoni articulates the intellectual puzzlement that is expressed by Torah scholars when they are faced with these verses. Nachshoni poses the questions that surely crowd the reader's mind: If God has appointed Moses as His messenger to Pharaoh and as the redeemer of the Hebrews, why then does God accost Moses on his way to Egypt and attempt to kill him? Was it, as some commentators say, that Moses faced the death sentence because he failed to circumcise his newborn son Eliezer? And if Moses and his wife have encountered some grave danger at the inn because he did not circumcise his newborn son, why then is it Zipporah – and not Moses – who circumcises the infant? And whatever can Zipporah mean by her first cryptic pronouncement *A bridegroom of blood are you to me!* when the death force is upon Moses, and her parallel remark after he has been spared: *A bridegroom of blood for circumcisions!* Furthermore, continues Nachshoni, it is unclear whom precisely the angel of God sought to kill; was it Moses or was it his newborn son? The commentary specifically acknowledges his thanks for the collected wisdom of the commentaries and the *midrash*, with whose help we can begin to make some sense of this incident at the inn.

According to Rashi the straightforward reading of the verses is that God sought to kill Moses because he failed to circumcise his newborn son while they were still all together in Midian. Because Moses delayed consecrating his newborn son to God, he faced dire punishment on the road to Egypt. The Talmud (Nedarim 31b) elaborates, saying that in those days circumcision was not a simple matter. What might appear to readers to be a simple course of action – Moses should have circumcised Eliezer in Midian and then left for Egypt – is in fact more complex. The Talmud presents Moses' dilemma: *If I circumcise Eliezer while I am still here in Midian, the boy is in danger if we travel immediately. I would have to wait here for at least three days afterwards to ensure his safe recovery. Yet God has commanded me to "Go, return to Egypt!" I am forbidden to delay setting out on God's mission.* Circumcise and wait, or leave for Egypt directly? Such was Moses' quandary according to the Talmud. In light of this, why then did Moses face punishment by death? The Talmud suggests that the inn itself holds the answer.

Akeidat Yitzchak explains that a very human Moses chose to delay the circumcision and to spend the night at the inn before pressing on toward Egypt. The reason for his choice was that Moses was not yet a man of God. He still desired his wife by his side, and he sought time for marital intimacy at the inn. The commentary says that had Moses been thinking logically he could have circumcised his son even when they had stopped at the inn. That he did not do so, but further delayed performing the circumcision, is the reason for God's wrath. Moses could have – and according to Akeidat Yitzhak Moses *should* have – circumcised Eliezer either before leaving Midian, or even upon arriving at the inn. In either case Moses then should have left the baby in the care of Zipporah, striking out alone for Egypt. That he did neither is the reason God confronts Moses *on the way at the inn.*

The Netziv explains this present confrontation between Moses and God as having its origins in Moses' spiritual transformation. According to the commentator, when Moses first confronted God at the burning bush in chapter 3 and removed his shoes out of respect for the holiness of the place, Moses began – perhaps unbeknownst even to himself – his ascent into holiness. God's intent was that from the encounter on Mount Horeb Moses would become the quasi-holy vehicle for the redemption of the Children of Israel. God would engineer the momentous event, and Moses and his brother Aaron would carry out God's wishes. The problem, according to the Netziv, is that Moses' spiritual transformation proceeded more slowly. In his human and thoughtful fashion, Moses was absorbing his new role, and after his discourse with God, he reluctantly assumed the mantle of redeemer. We must appreciate that back on the ground, so-to-speak, amidst his family in Midian, Moses was hard-put to remain entirely God's messenger. He was dutiful son-in-law, enamored husband, father of a newborn. His new mission was pulling him away from all that was familiar to him, and he was temporarily without moorings. Heeding God's command to hasten to Egypt, he postponed the circumcision of his newborn son, brought his small family along with him into the desert, and took comfort from the nearness of his wife in a desert inn. All of these behaviors were understandably human, and precisely what God did *not* require from the newly annointed redeemer.

God's confrontation of Moses at the inn that night was unexpected and very nearly fatal. Moses was completely unprepared for it. He was engaged in the prosaic acts of settling his family for the night. This is contrasted with the incident on Mount Horeb, where Moses, although surprised and awestruck at the vision of the burning bush, had been a solitary shepherd who spent his days in contemplation and meditation. He accepted God's presence there, and was as prepared on Mount Horeb as he would ever be to confront the Lord for the first time. Contrariwise, when God confronted Moses at the inn Moses' reaction was one of paralyzing fear. He quite simply did not expect God's abrupt appearance to him there. Moses was not in a state of readiness to meet God on His terms, having not yet made that critical transition from husband and father to Man of God.

Rabbi Adin Steinsaltz, in his commentary to the Talmud on this incident (Nedarim 31a), confirms the Netziv's understanding of Moses' near-fatal misstep. Says Steinsaltz, Moses was punished by God at the inn for the reason that instead of rising above his worldly and corporeal needs, Moses succumbed and allowed his own needs to control him. As God's anointed, He was expected to give priority to his spiritual self. Instead, his son remained uncircumcised, and he was dallying en route to Egypt.

Hama'or Shebatorah explains that one might think that as God's anointed, Moses could have delayed the commandment of circumcision with impunity, as he was already on his way to fulfill God's previously articulated command to return to Egypt. Had he stopped to circumcise his son he would have delayed returning to Egypt. Moses was in a seemingly impossible situation. But according to the commentary, because there *was* time to fulfill *both* of God's commandments, Moses was held to God's exacting standard.

Still, the textual difficulty is glaring: *God encountered him and sought to kill him.* Despite the wording, the commentaries reject the notion that God sought to eradicate the man He had selected and appointed redeemer of the Children of Israel. Rashbam laconically states that it was an angel, not God Himself, who encountered Moses at the inn. Sforno adds that the angel who encountered Moses was the designated angel of the *brit*, the angel of the covenant. This specific angel threatened Moses with death because he had bypassed the commandment to circumcise his newborn son and bring him into the covenant with God. Rashi names Eliezer, Zipporah and Moses' newborn, as the uncircumcised son whom God jealously desires to enter into the covenant, and the Talmud (Nedarim 32a) understands verse 24 to mean that God's threat was directed not against Moses, but against the uncircumcised newborn itself.

Contrariwise, Sha'arei Aharon posits that God is angry that Moses' and Zipporah's *firstborn* son, Gershom, was still as-yet uncircumcised. Readers will recall our discussion in chapter 22 that Yitro had required as a condition of Moses' marriage to Zipporah that their future firstborn son would be raised in Midianite tradition. Here, the commentary suggests that God is angered that Moses has not taken the first possible opportunity to circumcise Gershom now that he is out of Yitro's purview. The commentary suggests that Moses reasoned, "Since the *brit* has been delayed until now, I will wait until we arrive in Egypt and *then* I will circumcise him." We will see that it is this critical delay that nearly costs Moses his life.

Sha'arei Aharon explains that a close reading of verse 24 yields a hint to the reader that this was a terrifying *warning* to Moses rather than the angel of death come to exact *punishment.* The Biblical term for "God" in this verse, *YHWH*, is understood to represent the "*merciful* God." Had the verse used instead the word "*Elohim*" – the Biblical reference for "God of *judgement*" – our understanding of the verse would have been completely different. Thus, according to the *midrash*, the angel that encountered Moses was one of mercy, because it waited until Moses and his tiny caravan had reached the inn before accosting him. In contrast, the angel of judgement would have accosted Moses on the way, while he was trudging through the blistering sand dunes, and the danger to Moses in those circumstances would have been dire indeed.

Hama'or Shebatorah agrees, saying that the spirit that Moses encountered was surely the spirit of divine mercy. This merciful angel sought only to hurry Moses along, urging him to reach the sanctuary of the inn before complying with God's command to circumcise his newborn son. God's merciful angel did not seek to exact Moses' death. Nachshoni explains that the supernatural encounter was not intended as a sinister one; rather it was initially a divine phenomenon whose purpose was to signal that the time had come for the circumcision. Only when Moses apparently ignored the angel's presence did its mission revert to one of punishment.

This "angel of God," or manifestation of God's presence, caught Moses completely unaware. The *midrash* explains that Moses and his wife already had retired for the night. God's abundance concentrated itself in Moses' room at the inn, and quite literally filled it to bursting. Moses' only previous encounter with the spirit of God had been in the wild and barren spaces of the desert mountains, where Moses had been readying himself to accept God's presence in solitude and contemplation. Also, on the slope of Mount Horeb there was plenty of space for God's spirit to inhabit. Here at the inn, says Abarbanel, Moses is confronted by the enormity of God's presence after he has been busily occupied with the most mundane and corporeal of human needs. Not only is Moses unprepared for God to "find" him here, but God's abundant presence nearly suffocates him. An unready Moses is greeted by a virtual tidal wave of divine spirit, and he is paralyzed with fear. Says the commentator, at that moment Moses perceived his own imminent death. The lesson that Moses must absorb, teaches Abarbanel, is that as God's chosen prophetic messenger Moses was expected to exist in a solitude of contemplation so as to be prepared to accept God's revelations at any time, day or night, even at the inn.

What manner of physical or mental paralysis overtook Moses at the moment that *God encountered him and sought to kill him*? The commentaries present a picture of a stunned and shocked Moses, surprised into muteness and rendered nonfunctional in the overwhelming presence of God in the room at the desert inn. The thoughtful Bible reader might counter with the query that Moses already has stood in the presence of the Lord and conversed with Him on Mount Horeb; how, then, can we accept his utter paralysis here? The reader only has to envision Moses, Zipporah and the isolated desert inn, and if possible, imagine the sudden, unexpected manifestation of God's glory appearing in their room in the gloom of the desert night. Abarbanel laconically states that Moses panicked and went into shock. B'chor Shor explains that the circumstances instantaneously plunged Moses into a state of existential angst, so that he was as immobile as a corpse. The Netziv embellishes upon this and explains that the enormity of the glory of God appearing to Moses in the desert inn rendered him immobile. The commentator reminds us that Moses felt himself essentially unworthy of God's mantle, as was evidenced by his equivocation with God at the burning bush. God's sudden appearance to him at the inn was a burden he simply could not shoulder. It incited in Moses a radical alteration to his fundmental being, causing a paralysis born of terror, indecision and need. The Malbim summarizes Moses' physical and emotional state by saying that God's surprise presence to an unprepared and unholy Moses caused the man to shudder to his very foundations. In that split second Moses was rendered utterly unable to think or act.

The issue for the reader is how did Moses survive this brush with death?

The next verse presents the biblical reader with the undisputed champion of this episode, Moses' wife, Zipporah. *And Zipporah took a flint and cut the foreskin of her [newborn] son...* Moses is lying inert in their room at the inn, and Zipporah is in a turmoil of her own. She knows she must act to save her husband, but what should she do? The reader cannot but be struck by the contrast between Moses' disabled passivity born of his existential terror, and Zipporah's nearly instantaneous thought coupled with action. The Torah does not allow any hesitation between the words *He sought his death* at the end of verse 24, and the opening words of verse 25, *And Zipporah took a flint*...According to Abarbanel, in the instant between seeing her husband in the throes of a near-death experience and picking up the flint, Zipporah's ability to wisely, correctly and instantaneously infer both the causation and its antidote mark her as heroic.

What impelled Zipporah take the action she did (*and she cut the foreskin of her [newborn] son*)? It is undisputed that Zipporah was not privy to Moses' vision of God's exalted presence in their room at the inn. God revealed Himself only to Moses on that night. B'chor Shor explains that Zipporah's keen insight took over, so that she immediately began scrutinizing her husband's actions, searching for any act of his that might have led to his present predicament.

Sh'mot Rabbah (5:8) answers the question on every reader's lips: How did Zipporah know that Moses' life hung in the balance *because of a circumcision*? The *midrash* narrates the bizarre scenario. At that precise instant Zipporah watched in horror as God's messenger angel enveloped the supine Moses and swallowed him whole from the top of his head until his genitals. The Talmud (Nedarim 32a) narrates this same incident, adding that it was *two* angels of the Lord who assaulted the inert Moses: The angels of divine Wrath and divine Anger swallowed Moses' entire body, from his head down, and from his feet upwards, stopping suggestively at his genitals. Because Moses' genital area was the only part of his body exposed to her view, the rabbis explain that Zipporah was able instantly to infer that therein lay the essence of the problem, as well as the solution.

According to Alschich, Zipporah instantly deduced that Moses' dire predicament was due to one of two possibilities. Perhaps God was angered that Moses had wed her – a Midianite – thereby desecrating himself after having spoken face-to-face with the Lord at the burning bush. Alternatively, perhaps God's anger was incited by Moses' delay in conducting the ritual circumcision of their newborn son. She reasoned immediately that her best course of action was to perform the circumcision herself, and she fervently hoped that her courageous act would solve both exigencies. By performing the required *brit* she assumed that she would thereby nullify in God's eyes any unseemly aspect of her marriage to Moses; also, her consecration of their son via the *brit* would placate the Lord if the absence of the *brit* were the reason for Moses' punishment. Either way, Zipporah took the flint in hand and, in the process of consecrating her son, released Moses from his crisis.

Chizkuni adds that Moses' paralysis overtook him in front of Zipporah's eyes, and in a flash of prophecy it was revealed to her that *she* must be the one to act. The Talmud (Avodah Zara 27a) engages in a discussion about whether a *brit* performed by a woman is permissible. Rabbi Adin Steinsaltz's discussion of the Talmud's passage on this issue cites the Rambam's comment that a woman is fit to perform the circumcision in a situation where no male is present and able to act. The Talmud suggests that Zipporah might only have begun the circumcision and that Moses completed it after he recovered from his crisis. There are numerous opinions on the legal technicalities of such a circumcision. But a plain reading of the Torah text points to the essence of verse 25: *And Zipporah took a flint and cut the foreskin of her [newborn] son.* Moses' wife, Zipporah, daughter of the high priest of Midian, mother of Moses' two sons, performed the circumcision on their baby son while Moses lay incapacitated in the desert inn. It is undisputed that her bold action saved Moses' life.

And Zipporah took a flint and cut the foreskin of her [newborn] son, and she touched his legs… The Torah text seems clear at first reading: After Zipporah circumcized their son, she took the excised foreskin in her hand and placed it *at Moses'* feet. Says Rashi, Zipporah *threw* the skin at Moses' feet. We can appreciate that Zipporah, terrified that her action might not be in time to save her husband, threw down the foreskin almost like a gauntlet, implicitly saying, "It is done! The boy is now consecrated unto the Hebrew God! Now release Moses from your grip!" Ibn Ezra would agree, saying that Zipporah cast her baby's foreskin at Moses' feet so as to appease whatever evil spirit held him in thrall. Chizkuni adds that she might have intended that the blood of circumcision would atone for and expunge Moses' paralysis.

Because the Torah phrase is ambiguous – *whose* legs did Zipporah touch? – some commentaries suggest that the Bible's words might mean that Zipporah touched the legs *of her newborn son* during or after her act of circumcizing him. Chizkuni states that this interpretation naturally fills in the text's ambiguity, for of course she held the baby's legs while performing the *brit*. But Perush Yonatan also presents a third possibility; that Zipporah threw the baby's foreskin at the feet *of God's messenger angel* who appeared in their room at the inn that night. Zipporah's purpose was to present her baby's foreskin to the angel as an unambiguous offering: Her baby's covenantal foreskin in lieu of her husband's life. In a time-worn method of primitive exchange or appeasement of an angry deity, Zipporah boldly acted in the only way she knew.

These three interpretations are set out clearly in the Talmud

(Yerushalmi, Nedarim chapter 3:9). There the rabbis summarize the issue as follows: If the Torah text meant that Zipporah placed the foreskin at *Moses'* feet, she sought thereby to demonstrate to the angel of God that Moses' sin in failing to timely perform his son's *brit* in Midian has been expiated. If the Torah text meant that Zipporah tossed her baby's foreskin at the feet of *the angel,* her intention would have been clear to God's messenger: "Your mission is accomplished. Moses' son is now circumcized. You can leave Moses in peace and return to your Master!" And finally, if the meaning of the Torah text is that she touched the feet of *her baby son,* the crisis of ritual would have been averted by her bold act of performing the required circumcision itself, and her husband would have been released from his paralysis.

After Zipporah circumcised her son while Moses lay paralyzed, the Bible relates that she said, *"For you are like a bridegroom of blood to me."* This biblical phrase is strange and puzzling, and would seem to be nearly unintelligible. But we can appreciate the nuanced interpretations of the commentaries who assist the reader by parsing and examining this biblical phrase.

Of course, the first question on the reader's mind is *Who and what is the 'bridegroom of blood?'* Whom is Zipporah addressing? Rashi says that she is addressing her baby son Eliezer. Though this may seem strange at first, we can easily envision Zipporah comforting her baby son, cleaning up his blood after the circumcision, and saying, "My husband might have been killed tonight but for your blood that I have let!" In fact, Sh'mot Rabbah presents an embellishment to the Torah's mysterious phrase. The *midrash* allows the reader to see and hear as Zipporah addresses her baby while she swaddles him after the circumcision. According to the *midrash,* Zipporah is musing aloud to her baby saying, "With your blood, the blood of the *brit,* my bridegroom has been spared!"

Ibn Ezra confirms that the "bridegroom of blood" in our biblical verse is the newborn baby. The commentator, along with Sha'arei Aharon, explains that according to the rabbis, a baby boy on the day of his *brit* is referred to by his mother and the other women present as a bridegroom, or *chatan,* in honor of the consecrated new life that is symbolically beginning with the ritual circumcision.

Chizkuni, on the other hand, contends that it is Moses who is the "bridegroom of blood." When Zipporah says *"For you are like a bridegroom of blood to me,"* she is addressing her husband, and continuing in her heroic mode she takes the blame for this entire terrifying episode onto her own shoulders. Chizkuni places the emphasis on the Bible's phrase as follows: *For you are like a bridegroom of blood to me.* Zipporah is saying to her paralyzed husband that when he married her – a Midianite and not a Hebrew – he *became* her "bridegroom of blood." For by his continued act of having intimate physical relations with her, his Midianite bride, he has violated the code of the Hebrew God and may be is liable for death as a consequence. She is worried that the Hebrew God had placed a blood penalty upon Moses' head at the time he wed her, and that this near-death episode is therefore indirectly her fault.

Rashbam and Alschich summarize this episode and allow us to hear Zipporah's unrecorded thoughts and words: "This blood of our son's *brit* will serve to salvage my bridegroom from a death sentence. My husband kindled his God's wrath either because he delayed circumcising our son, or because he wed me. But whichever 'sin' brought him to this terrible state, this blood ceremony I have just performed will atone for it and return my husband's life to me."

The reader understands now that Zipporah's "bridegroom of blood" speech is her pronouncement that her bold act has caused God to spare Moses' life. The Torah's next verse – the third and final verse in this episode – confirms this understanding. The Bible tells us, *"Thence it instantly withdrew from him."* According to Abarbanel, the angel of death receded from Moses following Zipporah's wielding of the flint. The Netziv adds that Moses' awful encounter with God's angry and wrathful messenger angels is abruptly brought to a close after Zipporah's heroic act. Truly, then, Zipporah has saved the day. Sh'mot Rabbah states unequivocally that but for Zipporah's decisive act of wielding the flint, Moses would have been lost. Her bold action vanquished the spirit of a vengeful death by circumcising her son and thereby rescuing her husband.

Zipporah is justifiably jubilant after the departure of the angel of death, and the closing phrase in this episode at the end of verse 26 is, fittingly, in her voice: *And she said, "A bridegroom of blood for circumcisions!"* The simple reading of the text might interpret this as Zipporah's reiteration of her "bridegroom of blood" comment in verse

25, except for the fact that here in verse 26 the word "circumcisions" appears in the plural. Sforno and other commentaries interpret the phrase as referring simply to the two technical parts of the circumcision surgery itself.

Midrashically, we learn that an elated Zipporah first explains to her revived husband that she has performed the *brit* and chased away the angel of death. Thereafter, Zipporah marvels to her husband that the act of circumcision – a ceremony of blood – must have been the awaited antidote to his paralysis, because he returned to life immediately after she had performed it. According to Abarbanel the word "circumcisions" appears here in the *plural* because there were *two* opportunities for Moses to perform the circumcision on his son, and he missed both of them. Moses could have performed the *brit* either before he left Midian, or when they arrived at the inn. So important was this blood ritual of circumcision to the Hebrew God that even Moses – God's chosen messenger – was on the brink of death because he failed to perform it. According to the Torah text, that he did not succumb to the death-like paralysis that overtook him was due to Zipporah's quick thinking and bold action. She unquestionably saved his life. The Maharal states that the immediate departure of the angel of death following the *brit* confirmed for Zipporah that it was the importance of the circumcision – or its fateful absence – that lay at the essence of the night's bizarre happenings. And Zipporah, in her love for Moses, is relieved that it was the *brit* – and not his marriage to her – that was the cause of his crisis.

Thence, it instantly withdrew from him; thus she said, "A bridegroom of blood for circumcisions!" Before this terrifying episode draws to a close, the Torah allows us to infer that the angel of death had withdrawn *because of her.* It does this by the use of an often-overlooked, two-letter Hebrew word. The pivotal Hebrew word is *aZ,* meaning thus or therefore. The word connects in causality what comes before it in the text and what follows. Here, we are meant to understand that the angel of death's withdrawal and Zipporah's second "bridegroom of blood" pronouncement are connected causally. Torah Shlema presents a beautiful *midrash* about Moses' recognition of this causality, and the fulcrum is the word *aZ.* According to the *midrash,* we must jump ahead in the story of the redemption of the Children of Israel to the miracle of the splitting of the Red Sea. We see that the

Hebrews are able to cross the sea on dry land while Egyptian soldiers are drowned in the flood of the returning waters. Viewing the scene from the opposite shore, Moses and the Children of Israel break out in an exultant song of praise to God, affirming their spared lives and God's miracle of salvation. This Song of the Sea, presented in the Bible at Exodus 15:1–19, is delineated in the Torah scrolls by poetic indentation and special formatting. And the very first word of the Torah's narration of this song of exultation is the word *aZ*, the same word that the Bible uses here.

The *midrash* inquires, "Why did Moses begin the Song of the Sea with the word *aZ*?" The *midrash* responds that Moses is harkening back to his own salvation that night at the desert inn, when Zipporah saved his life by performing the *brit* on their son. "She gave me back my soul that night. For the Torah says, *Thus* [aZ] *she said*, [*you are*] *a bridegroom of blood for circumcisions!*" The careful Bible reader is led by the commentary to appreciate that in the near future Moses himself will acknowledge, via his echoing use of the word *aZ*, that Zipporah saved his life.

NOTES:

* This excerpt is taken from the authors' book entitled *Moses' Women*, (Ktav, 2008).

1. Readers will note that the Bible used the same root word, *PaKoD*, when it told us that "God remembered the matriarch Sarah" (Gen. 21:1) and opened her womb after she had endured decades of childlessness. The authors dealt with this issue in depth in Chapter 7 of their first book, *The Passions of the Matriarchs*.

2. Dr. Beth Samuels delivered a lecture entitled "Who is Serach Bat Asher?" at the 25th Anniversary Dinner of the Drisha Institute in New York City in May of 2004. This quote is drawn from her talk.

Tefilah:

FEELING THE PRESENCE OF GOD

Avraham Weiss

O ver the course of my rabbinate, I've met many wonderful people. Of these, one woman – Beth Samuels – personifies the theme of *tefilah*: feeling the presence of God. Beth was one of the most extraordinary individuals I've known. She died two years ago at a very young age, leaving her dear husband Ari and two small children, Danelle and Natalia.

I have so many memories of Beth. The time she rose on Shabbat morning in front of a packed synagogue and without a note, spoke brilliantly. One could feel the spirit of God coursing through her. Or in the Torat Miriam fellowship when participants were asked to share moments they felt the presence of God. Beth spoke poignantly about feeling God through her love for Ari.

Our liturgy on Shabbat refers to the Sabbath Bride, and in the *Midrash*, there is often discussion of angels walking on the earth. I have always wondered what these brides and angels look like. In Beth, I believe, we have found the answer. She was that angel walking on this earth, the Sabbath Queen herself. Beth was a genius of the intellect, a poet of the soul, all while feeling the presence of God.

The theme of this paper, feeling the presence of God in *tefilah*, reflects the very essence of Beth's life. May her memory forever be a blessing to her family, our people, and the entire world.

*   *   *

In the Psalms, King David declares, "I ask for one thing of the Lord." (Ps. 27:4) With David being under so much pressure, one would have expected him to ask for relief from King Saul with whom he constantly fought, or from the Philistines, the arch enemy of the Jews, or from the anguish of losing an infant child, or from the pain of his son Absalom's rebellion and ultimate death. The list goes on. David could have asked that God help him overcome Sheva ben Bikhri's revolt, or Adoniyahu's attempt to replace Solomon as David's successor.

Yet, with all these challenges, what David asks for is "to dwell in the house of the Lord all the days of my life; to behold the sweetness of the Lord, and to contemplate in His sanctuary." (Ps. 27:4) In short, David asks that he be able to feel the presence of God.

For Maimonides (Rambam) and Nachmanides (Ramban) this yearning constitutes the very essence of prayer.

I. *Maimonidean Prayer*

Maimonides records that the source of prayer is the Biblical verse "and you shall serve the Lord with all your heart." (Deut. 11:13) The Talmud records, "what is the service of the heart? This is prayer."[1]

In the words of Rambam,

> It is an affirmative commandment to pray every day, as it says, "And you shall serve the Lord your God." (Exod. 23:25) From tradition, we have learned that "service" is prayer, as it says "And to serve Him with all your heart (*ule'avdo bekhol levavkhem*)." (Deut. 11:13). The sages commented, "What is the service of the heart? This is prayer."[2]

Here, Rambam argues that prayer is fundamentally a function of *'avodat Hashem*, wherein the limited and finite person serves God – the unlimited and infinite source of all creation.

TSELEM ELOHIM

The key to understanding the idea of *'avodat Hashem* may be to analyze what is the most basic concept in the Torah. The Jerusalem Talmud records the following dispute between Rabbi Akiva and Ben Azzai:

> "Love your neighbor as yourself," (Lev. 19:18) Rabbi Akiva says this is the great principle of the Torah. Ben Azzai says, "This is the account of the descendants of Adam" (Genesis 5:1) is the great principle.[3]

The sentence quoted by Ben Azzai continues on to mention that the human being was created in the *demut*, or likeness of God. As the Torah states, "on the day that God created the human being, He made him in the likeness (*demut*) of God." (Gen. 5:1) Ben Azzai's understanding of the most basic concept in the Torah stems from this idea.

The Torah records, even before Ben Azzai's sentence, that God creates the human being in His image (*tselem Elohim*). (Gen. 1:27) This means that when we look at each other, what we see is the surface of a human being. But if we look deeply into each other, we should see a little bit of God. The word *tselem* comes from the word *tsel* which means shadow. Every human being is created in the spirit of God, in the image of God. In the words of the kabbalists, "*ḥelek Elohah mima'al*, [every person] possesses a piece of God Himself."

The concept of *tselem Elohim* yields crucial fundamentals about the value of the human being. It must always be remembered that *tselem Elohim* was not placed in the first Jew, but in the first human being from whom every human being comes. This means that every individual has a *tselem Elohim*. Bearing in mind that it is the *tselem Elohim* that makes human beings special, and bearing in mind that all human beings are endowed with the image of God, it follows, that all people are of equal value. Moreover, since the *tselem Elohim* is part of God, it follows that just as God is of endless value, so, too, every human being is of endless value. Also, as God is unique, the perfect One, so, too, every human being created in God's image is unique. No two people have the same fingerprints, the same consciousness, or the same soul prints.

The Mishnah in *Sanhedrin* makes these points when it asks why the world began with one person. Why did it begin with Adam?[4] The Mishnah gives us three reasons:

> To create peace amongst humanity, lest one say, "My grandparent is greater than yours…"
>
> To demonstrate that if one destroys a single soul it is as though he has destroyed the entire world. And if one saves a single soul, it is as if one has saved the entire world.
>
> To demonstrate the greatness of God. For a human being imprints many coins with one mold and all the coins look the same, while the Ruler of Rulers created all of humanity from the mold of Adam and not one is similar to the other.[5]

The world began with Adam to teach us three consequences of the reality of *tselem Elohim*. First, we are all of equal value, as we all come from the same source, from the same grandparent. Second, coming from Adam teaches that as Adam was of infinite value, after all, as the only human being alive, the future of the world depended on him, so, too, is every human being of infinite value. Saving one person, says the Mishnah, is tantamount to saving the world, destroying a person means destroying the world. Third, as Adam was unique, there was no one other than him, so, too, all human beings – Adam's descendants – are unique. No two people are the same. There is a popular saying that no one is indispensable. On one level this is true. But on the other hand, this Mishnah teaches that no one is dispensable. Everyone brings something to the table that no one else can bring. In a world of imitation, the Torah emphasizes individual creativity; doing our best to tap into our divine spark and find our unique voice.

It must be remembered, though, that *tselem Elohim* is potential. When God created Adam, God breathed into him His spirit. (Gen. 2:7) Whether Adam, or we his descendants, use or abuse that *tselem Elohim* is up to us. Note that after every creation the Torah records that "God saw it was good." (Gen. 1:10, 1:12, 1:18, 1:21, 1:25) After creating the human being, however, this declaration is omitted. Other creations have no freedom of choice, and, therefore, God can say at their creation, "it was good (*ki tov*)." But whether a human being is good or not depends on his or her deeds. *Ki tov* is a more appropriate refrain after the human being has lived a wholesome life, after having made the proper choices.[6] But no matter what we do or how we act, no matter how we've strayed, there is a profound Jewish belief that all human beings have the power to return to their inner true self, to the part of God in all of us.

REACHING IN AS A GATEWAY TO GOD

The idea of *tselem Elohim* is crucial to understanding the Jewish approach to *teshuvah* (repentance) and prayer. For Rabbi Avraham Yitzchak HaCohen Kook, *teshuvah* does not deal with a specific wrong. Rather it has to do with a general feeling of morose, of despondency, of alienation, of estrangement, of separation from God. *Teshuvah* means a return to the inner self, to the inner goodness and godliness inherent in every human being. Of course, we are responsible for our actions and must assume responsibility. But on a spiritual level the human being possesses inner purity. *Teshuvah*, whose root is *shuv*, to return, means to return to that inner purity, to that *tselem Elohim*, which makes us unique and of infinite value.

Rabbi Kook describes *teshuvah* in this way:

> A person does not conjure up the memory of a past sin or sins, but in a general way he or she feels terribly depressed. He feels himself pervaded by sin; that the Divine light does not shine on him; that there is nothing noble in him; that his heart is unfeeling. The primary role of penitence, which at once sheds light on the darkened zone, is for the person to return to oneself, to the root of his soul from where one can return to God (*umiyad yashuv el ha'Elohim*).[7]

Not coincidentally the instrument used to rally us to repent is the shofar. The sound of the shofar comes from the inner breath; it is a reversal of the breath God breathed into Adam – "and He breathed into him a spirit of life." (Gen. 2:7) The shofar sound breathes out the breath of God breathed into Adam, breathed into all of us. In the words of Sefat Emet, "The mitzvah of shofar [is the following]...through *teshuvah* we can stir the inner voice found in our souls."[8]

Our tradition maintains that anybody, no matter who they are or how far they've strayed, can always return to their inner, incorruptible goodness. The Talmud tells the story of Elisha ben Avuya, a devout and gifted scholar who had gone astray. Elisha's student Rabbi Meir implored him to repent. Elisha, who had become known as "Aher," which literally means other, or stranger, responded, "I cannot repent, because I heard a *bat qol*, a heavenly voice exclaim, repent, wayward children, except for Aher."[9] Rabbi Ahron Soloveichik explains that Elisha was called Aher, as he was a stranger to his true being. He did not repent because "Elisha was laboring under the erroneous conviction that he was corrupt, basically evil. But this was not true. Aher had failed to understand when he heard the *bat qol* that its message was: Aher cannot repent, but Elisha ben Avuya can."[10]

And here, Rabbi Kook argues, something powerful occurs. Once a person returns to his or her inner goodness, or inner godliness, one can return to God. This is what Rabbi Kook means when he writes that once a person returns to his/her inner true self, he or she will return to God "*umiyad yashuv el ha'Elohim*."[11] The primary role of penitence is for the person to return to oneself, to the root of his or her soul, from where one can return to God.

Thus, *teshuvah* contains two steps: moving inward, returning to the inner goodness and godliness; which then catapults us to move upward to God, to feel His presence. Note the flow of the verses dealing with *teshuvah* in the Torah.

> And it shall come to pass, when all these things are come upon you, the blessing and the curse, which I have set before you, **and you shall return to your heart.… And you shall return to the LORD your God**, and listen to His voice according to all that I command you this day, you and your children, with all your heart, and with all your soul. (Deut. 30:1, 2)

Note that the first part of the sequence of *teshuvah* here describes how one returns inward to one's heart. Only then in the second phase does the Torah speak of returning to God.

Prayer as a function of "*ule'avdo*," of serving God, of feeling God's presence, operates in a similar fashion. The first prayer accepted by

God was in the form of a sacrifice that Abel brought to the Lord.[12] One wonders why Abel's sacrifice, unlike Cain's, was accepted. Sefat Emet suggests an answer based on an insightful reading of the text. After Cain brings his sacrifice, the Torah states, "And Abel also brought [an offering]." (Gen. 4:4) Sefat Emet understands the text differently. In his words: "Abel brought himself [his inner I] with the sacrifice and, therefore, it was accepted before the Lord, may He be blessed."[13] Cain's sacrifice was external; it had no inner depth and was, therefore, rejected. Abel's sacrifice reflected an inner purity and was, therefore, received.

From this perspective, prayer is counterintuitive. It begins not by reaching up, but by reaching in. If prayer is transcendence, it is an inner transcendence that is at its source. Once the inner soul is revealed, we are in a better position to relate to the infinite God. This movement is recorded in the writing of Shem Tov ibn Falaquera who posits that by knowing the inner goodness and inner godliness, one can come to know God:

> They said that whoever knows his soul knows his Creator, and whoever is ignorant of knowing his soul is all the more ignorant of knowing his Creator. How can one believe that a person is wise concerning something else when he is ignorant concerning himself? Therefore, they said that the knowledge of the soul is prior to the knowledge of God.[14]

This, says Rabbi Kook, is the movement of prayer.

> Prayer rises up from down below to high above. How does this come about? From that source in our hearts which is filled with natural holiness, we draw out, we transform our refined feelings from potentiality to actuality.... And as we elevate ourselves, all the very sources of our existence, all the ramifications of our soul, all the life that pours out from our inner selves, and all the life-sources that gush over us, become elevated with us – until they make us reach the level of our own true selves. All becomes blessed; all becomes elevated; all becomes holy and exalted – all rejoices with righteous joy, all exults in holy gladness.[15]

In Kabbalistic thought, the goal of humankind is to achieve an all encompassing sense of unity. The world, say the Kabbalists, is in the state of *shevirat hakelim*, or broken vessels, wherein the human being is in tension, and oft times disconnected from all that surrounds him/her. The purpose of Torah according to this perspective is *tiqun* which literally means "fixing" or "repairing" or "uniting" the world on all levels. Specifically, this means that people should try to unite with the earth in perfect ecological peace; unite with each other in warm camaraderie; and unite with God in absolute harmony. *Tiqun* means also that the part of God in us should unite with the God above. In a certain sense, the soul and God above are like lovers yearning to be with each other. When the soul is kindled, it begins to soar like a flame leaping to connect to God. Without that rendezvous, the soul feels forlorn, like a lover bereft of his/her beloved.

Rabbi Abraham Joshua Heschel poetically captures this phenomenon:

> As a tree torn from the soil, as a river separated from its source, the human soul wanes when detached from what is greater than itself. Without the holy, the good turns chaotic; without the good, beauty becomes accidental. It is the pattern of the impeccable which makes the average possible. It is the attachment to what is spiritually superior: loyalty to a sacred person or idea, devotion to a noble friend or teacher, love for a people or for mankind, which holds our inner life together. But any ideal, human, social, or artistic, if it forms a roof over all of life, shuts us off from the light. Even the palm of one hand may bar the light of the entire sun. Indeed, we must be open to the remote in order to perceive the near. Unless we aspire to the utmost, we shrink to inferiority.
>
> Prayer is our attachment to the utmost. Without God in sight, we are like the scattered rungs of a broken ladder. To pray is to become a ladder on which thoughts mount to God to join the movement toward Him which surges unnoticed throughout the entire universe. We do not step out of the world when we pray; we merely see the world in a different setting. The self is not the hub, but the spoke of

the revolving wheel. In prayer we shift the center of living from self-consciousness to self-surrender. God is the center toward which all forces tend. He is the source, and we are the flowing of His force, the ebb and flow of His tides.[16]

It follows that while the movement of prayer begins inwardly, the ultimate goal is to reach upward. Were it to remain inward it could become a form of narcissism, of human beings becoming totally and completely self-absorbed. Thus, the source of prayer is "*ule'avdo bekhol levavekhem*, and to serve Him with all your heart." The goal is to serve Him, but the means to that service is with all our heart and soul – from the lower, to the higher.

RESPONSIBILITY

In the same breath, once kindled the soul not only soars from below to above, to connect with God, but also it moves outward – after all, in every human being there is a *tselem Elohim*. It follows, therefore, that prayer is not only vertical, but horizontal; it is not only directed toward God, but also towards our fellow person(s) who are created in His image.

Prayer is an example of a ritual which is God-centered. But that centeredness is not exclusive. In the end, prayer intersects with interpersonal relationships. It's a meshing of one's relationship with God with one's relationship with other human beings. Hence, when we begin our prayers, some have the custom to give charity. Some even recite the formula "behold, I accept upon myself the commandment to love my fellow person." Not coincidentally, virtually all of prayer is in the plural. When beseeching God, we speak not only for ourselves, but for the community.[17]

It follows that for Rambam, the motif of prayer is to feel the presence of God – in, up and out. Each of these directions reflect the value of assuming responsibility. Moving in involves contemplation of who we can become, and our responsibility to work on ourselves to become that person. Moving up makes us realize that we are connected and responsible to a Being far greater than we. Moving out establishes our relationship, indeed, our responsibility to our fellow person. These three themes are fundamental goals of prayer. They emerge from a common denominator – *ule'avdo*, to serve Him, or quite literally, "to work for Him," by doing our share to establish a world "that follows God's way of doing righteousness and justice."[18] (Gen. 18:19)

II. *Nachmanidean Prayer*

Nachmanides sees it differently. For Ramban, Biblical prayer is offered when being in distress. In his words:

> That we pray to Him in times of distress (*batsar lekha*), and that our eyes and hearts be directed towards Him as a servant to a master (*ke'einei 'avadim el yad adoneihem*). And this is the meaning of the sentence, "And when you come to war in your land against an enemy who has besieged you, and you will sound the trumpets and you will be remembered before the Lord your God." (Num. 10:9) And it is a commandment for every distress that comes upon a community to call out to God (*vehi mitsvah 'al kol tsarah vetsarah shetavo 'al hatsibur lits'ok*).[19]

SELF-TRANSFORMATION

Joseph Albo takes it a step further. For Albo, prayer has the power to influence God; that is, it functions as a plea to God to use His influence on the world to effect a change. This leaves us with the question of how this prayer mechanism may work. Albo argues that the key is once again to understand how *teshuvah* operates:

> In this way repentance benefits a wicked man, for through repentance he becomes another person, as it were, concerning whom no such decree was made.[20]

In other words, God decrees person X to suffer a certain fate. Once the person does *teshuvah*, the individual has been purified, and, in effect, has become a different person. Hence, the decree is inoperative, as person X no longer exists. Albo says it this way:

> This shows that when a decree is made upon a wicked person, it is conditional upon his maintaining his state of wickedness. But if he changes that state through repentance, he,

as it were, changes into another person upon whom that decree was not made.[21]

Prayer, Albo argues, operates in a similar fashion.

> In this way it is clear that prayer and proper conduct prepare a person to receive the good influence or to nullify the evil that has been decreed concerning him, because he changes from the evil state in which he was.[22]

According to Albo, God may have decided a certain fate for a particular individual. But after true, deep prayer, the individual has been elevated, and is no longer the same person. Hence, the decree is null and void. Albo concludes,

> That is, if you set your heart to pray and to improve your conduct, there is no doubt that through prayer and right conduct you will escape from these troubles. From this it is clear that prayer and right conduct are always helpful in nullifying a divine decree.[23]

Here, prayer and repentance (and for that matter good deeds) are all different sides of the same coin, as they both involve self-transformation resulting in a change of the decree.[24] From this perspective prayer and repentance are self transformative as one becomes a different person. The transformation may be minute, but still, the person is no longer the same. [25]

REQUEST DENIED

The idea that prayer changes our persona resulting in nullifying decrees is not simple, as the Bible includes many examples of sincere prayerful requests that were denied.

Consider the passage in the Talmud which posits that the three daily prayer services were introduced by the patriarchs.[26] Ironically, in each case, their prayers were not completely accepted. Abraham introduces the morning service when praying that the wicked city of Sodom be spared. This would include his nephew, Lot, who lived there. While Lot is saved, the city is destroyed. Isaac introduces the afternoon service, seemingly praying for a wife. Right then, he meets Rebecca and marries her. But their marriage has its ups and downs as they disagree on which of their sons should be the next patriarch, and Rebecca deceives her husband by instructing Jacob to take the blessings. Jacob introduces the evening service. As he leaves home, escaping from Esau, he prays for protection. He escapes Esau, but has to deal with Laban, his devious father-in-law. And years later, Jacob faces the difficult task of confronting Esau himself.

The Talmud considers Hannah as the paradigm of how one should pray.[27] She beseeches God for a child. Her request is granted as she gives birth to Samuel. Still, Samuel struggles; his children Yoel and Aviyah turn out to be evil, and the Jewish people rebel against Samuel, asking that he be replaced by a king (1 Sam. 1, 8).

Most telling, the very source of request in prayer is when Moses asks God that he be permitted to enter Israel. His plea is used by the Talmud to meticulously spell out how a request should be made:

> R. Simlai expounded: A person should always first recount the praise of the Holy One blessed be He, and then pray. From where do we know this? From Moses; for it is written, "And I sought out the Lord at that time," and it goes on, "O Lord God, You have started to show Your servant Your greatness and Your strong hand; for what god is there in heaven and earth who can do according to Your works and according to Your mighty acts?" And afterwards it is written, "Let me go over, I pray to You, and see the good land." (Deut. 3:23–25)[28]

In the end, Moses' request is denied. God does not permit him into the land. "Go up to Mount Nevo," God tells Moses, from there you will see the land. The people will enter but you will not. (Deut. 32:49, 52)

It seems, therefore, that prayer as a function of God responding to calls of distress is historically incorrect, as many such prayers were and continue to be rejected. In fact, the limitation of prayer, even the purest prayer, to always effect change may emerge from the Talmudic passage which declares, "length of days, children and prosperity, this does not depend on merit, but on *mazal*."[29] Here, the Talmud is suggesting that there are critical matters in life that depend on *mazal*; in other words no amount of prayer can alter the decree.

Yet another Talmudic passage expands on this idea and points out that each of us has been allotted a certain *mazal*. While that *mazal* cannot be absolutely cancelled, we have it within our power to change it to some degree, "If one is worthy years are added to one's life; if unworthy, the years of his/her life are reduced."[30] In simple terms, if we want to know how long we'll live, if we want to know if we'll be prone to depression, if we want to know if our children will have learning disabilities, a good start is to check out our pedigree. We are all born with certain predispositions, with a certain fate. But whatever the situation we are born into, we have it within our power to take precautions to improve upon our fate. How can we improve our physical well being? By seeking medical attention, eating the right foods, exercising properly. How can we cope with depression? By leading a life of emotional and spiritual inner peace and seeking professional help. How can we help a child with a learning disability? By being patient and giving time and love to our children. We may not be able to cancel out our fate, but we have it within our power to alter it to some degree.

Rabbi Yosef Dov Soloveitchik distinguishes between fate, *goral*, and destiny, *ye'ud*. Fate is God capriciously cast[ing] us into a particular dimension of life that we cannot control. Destiny, on the other hand, "is an active existence in which one confronts the environment into which he or she is cast." According to Rabbi Soloveitchik, "One's mission in this world is to turn fate into destiny, an existence that is passive and influenced to an existence that is active and influential."[31]

Esther Wachsman, mother of Nachshon, who was murdered in a terrorist attack in Israel, pointed out that after her son was killed, she was overwhelmed with grief. She was only able to move forward by reminding herself that she had a choice of either being a victim of her fate, or initiating a new destiny.[32]

Prayer, perhaps, is a pivot upon which this choice functions, as it is another formula through which fate can be changed. This may be the meaning of the Rosh Hashanah and Yom Kippur prayer "*uteshuvah utefilah utsedakah ma'avirin et ro'a hagezeirah.*"[33] This phrase is often translated, "repentance, prayer and charity remove the evil decree."

Were this the case, however, the Hebrew would read, "*mevatlin et hagezeirah hara'ah.*" *Mevatlin*, from the root *b-t-l*, is a strong verb meaning to cancel; *ma'avirin*, the verb found in the prayer, is softer, meaning to push aside. Moreover, *ro'a* is descriptive, meaning that acts of repentance, prayer, and charity temper or remove the harshness of the decree. In other words, through prayer (and for that matter, repentance and good deeds) we have it within our power to reshape, although not necessarily totally undo, our fate.[34]

It seems, therefore, that prayer as an airtight means of relieving distress is empirically and conceptually flawed. Of course, as Albo argued, prayer can be self-transformative. Still the transformation does not necessarily lead to God's intervention.

RELIANCE

In fact, a careful reading of Ramban reveals that for him, relief from distress is not the fundamental goal of prayer. To be sure, requesting God's intervention is a wish implicit in prayer; but it is not at its core. Rather, the foundation of Nachmanidean prayer may be that in distress we feel a deep sense of limitation, of loneliness. In response, we reach out in prayer to feel God's closeness, God's nearness, God's presence. Whatever the outcome, prayer allows us the possibility of forging an intimate relationship with God. Whatever the future brings, we are no longer alone.

It follows that the motif of prayer for Ramban is feeling God's presence. For Ramban, feeling that Presence is a response to distress. Hence, he writes that we are obligated to "call out to God in times of distress, *vehi mitsvah 'al kol tsarah vetsarah shetavo 'al hatsibur lits'ok.*"[35] The emphasis here is on calling out to God; there is no mention of God accepting our prayer.

This is also apparent in Ramban's concluding language on prayer:

> But certainly [daily] prayer is not obligatory, but it is a kindly trait of the blessed Creator who hears and answers (*sheshome'a ve'oneh*) whenever we call out to him.[36]

Here, Ramban is saying that God hears our prayers and that he answers our prayers, but there is no guarantee that God accepts them.

In the words of Rabbi Soloveitchik:

> Prayer finds its full exoteric expression in the spiritual act of lifting up one's eyes – the inner cry of dependence upon God, the experience of complete, absolute dependence portrayed by the Psalmist: "I lift my eyes towards the mountain, from where will come my aid?" (Ps. 121:1)
>
> When man is in need and prays, God listens. One of God's attributes is "*shome'a tefilah* – He who listens to prayer." Let us note that Judaism has never promised that God accepts all prayer....
>
> Acceptance of prayer is a hope, a vision, a wish, a petition, but not a principle or a premise. The foundation of prayer is not the conviction of its effectiveness but the belief that through it we approach God intimately and the miraculous community embracing finite man and his Creator is born.
>
> The basic function of prayer is not its practical consequences but the metaphysical formation of a fellowship consisting of God and man.[37]

This, for Ramban, is God's role in prayer. God is more a listener than a doer. Yes, prayer can impact a decree, God has the power to do as He wishes. But that is not the ultimate foundation of prayer. At its essence, the basic motif of prayer, according to Nachmanides, is to establish fellowship with God.[38] In short, prayer, according to Ramban, is a function of *batsar lekha*, of feelings of distress, inspiring a sense of dependence on God and our fellow person. Ramban's formulation "*ke'einei 'avadim el yad adoneihem*," quite literally, "as a servant in the hands of God" is an expression of this dependence, and has everything to do with feeling God's presence.[39]

III. *Feeling God's Presence*

The upshot is that for both Rambam and Ramban, the goal of prayer is to feel God's presence. For Maimonides, feeling that presence is *proactive*, to serve Him, every day, whether we are in need or not. For Nachmanides, feeling the Divine Presence is *reactive*, coming from distress.

Moreover, for Ramban, like Rambam, prayer may also be tri-directional – but the tri-directionalities differ.

For Rambam, they deal primarily with *responsibility*. Reaching in, we explore *who we can be*, and commit ourselves to realize that potential; reaching up, we feel part of something larger and resolve in thought and action to be true to that Being; reaching out, we challenge ourselves to do more for others.

For Ramban, the movement reflects our *reliance* on others. Reaching in, we come to grips with *who we are*, our limits and personal inadequacies; reaching up, we express our need for God's companionship; reaching out, we lean on others.

The interfacing of Rambam and Ramban is apparent when analyzing the language they use in their understanding of prayer. Rambam declares that it is a positive commandment to pray, as it says, "to serve Him with all your heart, *ule'avdo bekhol levavkhem*."[40] Ramban uses similar language when he writes that in distress, we turn to God, "as a servant to a master, *ke'einei 'avadim el yad adoneihem*."[41] Here, both Rambam and Ramban use the language of serving God.

However, *ule'avdo* as used by Rambam is a term that denotes daily responsibility, to work with God to make the world better. (The root *'e-v-d* means literally, "to work.") In contrast, *'avadim* as used by Ramban in the context of distress denotes reliance, dependence on God and others. (Here, the root *'e-v-d* means literally, a "servant" reliant on others.)

SYNTHESIZING MAIMONIDEAN AND NACHMANIDEAN PRAYER

Still, what unites Rambam and Ramban is much greater than what divides them. Whatever their specific understanding of prayer, it emerges from its foundation – an all encompassing deep, high and wide sense that God is near, within us, above us and in all directions.

For Rambam, however, recognizing God's presence impels us to *assert* ourselves and assume responsibility for ourselves, God and others. For Ramban, presence of God inspires an opposite feeling, one of *submission*, recognition of limitation, and dependency upon God and others.[42]

In the end, Rambam and Ramban may operate in dialectic as

there are times we are assertive, and other times submissive, and sometimes a combination of both. In fact, Rambam and Ramban may conflate as an understanding of who we can become makes one aware that achieving all our goals, realizing all our dreams, is often a daunting and impossible task. Conversely, recognition of limits can inspire one to overcome and improve.[43]

THE DIFFERENCE BETWEEN PRAYER AND TEFILAH

Truth be told, there is a great difference between prayer and *tefilah*, which is the Hebrew term commonly used for prayer. The English word "prayer" means to ask, to implore. The French word has the same root. The German word "beten" has the same meaning.

Tefilah means something very different. *Tefilah* may come from the root *nafal*, to fall before God, to yearn for Him, to feel His presence.

Note that as God changes Abram's name to Abraham and spells out his mission as the patriarch of Israel who will be an *"av hamon goyim*, a father of a multitude of nations," the Torah states *"vayipol Avram 'al panav*, Abram fell on his face." (Gen. 17:3–5) Here, *"vayipol"* is a form of *tefilah*, as Abraham assumes responsibility to fulfill his task. In doing so he recognizes the awesomeness of the task and his need for God's help. Similarly, after Sarai's name is changed to Sarah, indicating that she, too, is to be a leader, a princess for all of humankind, the Torah states, *"vayipol Avraham 'al panav*, Abraham fell on his face." (Gen. 17:15–17) Here again, in the same framework, *"vayipol"* is a form of *tefilah*.

On a deeper level, *"Panav"* may be in upper case, that is, Abraham falls on God's face, yearning and ultimately feeling God's presence as that is the ultimate motif of *tefilah*. This is no small matter, as feeling the presence of God, and for that matter bringing God into the world is the very mission of Judaism.

THE INTERFACE OF TEFILAH AND THE JEWISH MISSION

It is not a coincidence that in the early narratives of the Torah, sin results in estrangement from God. In the words of Nachmanides *"'ad shegiyreish oto het'o misham."*[44]

After Adam and Eve disobey God and eat from the tree the Torah states *"vayithabe ha'adam ve'ishto* **mipenei** *YHWH Elohim,*

Adam and his wife hid from the Lord God." (Gen. 3:8) Note the term *"penei,"* literally, they were hidden from the face of God; they no longer felt His presence. So too, after Cain murders Abel, the Torah says *"vayetseh Kayin mili[f]nei YHWH,"* literally, "Cain left the face of God." (Gen. 4:16) Again, in the description of the wrongdoings of the generation of the deluge, the Torah proclaims, *"vatishahet ha'aretz li[f]nei ha'Elohim,* the earth was corrupt before God," (Gen. 6:11) or more literally, the sins of the world were manifest in humankind turning away from the face of God.

And the story of the Tower of Dispersion reaches its crescendo with the words *"vayafets YHWH otam…'al penei kol ha'aretz,* the Lord scattered them on the face of the earth." (Gen. 11:8) This implies that they were no longer experiencing the face or the presence of God. In all these stories, the word *"penei"* plays a pivotal role in the description of the exile taking place – an exile from God's presence.

It is then that Abraham and Sarah come on the scene. Their mandate, and ultimately the mandate of the Jewish people is to bring God and God's system of ethics back into the world. This calling is in stark contrast to the people who lived during the Generation of Dispersion, who built the tower to make a name for themselves. (Gen. 11:4) In opposition, Abraham does not call out in his name, but "in the name of the Lord." (Gen. 12:8)[45]

This process reaches its crescendo as Jacob struggles with a mysterious being, just prior to his rendezvous with Esau.[46] As the struggle continues, Jacob is given an additional name, Yisrael. (Gen. 32: 29) The word Yisrael has many possible meanings, one of them being a compound of *shur* and *El,* or "to see God," to perceive God.[47] This becomes the name of the Jewish people, as our ultimate mission is reflected in the term Yisrael, to see God, to bring God back into the world.

The Torah goes out of its way to record the name of the place where Jacob's struggle took place, "Jacob called the place **Peniel,** for I saw the Lord face to face (*panim el panim*) and my soul was saved." (Gen. 32:31) Adam and Eve; Cain; the Generation of the Deluge; and the Generation of the Tower of Dispersion all turn against the face of God. Jacob/Yisrael sees God, embraces God – face to face.

No wonder King David under pressure asks for one thing – "to dwell in the house of the Lord all the days of his life, to behold the sweetness of the Lord and to visit His sanctuary." (Ps. 27:4) Rabbi Abba in the Midrash explains David's request as "*malkhut sha'al*,"[48] David asked like a king. He reaches high to realize the ultimate mission of Judaism to behold the Lord. Not only does David ask like a king, he literally asks for "*Malkhut*" (upper case *mem*); he asks to feel the presence of God Himself.

Thus, the mission of Judaism is to bring God, and God's system of ethics, into the world, and this mission is the ultimate foundation of *tefilah*.[49]

* * *

And this was the life and legacy of Beth. With all her heart, soul and mind – when she was well, and even when she became sick – Beth walked with the Lord, feeling enveloped by His Being, and exuding that spirituality to her family, her people and the world. May her memory forever be a blessing.

* * *

Rabbi Avraham (Avi) Weiss is Founder and President of Yeshivat Chovevei Torah – the Modern and Open Orthodox Rabbinical School. He is the Senior Rabbi of the Hebrew Institute of Riverdale, a Modern and Open Orthodox congregation and National President of AMCHA – the Coalition for Jewish Concerns.

NOTES

1. Taanit 2a
2. Maimonides, *Mishneh Torah*, Laws of Prayer, 1:1.
3. Jerusalem Talmud Nedarim 9:4
4. The mainstream opinion is that Adam was born male and female, with one side being male and the other female. The rib story according to this opinion is really the bifurcation of Adam into two distinct people – one male, the other female. See Ketub. 8a.
5. Sanh. 4:5. I've quoted the first two reasons of the Mishnah in reverse order to parallel our explanation of the fundamental values derived from tselem Elohim.

6. Nechama Leibowitz, *New Studies in Genesis*, (Jerusalem: Hemed Press). She writes "the phrase 'it was good' was omitted from man's creation because his good was dependent on his own free choice."

   See also Rashi to Gen. 1:26. Rashi notes that *veyirdu* may imply dominion as well as descending – this because *veyirdu* can either come from the root *y-r-d* or *r-d-h*. In Rashi's words: "if he is worthy he dominates over the beasts and cattle, if he is not worthy he will sink lower than them, and the beast will rule over him."

7. Rabbi Avraham Yitzchak HaCohen Kook, *Orot haTeshuvah*, (Jerusalem: Yeshivat Or Etsyon, 1992) ch. 3.

8. *Sefat Emet, Rosh Hashanah*, 5651, s.v. *mitsvat shofar*.

9. The Talmud records the story of Elisha ben Avuya. The English is the Soncino translation.

   > Our Rabbis taught: Once Aher was riding on a horse on the Sabbath, and R. Meir was walking behind him to learn Torah at his mouth. Said [Aher] to him: Meir, turn back, for I have already measured by the paces of my horse that thus far extends the Sabbath limit [2,000 cubits in all directions].
   > He replied: You, too, go back!
   > [Aher] answered: Have I not already told you that I have already heard from behind the veil: "return, you backsliding children" (Jeremiah 3:22) – except Aher. (Hagigah 15a)

10. Rabbi Ahron Soloveichik, *Jew and Jew, Jew and Non-Jew*, Jewish Life, Journal published by the Orthodox Union.

11. Rabbi Kook, ibid.

12. While there are no sacrifices today, many insights concerning prayer can be learned from the sacrificial service.

13. *Sefat Emet*, Genesis, *Bereishit* 5635, s.v. *besefer qol simḥah*.

14. Shem Tov ibn Falaquera, Introduction to *Sefer haNefesh*.

    See also Joseph ibn Saddiq in *HaOlam haKatan*. In his words: "By man knowing his own soul, he will know the spiritual world from which he can attain some knowledge of the Creator, as it is written, 'From my flesh I shall perceive God.'" (Job 19:26)

15. Rabbi Kook, *Sidur Olat Re'iyah*, p. 19.

16. Abraham Joshua Heschel, *God in Search of Man*, (New York, Farrar, Straus and Giroux, 1955) pp. 6–7.

    Sefat Emet argues that as we yearn for God, God reaches for us. He makes this point in his discussion of Jacob "encounter[ing] the place" as he flees from his parents' home "*vayifg'a bamakom*." (Genesis

28:11) "*Vayifg'a*" is a term for prayer. (Berakhot 26b) The Talmud (Hulin 91b) points out that the Torah uses the word *vayifg'a* and not *vayitpalel* (and he prayed) to denote that "the place (referring to Mount Moriah) jumped toward him (Jacob)."

In the words of Sefat Emet: "Since Jacob greatly desired to come to Mount Moriah, even as it was far away, Mount Moriah jumped to him." See *Sefat Emet*, Gen., Vayetze, 5634, s.v. be*Rashi vayifg'a*.

17. The idea that prayer, which seemingly centers on our relationship with God, is also interpersonal, extends to other rituals like Shabbat and kashrut. On its face, these are rituals that seem to be God-centered. But Shabbat can also foster meaningful family and community relationships. See Exodus 23:12 where the Torah states, "Six days shall you do your work, and on the seventh you shall rest, so that your ox and donkey may rest and your maidservant's son and the stranger may be refreshed." Note that the reasons given here for Shabbat are purely interpersonal. And kashrut can teach human beings reverence for the life of the animal killed by demanding humane slaughter and that we not consume blood as it is the very essence of life. (Lev. 7:11)

Reciprocally, Jewish law, which governs interpersonal relationships may also have something to do with our connection to God. After all, if I hurt another human being, I am also so-to-speak hurting God, as every person is created in His image. Keli Yakar, Rabbi Ephraim Lunschitz, makes this point when arguing that the Ten Commandments can be divided into horizontal pairs. For example, "*lo tirtzaḥ*, thou shall not murder," (Exod. 20:13) the sixth of the ten commandments, is found aside the first, "I am the Lord your God." (Exod. 20:2) For Keli Yakar, the two are interconnected, as killing another human being diminishes God, as the *tselem Elohim* within the human being has been destroyed. In his words,

> Thou shall not kill: After completing the five commandments that concerned the connection between God and the human being, the text lists another five corresponding commandments that concern interpersonal relationships as it is mentioned in the *Mekhiltah*. For example, the commandment "I am your God" parallels the commandment "Thou shall not kill," for if anyone spills blood, it is as though one is diminishing the form and image of God. (See *Keli Yakar*, Exodus 20:13)

18. One of the ways to realize this "common denominator" is through

song, especially participatory song. Song touches us inwardly, it ignites our inner spark of God; and song spans the chasm that separates heaven and earth by connecting us upward to God. Song also has a uniting quality that can move us outward to feel a oneness with our fellow person.

The prayer service is replete with instances when we recall our responsibility to ourselves and the larger world. At the outset of the morning service we list our interpersonal obligations in the *eilu devarim* prayer. And in the *Amidah*, when we, for example, ask God for healing, we ought to remind ourselves of our responsibility to do our share to help in the healing process. So, too, with all the other requests.

19. Nachmanides, *Sefer haMitzvot*, Positive commandment 5.

It is unclear whether Nachmanides means that in times of distress we are obligated to pray (*mitsvah ḥiyuvit*), or in times of distress when praying, one receives credit for having fulfilled a Biblical commandment (*mitsvah kiyumit*).

20. *Sefer haIkkarim, Book of Principles*, Joseph Albo, 4:18, translation by Isaac Husik. Albo offers several examples. He writes:

> Take the case of Ahab. The Bible says concerning him: "But there was none like Ahab, who did give himself over to do that which was evil in the sight of the Lord," (1 Kings 21:25) and a divine decree was made against him. And then, because he fasted, and covered himself with sackcloth, and humbled himself before God, it was said to Elijah: "Because he humbled himself before Me, I will not bring the evil in his days; but in his son's days will I bring the evil upon his house." (ibid 29)

21. ibid.

22. ibid.

23. ibid. For an analysis of the contradiction between God's omniscience and human freedom of choice, see Ralbag to Genesis 22:12, and *Responsa Rivash* n. 118. See also Hasdai Ben Abraham Crescas in *Medieval Jewish Philosophy* by Isaac Husik, (Philadelphia: Jewish Publication Society, 1958) p. 397. See as well Sa'adia Gaon in *Emunot Ve'Deot* 4:4; Maimonides, *Mishneh Torah*, Laws of Repentance, 5:5 and Ra'avad commentary as well as *Tiferet Yisrael* to Avot 3:99.

24. This may be the meaning of the prayer found in the Rosh Hashanah and Yom Kippur liturgy, "But repentance, prayer and charity cancel the stern decree." Through these acts, the person is altered; the decree

is, therefore, inoperative. An alternative understanding of this prayer will be discussed later.

The idea of self-transformation not only applies when we pray for ourselves, but when praying for others. Prayer operates in a holistic manner. Somehow through the process of prayer for another, that individual's persona changes. Self-transformation also applies to the communal aspect of prayer in the spirit of *'areivut*. In this sense we are inextricably bound to each other. Hence, when one improves himself/herself through prayer, the other by virtue of being part of community is also elevated.

See Rabbi Yosef Dov HaLevi Soloveitchik's "*On Repentance*" who understands *teshuvah* as having two elements, atonement from the sin, and purification of the heart. This is the meaning of the sentence recited in the Yom Kippur liturgy – "on that day God will offer you atonement, purifying you from all your sins." (Lev. 16:30) *Kaparah* is atonement for the deed. *Taharah* is purification of the heart. See Rabbi Yosef Dov Soloveitchik, *On Repentance*, edited by Pinchas Peli (Rowan and Littlefield: New York, 1984) pp. 49–52.

See also Rabbi Eliyahu Dessler, who comments in general terms on how every act has two elements: the act itself, and its impact upon the doer. For example, after stealing, one has stolen, but additionally, the thief is no longer the same person. The very act of stealing has impacted the personality, and made the person another, and for Rabbi Dessler, altered the "point of choice – *nekudat habehirah*" effectively changing the entire person. In his words as translated by Aryeh Carmell:

Everyone has free choice – at the point where truth meets falsehood. In other words, *behirah* takes place at that point where the truth as the person sees it confronts the illusion produced in him by the power of falsehood. But the majority of a person's actions are undertaken without any clash between truth and falsehood taking place. Many of a person's actions may happen to coincide with what is objectively right because he has been brought up that way and it does not occur to him to do otherwise, and many bad and false decisions may be taken simply because the person does not realize that they are bad. In such cases no valid *behirah*, or choice, has been made. Free will is exercised and a valid *behirah* made only on the borderline between the forces of good and the forces of evil within that person.

It must be realized that this *beḥirah*-point does not remain static in any given individual. With each good *beḥirah* successfully carried out, the person rises higher; that is, things that were previously in the line of battle are now in the area controlled by the *yetser hatov* and actions done in that area can be undertaken without struggle and without *beḥirah*. In this sense we can understand the saying that "one *mitsvah* leads to another." And so in the other direction. Giving in to the *yetser hara* pushes back the frontier of the good, and an act which previously caused one to struggle with one's conscience will now be done without *beḥirah* at all. The *yetser hatov* is no longer functioning effectively in that area. And so we have learnt: "One sin leads to another," and "as soon as one has committed a sin twice, it is no longer a sin for him."

See Rabbi Eliyahu Dessler, *Mikhtav MeEliyahu*, 1:113.

See as well Nechama Leibowitz, Sefer Shemot, *Vaera*, p. 115, her analysis of God hardening Pharaoh's heart.

25. This approach is very much in sync with Rabbi Samson Raphael Hirsch's understanding of *tefilah*, the Hebrew term for prayer. *Tefilah* for him comes from the root *p-l-l*, *palal*, to judge. Prayer is a process of self-judgment through which one evaluates oneself, improves, and emerges as another person. In his words:

> *Hitpalel*, from which "*tefilah*" is derived, originally meant to deliver an opinion about oneself, to judge oneself – or an inner attempt at so doing, such as the *hitpael* form of the Hebrew verb frequently denotes. In other words, an attempt to gain a true judgment of oneself. Thus it denotes to step out of active life in order to attempt to gain a true judgment about oneself, that is, about one's ego, about one's relationship to God and the world, and of God and the world to oneself. It strives to infuse mind and heart with the power of such judgment as will direct both anew to active life – purified, sublimated, strengthened. The procedure of arousing such self-judgment is called "*tefilah*." See Rabbi Samson Raphael Hirsch, *Horeb*, (New York: Soncino Press, 1962) p. 472.

26. See Ber. 26b. The entire passage reads:

> It has been taught in accordance with R. Jose b. Hanina: Abraham instituted the morning prayer, as it says, "And Abraham got up early in the morning to the place where he had stood." (Genesis 19:27) And "standing" means only prayer, as it says, "And Pinchas stood and prayed." (Ps. 106:30) Isaac instituted the afternoon prayer as it says, "And Isaac went out to meditate in the field at eventide" (Gen. 24:63) and "meditation" means only prayer, as it says, "A prayer of the afflicted when he faints and pours out his meditation before the Lord." (Ps. 102:1) Jacob instituted the evening prayer, as it says, "And he lighted upon the place" (Gen. 28:11) and "*pegi'ah*" means prayer, as it says, "Therefore do not pray for this people, neither lift up prayer nor cry for them, neither make intercession to Me." (Jer. 7:16)

27. ibid 30b, 31a.

28. Ber. 32a.

29. Moed Qat. 28b.

    Some suggest that *mazal* is an acronym of *makom* (the letter *mem*); *zman* (the letter *zayin*); and *la'asot* (the letter *lamed*); that is, to do what is proper in the right place at the right time. *Mazal* is, therefore, the good fortune, often having little to do with our forethought or pre-planning, to be in the right place at the right time. From this perspective, *mazal* can be loosely translated as "fate" something that occurs which is beyond our control.

30. Yebam. 49b. The entire passage reads:

    > For it was taught: "I shall fill the number of your days" (Exod. 23:26) refers to the years of the generations. If one is worthy one is allowed to complete the full period; if unworthy the number is reduced; this is the view of Rabbi Akiba.
    >
    > But the Sages said: If one is worthy years are added to one's life; if unworthy, the years of his life are reduced.

31. See Rabbi Yosef Dov Soloveitchik, *Kol Dodi Dofek, Listen – My Beloved Knocks*, translated by David Z. Gordon, edited by Jeffrey R. Woolf, (New York, Yeshiva University, 2006) pp. 5, 6.

32. Esther made this point in a commencement address she gave at Yeshiva University in 1995. The entire address was published by YU.

33. This phrase is found in the *Unetaneh Tokef* prayer of Rosh Hashanah and Yom Kippur.

34. This is not to say that prayer cannot at times be fully accepted. Sometimes our wishes are fully granted, and an evil decree is completely abrogated.

See Vayikra Rabbah 10:5. The English is the Soncino translation.

> From where is the view of R. Judah b. Rabbi that prayer effects complete pardon derived? From the case of Hezekiah. The original term of Hezekiah's kingship was only fourteen years, as it is written, "Now it came to pass in the fourteenth year of King Hezekiah." (Isa. 36:1) "In those days Hezekiah was deathly ill." (Isa. 38:1) But after he prayed, fifteen more years were given to him, as it is said, "Then came the word of the Lord...behold I will add to your life fifteen years." (Isa. 38:5)
>
> From where is the view of Rabbi Joshua b. Levi, who said that prayer effects half atonement, derived? From the case of Aaron, since at first a decree was pronounced against him, as it is said, "Moreover the Lord was very angry with Aaron to destroy (*lehashmido*) him." (Deut. 9:20) Said Rabbi Joshua of Siknin in the name of Rabbi Levi: Destruction (*hashmadah*) means extinction of offspring, as it says, "And I destroyed his fruit from above, and his roots from beneath." (Amos 2:9) When Moses prayed on his [Aaron's] behalf, half the decree was annulled; two sons died, and two remained. It is, therefore, written, "And the Lord spoke unto Moses, saying: Take Aaron and his sons." (Lev. 8:2)

See also Moed Qat. 16b. "The God of Israel said: I rule man. Who rules me? The righteous – for I issue a decree and he can annul it."

35. Nachmanides, *Sefer haMitzvot*, positive commandment 5.
36. ibid.
37. Rabbi Yosef Dov Soloveitchik, *"Worship of the Heart"* (Ktav: New York, 2003) p. 35.

A contemporary story illustrates this point. After Israeli soldier Nachshon Wachsman was kidnapped by terrorists in 1994, his parents asked that prayers be said on his behalf. In the end, Nachshon was killed. Journalists asked his father, a devoutly religious man, doesn't all this raise questions about God, and, more specifically, about the efficacy of prayer. You asked that people pray for your son. Sincere, powerful prayers were offered, and, yet God left them unanswered.

Nachshon's father responded that he believed God did answer the prayer, but His answer was "no." God's answer is not always "yes" but through the prayers recited by millions of people for Nachshon, a deep sense of fellowship with God and community was forged.

Interestingly, in Tanakh, God is viewed as a saving God. An example of this is the Psalmist's petition, – "when a person calls up to Me, I shall answer him, I shall be with him in his time of trouble, I shall grant him relief and honor." (Ps. 91:15) Here, "I shall be with him in his times of trouble" is redeeming. God is stating that if a person calls out to Him in distress, He will be there to save that individual.

In the Midrash, however, this phrase is the classic example, not of a saving God, but of an empathizing God. An example of this is the Midrash which seeks to explain why God appears to Moses from the lowly burning bush – telling him to demand of Pharaoh to let the Jewish people go. Why not from a taller more elegant tree? Says the Midrash as quoted by Rashi, "why in a lowly bush and no other tree, because 'I shall be with him in his times of trouble.'" (Rashi, Exod. 3:2 s.v. *mitokh haseneh*) In other words, as long as Jews are in slavery, God can only appear from a thorn bush, as God hears and feels and empathizes with the plight of His people.

This teaching is of great importance. Parents must know that at times they ought to listen to their children rather than offer advice. Rabbis, counselors and friends ought to also learn this distinction.

38. The danger of believing that appropriate prayer can always nullify a decree became apparent to me in the final days before Israel's withdrawl from Gaza. I spent those days in Netzer Hazani, one of the settlements in Gush Katif and witnessed as youngsters were told that if they prayed hard enough there would be no disengagement. Their prayers were pure, and yet, the disengagement took place resulting in countless crises of faith.

In a similar vein, in many communities today, women gather to recite Tehilim (Psalms), an act which is quite noble. Yet, if the only goal of these groups is that God grant our wishes through prayer, it can also prove to be problematic, as there is no guarantee that even the purest prayer will result in the changes we seek.

Truth be told, on Rosh Hashanah and Yom Kippur, days that are so identified with making requests for a better year, there are, in actuality, very few *bakashot* (requests). The central portion of prayer on Rosh Hashanah is *malkhuyot* – God rules, *zikhronot* – God remembers, and *shofarot* – God redeems. The central part of Yom Kippur is the *avodah*, the service in the *Beit Hamikdash*. Even the prayer *zakhreinu lehayim* – remember us for life – is found in the section of the service which is called *shevah* – praise of God.

39. Perhaps this is the meaning of Rivash, who writes:

> "I also have heard from Rabbi Shimshon of Kinon who was the greatest rabbi of his generation…he would say, 'I pray as if I am a child.'" (*Responsa Rivash* n. 157)

As a child is dependent upon others, so, too, do we stand before God, reliant on Him.

There are countless examples in the service of our standing before God, dependent upon Him. In the *Amidah*, we bow our heads as we make our requests. And in the *tahanun* that follows, we literally fall on our faces, recognizing that we are in God's hands.

40. Maimonides, *Mishneh Torah*, Laws of Prayer 1:1.

41. Nachmanides, *Sefer HaMitzvot*, positive commandment 5.

42. Rabbi Yosef Dov Soloveitchik reconciles the views of Ramban and Rambam by maintaining that both see prayer as meaningful only if it derives from a sense of *tsarah*.

For Ramban, *tsarah* "is an external crisis which arises independently of man. It emerges out of the environment and usually appears suddenly." The "surface *tsarah*" of Ramban arises only at particular moments.

Rambam regards "daily life itself as being existentially in straits, inducing in the sensitive person feelings of despair, a brooding sense of life's meaninglessness, absurdity, lack of fulfillment. It is a persistent *tsarah*, which exists *bekhol yom*, daily. The word *tsarah* connotes more than external trouble; it suggests an emotional and intellectual condition in which man sees himself as hopelessly trapped in a vast, impersonal universe, desolate, without hope." See Rabbi A. Besdin, *Reflections of the Rav*, pp. 79–82.

For Rabbi Soloveitchik, Maimonidean prayer reflects the ever present feeling of human inadequacy and inner struggle. The approach here suggests something different. For Maimonides, prayer is inextricably bound with an optimistic approach to life of positive resolve to make this world better.

43. See Rambam, *Mishneh Torah*, Laws [which are] the Foundations of the Torah, 2:2. There he distinguishes between *ahavat Hashem* and *yirat Hashem*. *Ahavat Hashem*, loving God, he defines as trying to emulate God. *Yirat Hashem* is awe of God, sensing ones limits in comparison

to God. In the end, *ahavat Hashem* and *yirat Hashem* lead to each other. Trying to emulate God precipitates awareness of that impossibility; being in awe of God could inspire one to do better and live a god-like life.

The Amidah may be an example of the dialectic of assertion and submission. On the one hand, our tone can be one of demand as we ask that our requests be fulfilled. On the other hand, it could be a tone of submission in recognition that, in the end, it's all up to God.

44. Ramban, Gen. 1:1.

45. Note the Bible's play on the word *shem*. In the Generation of Dispersion it refers to themselves. In Abraham and Sarah's it refers to God, as the name of God is added. I first heard this idea from Rabbi Menachem Liebtag.

46. The Torah describes this struggle with the words, "an anonymous man wrestled (*va-yei'avek*) with him." (Gen. 32:35) Rabbi Soloveitchik sees this struggle as a moment of *tefilah*. In his words, "this strange scene of Jacob wrestling with the angel is restaged in everyone's life." This is so, Rabbi Soloveitchik claims, because the human being is perennially in need, and in those moments God always welcomes his/her *tefilah*. See Rabbi Yosef Dov Soloveitchik, "*Worship of the Heart*" p. 35.

47. See Gen. 49:22 and Num. 24:17 where *shur* means to gaze or to see.

48. *Midrash Tehillim*, (Buber), Psalm 27.

49. I am deeply grateful to my students at Yeshivat Chovevei Torah Rabbinical School (YCT), the Bayit (Hebrew Institute of Riverdale) and the Wexner Heritage program, who have challenged me and offered insights that helped shape this paper. I am indebted to Shuli Boxer Rieser for her extraordinary help in typing and formatting this paper. And Dr. Elli Kranzler, *shliah tsibbur* of our Bayit, whose soulfulness and understanding of *tefilah* has profoundly impacted me.

From Fast to Feast

IN THE BOOK OF ZECHARIAH

Andrea Wershof Schwartz

T he construction of the Second Temple was a monumental national, political and religious project. That such a project would have been affected by myriad cultural considerations is not surprising. Even so, students of the Bible often overlook the ways in which the various passages of the Bible that describe different periods and perspectives on this construction provide an opportunity to capture the importance of this moment for biblical theology. In this article, I will examine the ways in which two Jewish holidays, Sukkot and the Ninth of Av, are reframed in the biblical book of Zechariah. It is well known that the holidays of the Jewish calendar year bear diverse meanings. While the observance of a single Jewish holiday in a specific historic period may draw energy from multiple symbolisms simultaneously, it is often the case that the different symbolisms attached to a given holiday are a byproduct of historical transformation. The reframing of Sukkot and Tisha B'Av in the book of Zechariah, I will show, is an example in which historical circumstances led to a refocusing of the holiday's symbolic meaning.

When Zechariah prophesies about the future, he refers to two changes that will affect these Jewish holidays: the fast of the ninth of Av will become a day of celebration, and the festival of Sukkot will become a universalistic holiday for all nations. Specifically, in addressing a group of Israelite leaders who have come to inquire about the role of the fast of the ninth of Av during the construction of the second Temple, Zechariah predicts that the four Jerusalem-related fast days,[1] will become days of celebration. He states, "The fast of the fourth month, the fast of the fifth month, the fast of the seventh month, and the fast of the tenth month shall become occasions for joy and gladness, happy festivals for the House of Judah" (Zech. 8:19), alluding to a fundamental shift in the symbolism of the fast days from occasions for national mourning to days of rejoicing. Regarding the festival of Sukkot, in the last chapter of the book, Zechariah foretells that "all those nations that came up against Jerusalem shall make a pilgrimage year by year...to observe the Feast of Booths" in the end of days (14:16).[2] He predicts that the very nations who fought against the Israelites in the past will come to celebrate Sukkot together with the Israelites in the city of Jerusalem.

Each of the prophecies about these holidays refers to a change in their future observance, with the fast days changing their very nature from days of sorrow to days of happiness, and the feast of Sukkot shifting from a particularistic pilgrimage festival to a universalistic holiday. What do these two passages have in common, and what does a close reading of each reference reveal about the theological message of Zechariah's prophecy, in the setting of the rebuilding of the second Temple in Jerusalem?

The final literary section of what scholars consider the first part of the book of Zechariah[3] begins with the arrival of a delegation of Israelite leaders to Jerusalem, where the construction of the second Temple is underway, under the reign of King Darius of Persia. The delegates ask Zechariah about the liturgical calendar, questioning the necessity of continuing to mourn the destruction of the Temple in the month of Av, now that the Temple's rebuilding is in progress. "Shall I weep and practice abstinence in the fifth month?", they ask the prophet (7:3). Zechariah answers the group with a lengthy response and explanation of his rationale (7:4–8:18), which culminates in his above-quoted statement that the four fast days will become "occasions for joy and gladness" (8:19).[4]

The passage itself presents several difficulties. First, why does the question of the delegates (7:3) refer only to the fast of the fifth month, namely, the Fast of Av, while Zechariah's response in 8:19 mentions four dates? Second, Zech. 7:1 indicates that the delegates arrived "in the fourth year of King Darius," two years after the construction of the Temple had begun, and in "the ninth month, Kislev," more than eight months in advance of the fast day in question. What is the significance of this timing? And third, what purpose does the intervening sermonic material in the prophet's response serve (7:4–8:18)?

That the fifth month, presumably referring to the fast of Av, is the sole focus of the delegates' question leads to the assumption that it had already, in the 6th century BCE, achieved its status as one of the most significant fast days observed in Jewish tradition of the time.[5] Since the ninth of Av would eventually come to serve as a symbol for all the persecution and misfortunes of the Jewish people,[6] one can assume that the subsidiary events mentioned in 8:19, including events leading up to the destruction of the Temple such as the breaching of the walls of Jerusalem,[7] are included under the general heading of this fast. Scholars note that these four fasts recall the beauty and grandeur of the Temple and the disgrace of the Israelites since its destruction,[8] while the number of fast days attests to the important influence of the destruction in the collective memory of the Israelites.[9] In this context, fasting represents a measure of self-denial and mourning introduced post-exile, lest the tragedy of the destruction of the Temple be forgotten.[10]

Perhaps the timing of the question can be explained by the imminent fast of Tevet, less than a month away, which marks the beginning of Nebuchadrezzar's siege on Jerusalem (2 Kgs. 25:1–2; Jer. 39:1). However, one must still examine why the delegation comes less than a year after Temple's re-foundation, which scholars situate in 518 BCE, in the second half of Darius's fourth year as king.[11] Historical data indicates that during this period Darius had instituted his policy of using traditional native collections of legal materials to encourage local social order and thus stabilize the Persian Empire.[12] Darius was interested in granting semi-autonomy to Jerusalem, and therefore promoted the legitimization of local figures of authority. This strategy could account for the importance of Zechariah's role as prophet.

Perhaps the impetus that prompted the people to approach Zechariah was the return to Zion itself and the rebuilding of the Temple, and a hope that the promised redemption was at hand.[13] The return to Zion, however, was not necessarily a period of obvious deliverance, but rather a difficult and tumultuous time in which the ultimate outcome of the apparent redemption was unclear. If the situation in Jerusalem had been unequivocally good, the question of the Israelite leaders would have been unnecessary, as there would clearly have been no need for continued mourning.[14] Given this context, the delegates may have doubted that the promised age of redemption had actually arrived. Additionally, they may have been concerned that the construction would be halted as it had been after the return from Exile during the time of Ezra, in 538 BCE under King Cyrus, when it ceased due to interference from "adversaries of Judah and Benjamin" (Ezra 4:1).

Several other reasons may have led the delegates to doubt that they were experiencing a redemptive process. First, the relative inferiority of the Second Temple compared to the First may have led to skepticism: according to Babylonian Talmud, the *Shechinah*, God's presence, did not dwell in the Second Temple as it had in the First.[15] Second, this period was struck by a series of economic and military crises as cited by contemporary biblical prophets: Haggai records agricultural problems, lamenting, "you have sowed much an brought in little" (Hag. 1:6), Nehemiah warns that when the nations "heard that healing had come to the walls of Jerusalem…they all conspired together to come and fight against Jerusalem" (Neh 4:1-2), and Zechariah states "the earnings of men were nil, and profits from beasts were nothing" (Zech 8:10). Third, beyond the economic and military instability, the Israelite nation remained very divided and fractious, perhaps due in part to the fact that many of the exiles chose not to return from Babylonia. And finally, the delegates may have been anxious for the pitiful state of a people living under fickle Persian rule; the state of the Jews was so perilous under the Persians that, according to the book of Esther, there could even be an attempt from the Persian capital, Shushan, to annihilate the entire nation.[16]

Thus perhaps the harsh reality of that time led the Jews to

hesitantly inquire of the prophet if this was indeed the true redemption. Their question was not merely about halakhic practice: they expected a concrete prophetic response to their uncertainties. In what Ralph L. Smith calls "a decalogue of promises…of salvation, hope, and forgiveness,"[17] Zechariah addresses these concerns, reassuring the Israelites that God has "returned to Zion, and [God] will dwell in Jerusalem…the City of Faithfulness" (8:3). Zechariah paints a hopeful picture of the future, prophesying that the city streets will once again be filled with young and old (8:4–5), promising blessings of longevity and continuity, and reassuring that more exiles will return (8:7–8). In response to the delegates' implied fears about the economic reality, Zechariah says "what [the people] sows shall prosper", affirming that there will be agricultural fertility (8:12).

Zechariah reassures the Israelites: "Have no fear!" for God will not reconsider the decision to do good (8:13–15), promising that the building will continue uninterrupted. However, the prophet tempers these statements of comfort with the admonition that the Israelites must "render true and perfect justice" (8:16). Zechariah concludes his response with the promise that these fasts will, in the future, "become occasions for joy and gladness, happy festivals for the House of Judah," promising that conditions will improve as long as the Israelites indeed "love honesty and integrity" (8:19).[18] The fulfillment of the covenant will then cause the nations of the world to recognize the supremacy of God and Israel, climaxing in the declaration, "We have heard that God is with you" (8:23).[19]

Zechariah's depiction of Sukkot at the end of days helps elucidate the nature of the theological change occurring with the transformation of the ninth of Av. The image of the nations joining the Israelites in Jerusalem in peace that concludes Zechariah's description of the future fast days reflects the hope of shifting from warriors to peacemakers expressed in the prophets.[20] This peaceful image, however, contrasts sharply with the depiction of the nations fighting against Jerusalem in Zech. 14:2, which introduces his description of the observance of Sukkot at the end of days. In this passage, the prophet states that in the end of days God will "gather all the nations to Jerusalem for war" (14:2). The account of God's "day of battle" against Jerusalem (Zech. 14:3) is replete with language of recreation, such as "in that day, there shall be neither sunlight nor cold moonlight, but there shall be a continuous day" (14:6–7) implying that God will create a new world order that will place the Israelites in a position of power over the other nations.[21]

The upheaval that will precede the days of redemption and renewal is thus a necessary antecedent for the inauguration of a new era that will lead to the ultimate universalization of God's Kingship (14:9), culminating in a celebration of Sukkot in Jerusalem by all the nations. Jeffrey Rubenstein suggests that Zech. 14 presents "an ideal vision of…the temple-city," affirming God as Lord of all the earth (4:19), worshipped by all human beings, as evidenced by this universalistic celebration of Sukkot.[22] In fact, Sukkot remains in the Rabbinic imagination as a holiday in which the other nations are welcomed into the service of God: in Tractate Sukkot of the Babylonian Talmud, the Rabbis describe the 70 bulls of the Sukkot sacrificial ritual as being offered on behalf of the 70 nations (Sukkot 55b).[23]

Why does this chaos of re-creation culminate in the observance of this holiday in particular? The different aspects of Sukkot range from the agricultural aspect of the Feast of Ingathering (Exod. 23:16, 34:22), to the historical element of the Feast of Booths, which recalls the sojourn of the Israelites in the desert (Deut. 16:13–17), to the divine enthronement theme of the Festival of the Lord (Lev. 23:39–43). Sometimes referred to simply as "The Festival,"[24] Sukkot can be considered the preeminent pilgrimage festival, as well as a celebration of the renewal of the covenant.[25] For instance, Moses commands Israelites to read the Torah at a public gathering every seven years on Sukkot to "hear and so learn to revere the Lord" (Deut. 31:12). The sukka itself can be viewed as evidence of God's protection,[26] as a sign of God dwelling amongst the people, and even as a symbol of the Temple.[27] Thus by participating in this multi-faceted holiday of pilgrimage, the nations join with the Israelites in recognition of God and acceptance of God's blessing.

The references to the fast days and Sukkot, then, are tied together by the nations' acknowledgement of God's sovereignty and their affirmation of Israel's unique role. The conclusions of each section of the book of Zechariah thus present a transformation of an Israelite holiday coupled with a description of a universal longing for God. However, the promise of blessing to the nations is dependent on Israel behaving in a way that reflects the justice inherent in the divine message. Only by fulfilling the covenant with God, will the Israelites have the potential to transform their holidays into occasions for universal worship and peace.[28] Thus after the difficult years of exile, Zechariah uses the eschatological holidays to offer a challenge to the Israelites that will be rewarded with the promise of redemption. He promises that the nations will join the Israelites in worship of God, and that the fast days will become days of joy, if the Israelites "love honesty and integrity" (8:19). This promise transcends national boundaries, placing Jerusalem and the people of Israel at the center of a world of peace in which "there shall be one Lord with one name" (Zech. 14:9).

Andrea Wershof Schwartz
MA, Jewish Theological Seminary
MD Candidate, Mount Sinai School of Medicine

NOTES

1. The fast days mentioned in Zech. 8:19 are understood by Carroll Stuhlmueller and others to be the four dates associated with the destruction of the Temple of Jerusalem in 586 BC (Carroll Stuhlmueller, *Rebuilding with Hope: A Commentary on the Books of Haggai and Zechariah* [Grand Rapids: Wm. B. Eerdmans Publishing Co.; Edinburgh: The Handsel Press Ltd., 1988], 103). The fast of the fourth month, counting Nissan as the first month, refers to Tammuz, when the wall of Jerusalem was breached, leading to the capture of the city (Jer. 39:2, 52:6). The fast of the fifth month commemorates the ninth of Av, on which day the Temple was burned (2 Kgs. 25:8–9), and the fast of the seventh month, Tishrei, is in memory of the assassination of the governor of Judah, Gedaliah ben Ahikam (2 Kgs. 25:25; Jer. 41:1–2). The fast of the tenth month, Tevet, marks the beginning of Nebuchadrezzar's siege on Jerusalem (2 Kgs. 25:1–2; Jer. 39:1).

2. All Biblical translations follow *Tanakh: The Holy Scriptures: The New JPS Translation According to the Traditional Hebrew Text* (Philadelphia: Jewish Publication Society, 1999). Unless otherwise indicated, all chapter and verse references are to Zechariah.

3. See, for instance, David L. Petersen, *Zechariah 9–14 and Malachi: A Commentary* (Old Testament Library; Louisville: Westminster John Knox Press, 1995), 2ff.

4.   Carol L. Meyers and Eric M. Meyers, *Haggai, Zechariah 1–8* (Anchor Bible 25b; Garden City, New York: Doubleday, 1987), 386.

5.   A series of calamities justified the ninth of Av as the major day of mourning in the Jewish calendar. According to the Mishna (Ta'an. 4:6), not only was the First Temple destroyed by the Babylonians on the ninth of Av in 586 BC, but the burning of Second Temple by Titus also occurred on this date in 70 CE. In 135 CE the second war of independence against the Romans, under Bar Kochba and Rabbi Akiba, ended with the fall of Betar on the ninth of Av in 135 CE, and the expulsion of the Jews from Spain began on the same day in 1492 CE. See "Av, the Ninth of" in *Encyclopedia Judaica*, Volume 3. (Jerusalem: Keter Publishing House, 1972), 936.

6.   See note 1 for a discussion of the historic events associated with each fast day. The fast of the seventh month could theoretically refer to the day of Yom Kippur, but fasting on this day is not mentioned explicitly, only that one should "practice self denial" (Lev. 16:29) See Ralph L. Smith, *Micah – Malachi*. (Word Biblical Commentary 32; Waco, TX: Word Books, 1984), 222.

7.   Gershon Porush, "'Shall I Weep in the Fifth Month?' Understanding Zecharyah 7–8." *Jewish Thought: A Journal of Torah Scholarship* 5:1 (1998), 22.

8.   Meyers and Meyers, *Haggai, Zechariah 1–8*, 392.

9.   In the Bible, fasting has several different functions. It is used as a "praying practice or as an intercessory measure" (Ibid., 388) (as in David's attempt to save the life of Bathsheba's child in 2 Sam. 12:16), as a measure of piety (as in Moses on Mount Sinai in Exod. 34:28), as atonement for sin (as in the Israelites' fasting after the capture of the Ark in 1 Sam. 7:6) or to rid wickedness (as in God's rebuke of insincere fasting in Isa. 58:5–7). In Zech. 7:3, fasting functions in response to loss and has shifted from the "arena of popular piety (non-Torah, non-temple oriented) into the official religion of Israel by force of the circumstances of later Israelite history" (Stuhlmueller, *Rebuilding with Hope*, 105).

10.   Meyers and Meyers, *Haggai, Zechariah 1–8*, 380. The fact that the reigning dates of Persian rulers, not Israelite, are used to mark time may indicate an acceptance by the prophet, however reluctantly, of Persian rule.

11.   Ibid., 390.

12.   Stuhlmueller, *Rebuilding with Hope*, 105.

13.   Porush, "Shall I Weep," 23–24.

14.   Yoma 21b.

15. Esther 3:13.

16. Smith points out that each promise is introduced by the superscription "thus said the Lord of Hosts," כה אמר יהוה צבאות. See Zech. 8:2 for an example. (Smith, *Micah – Malachi* 231).

17. The Babylonian Talmud declares on the basis of this verse that as long as there is no peace, the fast day of Tisha B'Av will remain a day of mourning (Ros. Has. 18b). Rashi (Rabbi Solomon ben Isaac, 1040–1105) comments on this passage that "peace" refers to the time "when the hand of the nations is not over Israel" (Rashi on Ros. Has. 18b. in I. Epstein, ed. *Hebrew-English Edition of the Babylonian Talmud*. [trans. M. Simon; London: Soncino, 1983], 35), while Ramban (Rabbi Moses ben Nahman, 1194–1270) understands "peace" as a reference to the day when the Temple stands rebuilt (Nahmanides, *Torat Ha'Adam*, RN"D). Both of these interpretations fit Zechariah's depiction of the eschatological holidays when Israel's glory will be restored through the rebuilding of the Temple and the reinstatement of her autonomy.

18. Zech. 8:23 echoes both Isa. 45:14 and the words of Abimelech to Abraham in Gen 26:28.

19. See Isa. 2:1–4 and Mic. 4:1–5: "They shall beat their swords into plowshares…"

20. Walter Harrelson. "The Celebration of the Feast of Booths according to Zech. 14,16–21," in *Religions in Antiquity*, ed. J. Neusner (Leiden: Brill, 1968), 95–96.

21. Jeffrey L. Rubenstein, "Sukkot, Eschatology and Zechariah 14," *Revue Biblique* 103:2 (1996), 186–7.

22. Jeffrey L. Rubenstein, "An Eschatological Drama," *AJW Review* 21/1 (1996), 1–37, 32.

23. See 1 Kgs. 8:2, Ezek. 45:25, Neh. 8:14, and 2 Chr. 5:3.

24. George W. MacRae, "The Meaning and Evolution of the Feast of Tabernacles" *CBQ* 22 (1960), 261.

25. Psalm 27:5 reads, "He will shelter me in His pavilion (בסכה) on an evil day."

26. MacRae, "The Meaning and Evolution of the Feast of Tabernacles," 271.

27. Joyce G. Baldwin, *Haggai, Zechariah, Malachi: An Introduction and Commentary*. (Tyndale Press: Downers Grove, IL, 1972), 155–6.

Interrupting Birth Control:

RE-READING A FAMOUS *BERAITA*

Barry S. Wimpfheimer

F ew beraitot have garnered as much attention in traditional and academic Rabbinics as the beraita about three women's use of contraception found at Tosefta Niddah 2:4. Readers of all types are fascinated by this text's notably explicit comment on a subject that is titillating and nearly silent in ancient literature: the mechanics of sexual congress and efforts to circumvent conception.[1] The increasing transparency with which all aspects of sexuality have been treated in modernity has led scholars in various disciplines to the beraita; it is not unexpected that scholars working within the contemporary setting often project their own politics and interests onto such a text. In this article, I will attempt to relocate a contemporaneous context for this beraita and comment upon its original purpose. In the process of that relocation, I will note various ways in which some of the multi-vocal and multi-generational redactive texture of the beraita has been overlooked in previous readings. The ungrammaticalities that form the basis for higher criticism will contribute to a reading that understands the beraita as remarkable not for its contraceptive advice per se, but for the way that advice demonstrates a bioethical concern for new life that is uncharacteristic of its time. My reading highlights the way in which a single rabbi, the tanna R. Meir, is responsible for initiating an advocacy program for newborns that begins as radical advocacy before its absorption into mainstream halakhah.

The beraita under discussion, found at Tosefta Niddah 2:4, reads as follows:

Three women are using a *mokh*:
1. A minor
2. One who is pregnant
3. One who is nursing

1. A Minor lest she will conceive and she will die
    a. Who is a minor? Between eleven years and one day and until twelve years and one day.
        i. Less than this and greater than this he has normal intercourse and does not worry
2. One who is pregnant lest she will transform her fetus into a "*Sandal*."
3. One who is nursing lest she will kill her child.
    a. For Rabbi Meir used to say he threshes inside and winnows outside.[2]
    b. But the Sages say he has normal intercourse and [the almighty][3] is watching over his hands as it says, "God watches fools."

The outline presentation of this beraita demonstrates the text's blatant structure.[4] The opening sentence of the beraita declares that three women are using a *mokh*. The *mokh* is an occlusive pessary composed of hackled wool or flax.[5] Though medieval commentators debate whether it is inserted before or after intercourse, other sources indicate that the *mokh* is best understood as an occlusive device used during intercourse.

While the definition of the *mokh* is easily enough established, of greater concern is the opening sentence's verb. The beraita employs an active participle, best translated as "are using." It is not entirely uncommon for mishnah-form texts to employ participles, but such verbs often leave ambiguities in their interpretation because they are better suited for descriptive rather than prescriptive purposes. To say that certain women "are using" something does not articulate whether this use is mandatory or optional or whether such use is unusual for these or other women. In his work on birth control in Jewish law that began with a 1966 Hebrew dissertation entitled, "Three Women Employing a *Mokh*," and continued with his English monograph *Birth Control in Jewish Law*,[6] David Feldman utilizes the ambiguity of the beraita's active participle as a crux through which to structure significant debates within medieval and modern rabbinic treatments of contraception.[7] Some authorities, Feldman observes, translate the active participle as mandatory language: "three women *must* use a *mokh*," while other authorities translate it as optional language: "three women *may* use a *mokh*." While these translations have implications for the beraita's three categories of women, they also have implications for the larger number of women who fall outside these categories. The authorities who read the verb as licensing optional use of a *mokh* by the three categories of women in the beraita do so by presuming a halakhic backdrop in which such use is prohibited to other women, while those who read the beraita as mandating use of the *mokh* by the three categories of women in the beraita presume a halakhic backdrop in which such use by other women is either optional or prohibited.

Both Feldman's Hebrew dissertation and his English monograph on birth control in Jewish law have a complex relationship with rabbinic law as they strive to simultaneously survey the broad (from the Mishnah to the present) history of their topic as a textual critic while participating in the traditional discourse and attempting to stake a halakhic position on the issues. Both works foreground the beraita under discussion in an attempt to fuse rabbinic law behind a single source so that a strong reading of this source can definitively determine Jewish law's perspective on birth control. A critical approach to both this source and its subsequent traditional scholarly readings leads to Feldman's permissive attitude towards the use of woman-initiated contraceptive techniques that are analogous to the pessary of the beraita.

Feldman's decision to participate in the living discourse of halakhah dulls some of his best critical work. In his dissertation,

Feldman claims that the intent behind the beraita's composition was not that of a statutory legist's commanding or prohibiting behavior with the force of law, but of officials' advocating practices for the public health benefit of individuals within the community.[8] The upshot is that tannaitic literature *does not legislate* about specific contraceptive practice. This significant claim is obscured, though, by Feldman's broad focus on the history of rabbinic legal interpretation as it has redounded to the present day.[9] Despite his insight in the beraita itself, Feldman defaults into the traditional discourse's reading of the beraita against a background of legislation. Against Feldman's critical instincts, the beraita becomes a statutory legal text that functions like other such texts within his reading.

Furthermore, by participating in the traditional discourse, Feldman follows its lead in reading Bavli ideas back into the tannaitic sources. Most traditional rabbinic interpreters privilege the Bavli in their scholarship. For this reason, the idea of wasted male seed as a locus of legal interest as found in the Bavli becomes the basis for reading the beraita. The Bavli tradition of wasted seed as the basis for moral opprobrium and legislation is turned into the context for reading the beraita in many traditional readings. Despite his own feeling about the beraita's compositional intent, Feldman allows this traditional retrojection onto the beraita and situates his discussion of birth control within a world conceptually dominated by wasted seed. This allows Feldman to marry the most explicit conceptual prohibition related to discrete sex acts (wasted seed) to the most explicit rabbinic text about the mechanics of contraception (the beraita). In the process, Feldman loses sight of his own critical reading of the beraita.[10]

Feldman finds the beraita helpful as a taxonomic tool for surveying a litany of traditional legal readers. These readings, Feldman argues, can be structured around two debates: the aforementioned interpretive debate about the active participle and a debate about whether the *mokh* is designed for pre-coital or post-coital use.[11] Remarkably, Feldman brackets his own intuitions both regarding the meaning of the beraita in its original context and regarding important details like the mechanics of a *mokh*, in order to preserve the discursive realities of traditional rabbinic responsa.[12] In the process, Feldman ends up reifying some of the tendencies of the discourse against his better judgment; most notably, Feldman reads the beraita in light of the presumption that tannaitic law operates with the notion of wasted seed and its concomitant opprobrium and legislation in mind.

The presumption that wasted seed is the fundamental basis for all rabbinic texts regarding birth control in rabbinic law is the basis for Michael Satlow's strong historicist critique of both traditional readers and Feldman for his complicity in their discourse.[13] With Feldman as his straw man, Satlow reviews rabbinic sources to determine if they, in fact, reflect the traditional presumption of wasted seed as the ideational core of the legal program.[14] Satlow draws attention to the very limited treatment of wasted seed in rabbinic literature. The notion of wasted seed appears in a single Bavli Sugyah at Niddah 13. As we will discuss in greater detail below, Satlow asserts that wasted seed is an idea important to the Stammaim responsible for composing that Bavli Sugyah and retrojected onto earlier source material utilized in the construction of that pericope.

With respect to the beraita we have been discussing, Satlow parts company with Feldman and extracts himself from the traditional discourse. This is most significant for the legal application of the beraita to women who are not explicitly included within one of the beraita's three categories. While Feldman jumps into a discourse that takes it on faith that the beraita has omnisignificant meaning as a canonical source, including ramifications for women other than the three explicitly discussed, Satlow declares simply that "reading a ban on other women's use of the mok[h] in this passage is not warranted."[15] Satlow justifies this declaration by noting that the beraita's opening statement is elaborated upon in the subsequent structure of the beraita and the recommendation of the *mokh* is based upon health risks specifically associated with these three women.

While I agree generally with Satlow's approach, I do not consider his justification sufficient since a statement articulated about a sub-class of women (three categories) can naturally shed light on the larger class of women in general. Even if the intent of the beraita is to offer advice regarding health risks, that advice can project an image of the legal context in which it is offered. To say then that this beraita has no light to shed on the legal circumstances of women in general, one must say (elaborating on the work of both Feldman and Satlow) that women in general do not exist as a legal category for purposes of contraception since tannaitic law *takes no interest* in legislating such behavior. Pushing the argument further, not only does tannaitic literature not legislate about contraception, it also does not attach any moral opprobrium to the practice.[16]

The distinction between specific legislation and moral opprobrium is not insignificant when speaking about rabbinic literature. One often encounters rabbinic texts that reflect a moral position without staking that position to a specific legal responsibility or to jurisprudential consequences.[17] What I am noting here is that tannaitic literature not only does not legislate about contraception, it also does not moralize regarding contraception. There are, of course, tannaitic texts that present procreation both as a moral imperative and as a specific legal obligation. Yet none of these texts focuses on discrete sex acts and requires specific mechanics in a married couple's intimate life.

In his treatment of 'wasted seed,' Michael Satlow claims that the rhetoric of wasted seed as a driving force in Jewish considerations of contraception and masturbation is the invention of the Stammaim responsible for the Sugyah at Niddah 13.[18] Despite the fact that the Sugyah attributes several of its important statements that utilize wasted seed as a concept to early (and even Palestinian) Amoraim, Satlow is compelled by the absence of this concept in tannaitic or Palestinian literature to attribute this innovation to the Stammaitic layer. Though I believe that Satlow overreaches when he allows his thesis to dictate the notion that the Stammaim are entirely responsible for the notion of wasted seed, there is little doubt that he is correct regarding tannaitic sources.[19] Any reading of tannaitic sources in light of wasted seed is anachronistic.

Taking Satlow's idea a bit further, it is not the Bavli itself but the post-Bavli legal discourse that is responsible for treating wasted seed as a discrete issue worthy of incorporation into a legal code. Within the very Nedarim 13 Sugyah that Satlow uses as the crux of his argument, the sources that employ wasted seed are sources that indicate moral opprobrium, but they are not specific and enforceable legal statutes. That such a distinction within the Talmudic sources is not anachronistic is apparent from the way in which that very Sugyah treats a tannaitic source.

The Mishnah *ad loc* declares that a man who checks for emissions too often should have his hand cut off. The Bavli's discussion of this Mishnah questions whether the mishnaic phrase is to be understood as a legal statute or a curse. The Bavli's attempt to take this evidently hyperbolic statement as a statutory instruction is comical and the Bavli basically rejects this possibility by *reductio ad absurdum*.[20] While it is absurd to take this violent statement in the Mishnah as normative statute, it is clear from both this discussion and the rest of the Sugyah that the Stam incorporates hyperbolic normative statements into its discourse of precedent, distinguishing between such statements and either formal statutes or other such indicators of normative behavior.[21] This process begins the transformation of wasted seed from hyperbole to normative statute. Within the post-Bavli halakhic discourse, there is little recognition of the fact that these ideas originated in the context of hyperbolic declarations of moral opprobrium. The Stam's apparatus for comparing earlier texts succeeds in preparing the transformation of wasted seed from a morally reprehensible but unlegislated act to one incorporated within the legal code.[22] This transformation of wasted seed prepares the way for traditional readers to look backward at our beraita from within that context and assume that the beraita anachronistically legislates (even when it is only advocating a health precaution) against its prohibitive backdrop.

We have noted thus far that though contraceptive practice is what makes the beraita interesting, that practice is not the originally intended context of the beraita's composition. To retrieve that compositional context, we need to return to the compositional clues available within the beraita.

There are various critical issues within the beraita that draw our attention to one particular category of women among the three mentioned in the beraita: the nursing woman. At the level of the potential risk, the nursing woman seems the least directly vulnerable; after all, lactation reduces the possibility of conception and wet nursing was a prevalent practice in the larger culture.[23] And yet, the beraita utilizes its strongest rhetoric in expressing this risk: "lest she *kill* her child." On a structural level, the nursing woman is the only category of woman in the beraita that is justified not only through a statement explaining the risk involved, but also through the citation of a tannaitic debate that transpired before the period of the beraita's redaction. Perhaps most significantly, this beraita is located within a series of beraitot that can be considered its own small sub-tractate on nursing.

Scholars have long been aware of textual groupings whose unity predates the redactive setting in which we find them.[24] Whether the impetus for such organization was that topics were studied in this way or that this organization aided memorization, there is no denying that such units exist. Tosefta Niddah 2:1–7 is a small unit of tannaitic texts about nursing triggered by a mishnaic comment about nursing women. Though some of these texts are paralleled elsewhere in rabbinic literature, others make their sole appearance in this context. Given the placement of the beraita of the three women within this grouping, it is fair to assume that the beraita was originally understood (if possibly not composed) within the context of nursing and helps explain why the beraita seems weighted towards its nursing example.

It is within the nursing context that I would like to narrativize this beraita diachronically, and imagine the ways that its recommendations and disagreements map onto historical realities. In the ancient world, nursing was an activity performed sometimes by mothers and sometimes by nurses. There are wet nurses referenced in the Hebrew Bible and rabbinic literature refers to the wet nurse on several occasions. At Rome, wet nursing was more common in higher social classes than maternal nursing, and was widely practiced across all classes.[25] Keith Bradley has suggested that the prevalence of wetnursing stemmed from paternal detachment from their newborns borne of anxiety regarding the high rate of infant mortality.[26]

Roman legislation and literature parallel to the tannaitic period paints the picture of a society in which many if not most individuals were reluctant to beget and support children.[27] Roman families, especially those of the aristocracy, were often comprised of fewer than three children despite legislation designed to incentivize fecundity and punish family planning. Within this world, techniques for family planning included both infant exposure and infanticide.[28] While such practices came in for moral condemnation from various circles, their prevalence demonstrates the degree to which newborns were not considered to have basic rights to life and certainly no claim to parental resources.

Scholars have noted that Hellenistic Jewish sources represent some of the most rhetorically vituperative ones vis-à-vis these anti-child practices. Philo, for example, refers to the practice of infanticide and exposure as murder of the highest order.[29] Scholars have often presumed, on the basis of Philo and other Hellenistic sources, that the Jewish context was different than the larger societal one. John Boswell writes:

> Although no scriptural or rabbinic text in fact required this, it is possible that it was a cultural expectation among Hellenized Jews, and that Jewish writers of the time re-garded it as a part of oral tradition.[30]

But just as the official Roman sources legislating and promoting child-friendly practices testify to an opposite world reality, so the Hellenistic sources must be read complexly to recognize that Jewish culture was part of the larger society and struggled with many of the same cultural conflicts that affected prospective Roman parents. The evidence of exposure in tannaitic sources testifies quite clearly to the existence if not the prevalence of this practice within tannaitic culture.[31]

To properly situate our beraita in its historical context, I would like to suggest that we read R. Meir as a rabbinic Favorinus. The Hadrianic philosopher Favorinus (80–160 CE) is cited in Aulus Gellus as attempting to convince new parents that they should not assign infants to a wet nurse but insist that the mother nurse the infant her-self.[32] The tanna R. Meir is a contemporary of Favorinus and seems similarly compelled to encourage maternal nursing for the sake of the newborn's wellbeing. It is within the mindset of protecting new life that R. Meir advocates *coitus interruptus* as the intercourse practice of the nursing woman.

We often approach rabbinic literature with skeptical, especially feminist, eyes. The scholar must be wary of the androcentric nature of a literature that talks about, but not with, women. My own feminist impulse originally suggested to me a reading of R. Meir based on a male attempt to control the mysterious power of female reproduction through legislation.[33] It is the same impulse that leads Michael Satlow to assume that the purpose of this beraita is to protect the property interest that a man has in offspring and potential offspring.[34] But both of these readings are guilty of over-skepticism and turn R. Meir into the fantasy of a late antique male as imagined by a contemporary scholar. They each read too much misogyny into the rabbinic text. In this reading, I argue that R. Meir is stridently proactive with respect to contraception as a public health advocacy in order to protect the wellbeing of new life. This I will corroborate on the basis of several other texts attributed to R. Meir.

Just as there is no evidence that tannaitic or prior Jewish law took an interest in discrete acts of contraception, so there is no evidence from other sources that the tannaim took a protective interest in the health of women.[35] But this beraita is not about women's health; it is about newborn survival. That is not to ignore the fact that any discourse of fetal and/or newborn health is automatically related to women's health and almost always involves some degree of paternalistic controlling of women's bodies. But if we are pursuing authorial intent and the original context of composition, it is important to place emphasis on the programmatic purpose of the beraita to protect new life.

In our contemporary world, public health risks do not emerge as broadly accepted phenomena overnight. Rather, a phenomenon is initially identified by research as a danger. Advocates raise public awareness by making noise and are sometimes able to generate consensus surrounding the risky activity. When some consensus is reached, attempts are made to legislate to protect society from the risk and/or repair damage already caused. But legislation does not, in and of itself, change practice. Evolutions in personal practice are slow, and many are reluctant to alter habits even once a broader consensus has been established. There is little reason to assume that circumstances in Late Antiquity were much different.

In his legislation vis-à-vis the nursing infant, R. Meir reflects the passionate commitment of an early advocate fighting against consensus. Like his contemporary Favorinus, R. Meir pushes maternal nursing within a culture in which the practice is threatened by cultural and economic considerations.

Much of tannaitic halakhah develops within *apriori* biblical legal categories. This is not to say that the Bible fully categorizes its law, only that the rabbinic categories originate in biblical ideas. But the public health basis for the laws of this beraita makes this beraita's genealogy somewhat abnormal, though certainly not unique. Rather than emerging from a pre-existent biblical notion of birth control to save certain women, this emerges from a rabbinic perception of health risk. How does such a perception evolve into a legal category and become included within a rabbinic statute?

It is my contention that the pre-history incorporated in the beraita provides evidence for the fact that R. Meir initiated the notion of birth control for the nursing woman through his suggestion of interrupted intercourse for a couple in that situation. Prior to R. Meir, the nursing woman would not have been differentiated from women in general for purposes of contraception. R. Meir's public health suggestion intervened within a world in which nursing women were not engaged in special birth control practices; R. Meir suggests that they engage in *coitus interruptus*.

With this in mind, we can understand the anonymous collective of Sages in a more nuanced way. While the typical reading might imagine the anonymous "Sages" as a signifier for one of R. Meir's named contemporaries, I would like to understand "Sages" as reflecting the default sexual practice in which R. Meir intervenes. The anonymous collective known as the "Sages" represents the *status quo ante*. In other words, R. Meir suggests a public health intervention within a world in which the nursing woman is not taking any contraceptive precautions. Though he may have been somewhat influential, R. Meir would not have been able, as the contemporary example of the Surgeon General might demonstrate, to immediately transform general practice. Because there were those who still acted in the default fashion, a tanna formulates the position of R. Meir's opponents in a way that provides a positive rationale for the default practice. By my reading, the reason R. Meir's position was not fully accepted was not necessarily because of ideological opposition; rather, his was the fate of all radical advocates who call attention to a hitherto unidentified risk. That a contemporaneous culture that regularly disposed of newborns and aborted fetuses would not immediately acquiesce to R. Meir's identification of a risk is not shocking. But despite the radical nature of R. Meir's initial advocacy, his efforts are not in vain. By the time of the beraita's final redaction, the notion of the nursing woman as an at-risk category had reached consensus and the anonymous (presumably unanimous) position of the beraita's opening statement legislates to avoid this risk. Furthermore, R. Meir's initiative in the case of the nursing woman leads the beraita's redactor to extend protection to two other categories of women whose risk is more immediate than that of the nursing newborn.

This historical narrative of the evolution of the notion of risk in this case helps to explain the glaring strangeness of the Sages' position not to protect against a threat to infant mortality. If, in fact, the nursing child is a health risk, the position of the Sages is at odds with the general tone of the beraita; where the beraita is concerned for the health of the mother and/or child, the Sages are lackadaisical in suggesting a passive theological acceptance of biological fate. In this reading, the Sages' position is a rationale provided to justify the status quo. Rather than reading trust in God as a strong statement of belief, I take it to represent both a cynicism about the alleged risk and a rabbinic fatalism regarding the transformative power of a halakhic suggestion. As the Bavli's version of this formulation[36] often puts it, "Since many have traversed this path, God watches over fools:" Rabbinic authoritative impotence leads to a statement of theological faith.[37]

With this explanation, I am suggesting that the beraita points to the pre-history of the debate between R. Meir and the Sages because that debate reflects an emerging understanding of the nursing child as someone in need of protection and the nursing woman as someone who might employ birth control. That R. Meir is responsible for this emerging understanding can be demonstrated through the remarkable number of tannaitic texts that attribute strong halakhic protections for the nursing child to the view of R. Meir.[38]

R. Meir's Reforms

Among the amoraim, R. Meir is known for his *Gezeirot*, a term that (like our above suggestion regarding public health) implies a rabbinic authoritative proclamation whose basis is the subjective logic of the person making the decree. Within various statutes related to issues of marital law, especially related to the fetus, R. Meir demonstrates a consistent desire to protect newborns and a suspicion of all those who might be motivated to do harm to newborns.

R. Meir's most explicit suspicion is directed at pagan women who act as midwives for Jewish women. R. Meir bans such a practice. Mishnah Avodah Zarah 2:1 prohibits Jewish women from mid-wifing or nursing pagan babies, but permits pagan midwives and wet-nurses for Jewish babies. The related passage at Tosefta 3:1 differs slightly:

> A Jewish woman should not nurse a pagan child for she is raising a child to idolatry, but a pagan woman may nurse the Jewish woman's child.
>
> "A Jewish woman should not midwife a pagan woman for she raises a child to idolatry, and a pagan woman should not midwife a Jewish woman because they are suspected of murder."
>
> These are the words of R. Meir,
> but the Sages say "a pagan woman may midwife a Jewish woman when others are standing on top of her, but not privately because they are suspected of murder."

The Tosefta represents the issue of whether a pagan woman can midwife for Jewish women as a debate between R. Meir and the majority of Sages. R. Meir prohibits a Jewish woman from retaining a pagan midwife because pagan women are suspected of murder; the Sages permit the Jewish use of a pagan midwife, but only under supervision. Because the relationship between Mishnah and Tosefta is complex, we generally cannot assume that either text is prior to the other. And yet, the attribution of the prohibitive position to R. Meir in the Tosefta suggests that the debate between R. Meir and the Sages in Tosefta is prior to the anonymously stated unanimous position of the Mishnah. This gives the impression that an historical narrative similar to that of our beraita transpires in this context. R. Meir introduces concern for the pagan midwife into the discourse because of his suspicion and forces the consensus to respond to him. His contemporary sages, Tosefta indicates, meet him halfway by accepting his suspicion and requiring supervision for the pagan midwife. But the redactor of this Mishnah includes no such provision, permitting pagan midwives along with pagan nurses.

The historical narrative of pagan midwifery provides a contrast to that of our beraita. In the case of nursing, the risk advocated initially by R. Meir becomes consensus and is reflected in the majority's legal literature. In the case of pagan midwifery, R. Meir's suspicion of the pagans of murder does not reach consensus and though it occasions some response from his contemporaries, it eventually disappears from the legal mainstream. R. Meir's suspicion of midwives sounds hyperbolic to our own ears but is arguably reflective of some of the contemporaneous circumstances discussed above. Within a Roman pagan society rife with infanticide and exposure, R. Meir is suspicious of pagan's under-valuing of infant life.

But R. Meir is not only suspicious of the pagans. R. Meir's fear for newborn survival also encourages suspicion of *Jewish* women. Within a beraita quoted several times in the Bavli, R. Meir insists that the law that prohibits a widow to remarry for three months after her husband's death applies without exception.[39] Even those women whose personal circumstances deny the possibility of pregnancy are also required to wait the three months. Though it is possible to understand this principle on the basis of a need to create unexceptional laws, I contend that the basis for this is suspicion. R. Meir includes in his list of women who might make a case for remarrying immediately two women who were having marital issues with their respective spouses. I interpret R. Meir's insistence on three months as a disincentive because of the suspicion that such women might be responsible either for the death of their husbands or of danger to their fetuses.

R. Meir's heavy activity within laws pertaining to the nursing woman demonstrates his strong suspicion that these women do not have their children's best interests at heart. In this regard, R. Meir revives an earlier minority opinion (attributed to Beit Shammai) that extends the ban on a nursing widow's remarriage to twenty-four months.[40] If a woman violates this prohibition and marries anyway, R. Meir strips her of the protection of the Ketubah. R. Meir also uses the laws of Niddah to incentivize nursing and punish weaning.[41] Since a nursing woman receives a more lenient treatment vis-à-vis the rabbinic science of blood identification, R. Meir insists that this status is tied not to parturition, but to actual nursing. Thus a woman who does not nurse is not offered the benefits of being considered a nursing mother, and a woman who nurses, even beyond the minimal timeframe of twenty-four months, gains this benefit for as long as she nurses. Since a different statute (in this very chapter)[42] has a rabbinic debate regarding the duration of time it is appropriate for a woman to nurse (with some thinking that twenty-four months is an outer limit), it is particularly noteworthy that R. Meir is willing to encourage women to nurse their children even until age five by extending the Niddah benefits.[43]

Were these the only examples of R. Meir's approach to family law, we could accuse R. Meir of rank misogyny because of his suspicion of the infanticidal tendencies of women both pagan and Jewish. But R. Meir also extends his suspicion to predatory men who take a sexual interest in nursing or pregnant women that is to the detriment of fetus or child. In this example, R. Meir is not solely responsible for this suspicion, but he is notable for his contribution to its increase. An anonymous statute in this chapter of Tosefta states that a man should not marry a pregnant woman or a nursing woman. A beraita at Bavli Sotah 26a cites R. Meir as saying that a man who married a pregnant or nursing woman must divorce her immediately and can never remarry her.[44] A further extension of this penalty is attributed to R. Meir by Mishnah Sotah 4:3 which cites R. Meir's opinion that the woman in this marriage, should it continue, does not receive Ketubah benefits and the man is not able to employ the Sotah ritual; in other words, though there is no mechanism to prevent such a marriage from remaining binding, R. Meir removes two protections attached to marriage from this union. What is remarkable about the removal of the Sotah possibility is that Sotah is a biblical ritual and the prohibition on marrying a pregnant or nursing woman is rabbinic at best. This raising of the stakes of the prohibition further evidences our picture of R. Meir as a passionate advocate.

In her work on nursing in Rabbinic literature, Gail Labovitz has pointed to the fact that the Tosefta passage regarding nursing differs from many other rabbinic texts because it is motivated by the best interests of the child rather than by the rights and responsibilities of husband (father) and wife (mother) in the marital relationship.[45] It is not surprising that three (including our beraita) of our examples of R. Meir's active reform on behalf of the well-being of the infant are cited in this nursing unit of Tosefta Niddah.

One aspect of our narrativization of the beraita remains to be explained. Why is it that there is a development away from the *coitus interruptus* suggested by R. Meir and towards the *mokh* advocated by the opening anonymous statement of the beraita?[46] Though this is not a question of legal distinction (why is the law different in these two scenarios) it can be answered in many of the same ways that the question of legal distinction (the contradiction between the beraita and other halakhic texts) has been answered in the traditional responsa. Some traditional readers distinguish between the cases because of the actor responsible (man/woman) for the contraception while others talk about the *mokh* as permitting regular intercourse and *coitus interruptus*, as its name suggests, as interrupting the normal course.[47] Either of these might have motivated the transition from *coitus interruptus* to the *mokh*. Alternatively, it is possible that the *mokh* was preferred for more mundane practical reasons: *coitus interruptus* requires a certain skill level for the participant and accidents might happen. I would also suggest that *coitus interruptus* allows the fact of contraception to intrude on the act of sexual intercourse in explicit ways. In his writing about the discourse of sex in the nineteenth century, Michel Foucault talks about the clash between *eros* and *thanatos* inherent in the sex act and describes the way *coitus interruptus* encapsulates this conflict:

> The most notorious of "frauds," *coitus interruptus*, represented the point where the insistence of the real forced an end to pleasure and where the pleasure found a way to surface despite the economy dictated by the real.[48]

One final explanation for the transition from coitus interruptus to the *mokh* in the beraita may be that coitus interruptus was negatively valenced through its association with Er and Onan, as we will discuss below.

I have thus far used the texture of the beraita to provide a narrative history for the issue of contraceptive use for the nursing woman. Within a world in which the survival of newborns was threatened by circumstances both controllable and not, many in Roman society took the tack of diminishing the value of newborn life. Some Roman intellectuals decried this situation, but seem to have been fighting (until the rise of Christianity) a losing battle. In this context, R. Meir advocated for *coitus interruptus* as a contraceptive practice as part of a program committed to the survival and wellbeing of newborn infants. His contemporaries were not immediately won over and resisted this approach, justifying their intransigence with theology. Over time, though, a consensus built around the notion of advocating contraception as a public health suggestion when failure to use such could be fatal. The method of contraception advocated for the public, though, was the *mokh* rather than *coitus interruptus*. What we have demonstrated, then, is that while the beraita is often read as significant for what it tells us about contraception as a moral and legal issue in Jewish law, the original context was not one that considered contraception either as a subject of legislation or moral opprobrium. Rather, the beraita demonstrates a rather remarkable advocacy project for newborns within a world in which infant mortality led to a general malaise and indifference with respect to new life.

The Beraita in the Bavli

The birth control beraita found in Tosefta is explicitly cited in five contexts in the Babylonian Talmud. Each of these contexts includes a discussion of a minor female and her ability to conceive.[49] One of the contexts focuses on the equivocal language "*maybe* she will conceive and die" to infer that there are minors who *can* conceive and carry their babies to term. The other four contexts look to the beraita to represent the view that minors *cannot* successfully carry a baby to term. The distinction between these Bavli texts is not driven by any scientific disagreement on the part of the various Stammaim, but by the local redactoral needs and the rhetorical tendency of the Bavli to structure its sources in question-and-answer format.

Despite the five different contexts, the text of the beraita in the Bavli is remarkably uniform:

R' Bibi recited before R' Nahman:

Three women are using a *mokh*: 1) A minor 2) One who is pregnant 3) One who is nursing

1. A minor lest she will conceive and lest she will die
2. One who is pregnant lest she transform her fetus into a "*Sandal*".
3. One who is nursing lest she *wean her child and it will die*.
   a. And who is a minor? Between eleven years and one day until twelve years and one day.

> Less than this and more than this *she* has normal in-tercourse *as usual. This is the opinion of R' Meir.*
>
> But the sages say *this one and this one (she)* has nor-mal intercourse *as usual and heaven will have mercy* as it says, "God watches over fools."

There are several significant ways in which the Bavli beraita differs from its Tosefta parallel. First, this version does not tolerate interruptions within its structure. The opening statement's three categories of women are immediately followed by the one-line rationale for each of these. The beraita only cites definitions and controversies (structural level three) after reciting each of these rationales. Second, the two third-level comments of the Tosefta version (the definition of a minor and the prehistory of controversy regarding the nursing woman) are combined in the Bavli version. Third, the agent of this third-level legislation is of a different sex; while in the Tosefta version the prehistory targets the male, the Bavli version of the controversy targets the female. Fourth, within the case of the nursing mother, the Bavli version tones down the rhetoric of its rationale; where the Tosefta version suggests the *mokh* because the nursing mother might *kill* her child, the Bavli version argues that failure to use the *mokh* might result in the possibility that *she will wean the child and it will die.*

The general approach of scholarship in treating parallels of this nature is to privilege the version found in the earlier redacted Tosefta over the version found in the later redacted Bavli. The assumption behind this approach is that Bavli tradents altered the text of this beraita for their own purposes. A site-specific lower critical evaluation in this case dovetails with this general approach. *Lectio difficilior* indicates that the interrupted structure of Tosefta is likely the uncorrected original, the rough combination (see below) of the two third-level comments is a strong higher critical argument for editing, the transformation of the sex of the legal subject is an attempt to fix a problem within the Tosefta's version and the rhetoric of weaning is an attempt to soften the strangely violent suggestion that a nursing woman who has sex is "killing" her child. These arguments all move in the direction of arguing that the Bavli tradents altered their received beraita to smooth out interruptions in its structure, complexities in its logic and perceived ungrammaticalities.

The Bavli tradents indicate their desire to clean up the beraita in various ways. For one, the structure is insisted upon and the rhetoric is toned down. The Tosefta version presents tension between the beraita's legal layer and its pre-history layer since the redactive position suggesting a *mokh* does not cohere with either the view of R. Meir advocating *coitus interruptus* or with the view of the Sages suggesting no intervention at all. The Bavli tradents are particularly motivated to clean up the prehistory of the Tosefta because within that prehistory (according to both views) the legal subject is the male (he threshes, he has normal intercourse) while the legal subject of the beraita is the female (three women are using a *mokh*).

The final product of the Bavli's combination efforts is marked with the types of redactive sticking points typical for such combinations. R. Meir and the Sages are said to be arguing within the category of the minor rather than the nursing woman. But in combining the two different phrases the Bavli tradents restructure the combination around the similar sounding phrases (פחות מכן ויתר על כן משמש כדרכו ואינו חושש) and (וחכמים אומרים משמש כדרכו) while altering the gender of the legal subject. This creative act of composition leads to the insertion of a term within the position of the sages (אחת זו ואחת זו) that is not ideally appropriate for this kind of argument. Since the definition creates three categories of minor (before 11, between 11 and 12, after 12), the use of a term that refers to two categories is strange. (It is possible that the restructuring is designed to make R. Meir and the Sages agree)

I argued above that R. Meir's activity within the Tosefta's prehistory is of a piece with his suspicions of both women and men regarding infant wellness. It is this suspicion that results in the rhetoric of murder "lest she kill her son." The toning down of the rhetoric brings the example of the nursing women in line with the other two categories of women in the beraita.

In the Tosefta's beraita, R. Meir advocates *coitus interruptus* for a man who is having sex with a nursing woman. The disagreeing position of the Sages, I suggested above, reflects less a reasoned argument and more a de facto defense of the *status quo*. By the time of the beraita's redaction, though, R. Meir's concern for the nursing woman had elevated her to the category of at-risk and triggered her inclusion within the group of those whose intercourse was life-threatening and had to be modified accordingly. Once the possibility of a *mokh* exists, though, there is something strange about R. Meir's suggestion. After all, why advocate *coitus interruptus* for the nursing mother and not for the minor or the pregnant woman? The elimination of *coitus interruptus* from the beraita might therefore also be related to the sense that the original beraita strangely reserves its strongest recommendation for its least risky category. Since the diachronic development of and historical context behind R. Meir's suspicion was lost upon the Bavli tradents, the uneven treatment of the nursing mother as the riskiest category was modified.

In his work on wasted seed, Michael Satlow has emphasized a single discrepancy between the two beraitot. The reformulated beraita in the Bavli, Satlow notes, has no mention of the practice of *coitus interruptus*. Babylonian tradents, Satlow argues, needed to delete this sentence because it flies in the face of the late Bavli emphasis on wasted seed.[50] Furthermore, another Bavli beraita situates the missing line within a context that demonstrates its controversial nature:

> All twenty-four months he threshes inside and winnows outside," [these are] the words of R. Eliezer, but they said to him, "Are these not like the acts of Er and Onan?

The position of R. Eliezer is verbatim that of R. Meir in MS Vienna of Tosefta. The assumption has been that the beraita is a Babylonian beraita created on the basis of the original line removed from Tosefta. There are only two direct text witnesses to the Toseftan beraita, though, and the *editio princeps* of Tosefta cites R. Meir as quoted above *without* the reference to a time period. Given the general lower critical inclination to assume that text is added rather than removed, it is fair to assume that the verbatim overlap of the Toseftan beraita and the Bavli is a function of a tradent who inserted the extra words *into Tosefta* on the basis of the Bavli.[51] Even so, the two statements overlap in their suggestion and raise some possibilities.

Since Satlow assumes that the deletion of *coitus interruptus* from the beraita is a function of the agenda to promote wasted seed as the dominant issue governing contraception, he has little use for the Bavli beraita other than as evidence for resistance to *coitus interruptus*. I would like to bracket the wasted seed issue and pursue the evidence of the beraita itself. The beraita claims to record not just a legal debate, but the performative instance of such. R. Eliezer claims that a man engaged in a sexual relationship with a nursing woman should practice *coitus interruptus*. An anonymous third person plural is outraged by this suggestion since it is reminiscent of the actions of Er and Onan. The outrage at the suggestion suggests that the act of *coitus interruptus* has reached, at the moment of the beraita's redaction, a degree of moral opprobrium.[52] There is no need to read into this beraita an entire legal category of contraception or that the law, on the basis of Er and Onan, takes an interest in discrete acts of a couple's sexual relationship. Even so, the beraita is evidence that moral opprobrium is in the process of developing around specific sexual practices. This Bavli beraita suggests that the deletion of *coitus interruptus* from the Bavli's version of the beraita is a function of a developing antipathy towards certain modes of sexual activity. The text richly describes a developing communal moral opprobrium against certain practices and links that antipathy to a pair of biblical villains. The association of Er and Onan with *coitus interruptus* is not surprising since the simplest reading of the biblical story of Onan implies that this was Onan's regular practice and since Genesis Rabbah 85 utilizes the same euphemism as both beraitot to describe the practice.[53]

There is little possibility of determining whether R. Meir's suggestion of *coitus interruptus* occurred prior to the association of that practice with Onan. But even such an association does not guarantee that the practice would be treated with opprobrium. After all, most ancient interpreters understood the mechanics of Onan's act but did not focus on these, presuming that his crime lay with his refusal to participate in the requirements of levirate marriage. As with the requirements of procreation, tannaim did not look at discrete acts of intercourse, but at the programmatic commitment to raise a son for a dead brother. The Bavli beraita tracks the development of a consciousness of the discrete act that would lead eventually to legislation. But as I noted above in the discussion of wasted seed, even at the close of the Bavli, there is not a fully developed category of legal prohibition built around wasted seed. Rather, there is a homiletic and hyperbolic demonstration of moral opprobrium around wasted seed. And here I would offer a possible correction to Satlow's thesis regarding wasted seed. What occurs in the post-tannaitic period is the development of moral opprobrium around discrete sex acts and associated with specific modes of sexual activity. This results in an interpretation of Er/Onan that attends to their specific mechanics (Genesis Rabbah) and a moral revulsion at the suggestion that someone, even with warrant, would perform such an act.

In conclusion, I have attempted to contextualize the beraita of birth control within the cultural context of its period of production. I have argued that the Greco-Roman evidence points to a culture in which infants often had poor prospects for survival both because of natural conditions and because of cultural responses to those natural conditions. Infanticide and exposure can be understood as cultural responses to dim survival prospects; simply put, new life was not as valued as established life. Within this world, R. Meir advocated for maternal nursing through various enactments. One of these was his advocacy of *coitus interruptus* as the contraceptive practice of a nursing woman. Over time, R. Meir's concern for the infant became consensus and the *mokh* was substituted for *coitus interruptus* as the preferred contraceptive technique. The disappearance of *coitus interruptus* coincides with the increasing rabbinic attention to discrete sex practices. This begins with moral opprobrium attaching to certain practices. It is within this developing moral relationship with specific sex practices that the biblical story of Er and Onan begins to be analyzed for its specifically described practices and eventually some rabbis begin focusing on wasted seed. Wasted seed becomes the program for the Stammaitic treatment of the topic at Niddah 13, a treatment that does not itself turn wasted seed into legal statute but prepares the way for the post-talmudic literature to do so. The post-talmudic halakhic discourse reads the beraita not as an instance of rabbinic health advocacy, but as a statute legislating against a backdrop of wasted seed.

Department of Religion
Northwestern University

NOTES

1. The beraita or its Bavli parallel is treated in John Boswell, *The Kindness of Strangers: The Abandonment of Children in Western Europe from Late Antiquity to the Renaissance* (Chicago: University of Chicago

Press, 1998), 150 no. 44, K.R. Bradley, "Sexual Regulations in Wet-Nursing Contracts from Roman Egypt," *KLIO* 62, no. 2 (1990): 323–24, Robert Étienne, "La Conscience Médicale Antique Et La Vie Des Enfants," *Annales de demographie historique* (1973): 25, Norman E. Himes, *Medical History of Contraception* (New York,: Gamut Press, 1963), 71–75, Keith Hopkins, "Contraception in the Roman Empire," *Comparative Studies in Society and History* 8, no. 1 (1965): 142–44, John Thomas Noonan, *Contraception: A History of Its Treatment by the Catholic Theologians and Canonists* (Cambridge, Mass.: Belknap Press of Harvard University Press, 1986), 10–11, 20, 50–51, John M. Riddle, *Eve's Herbs: A History of Contraception and Abortion in the West* (Cambridge, Mass.: Harvard University Press, 1997), 73–75.

2. MS Vienna inserts "All twenty four months" within R. Meir's statement. If we follow the *editio princeps*, though, the debate between the two authorities could reference all three cases.

3. The implicit bracketed noun is explicated in MS Vienna. Its absence may suggest that the sages are referencing a proverb משמש כדרכו משמר על ידיו since the term "משמר על ידיו" is somewhat strained and might be chosen for symmetry with "משמש כדרכו". *Lectio Difficilior* suggests that MS Vienna's "משמר עליו" is a correction.

4. While an implied structure and a rigid outline are somewhat different, any method of reducing oral writing into text involves some measure of interpretation.

5. Himes, *Medical History of Contraception*, 74, Riddle, *Eve's Herbs: A History of Contraception and Abortion in the West*, 74. Riddle critiques David M. Feldman, *Birth Control in Jewish Law: Marital Relations, Contraception, and Abortion as Set Forth in the Classic Texts of Jewish Law* (Northvale, N.J.: J. Aronson, 1998) for the latter's definition of a *mokh* as wool or cotton. Feldman gets the notion of cotton from Rashi's commentary to the Bavli version of the beraita.

6. The work has also sometimes been published under the title: "Marital Relations, Contraception, and Abortion."

7. David M. Feldman, "Three Women Are Employing a Mokh: The Beraita and Its Commentary in the Writings of Medieval and Modern Rabbis (Hebrew)" (The Jewish Theological Seminary of America, 1966), Feldman, *Birth Control in Jewish Law: Marital Relations, Contraception, and Abortion as Set Forth in the Classic Texts of Jewish Law*.

8. Feldman, "Three Women Are Employing a Mokh: The Beraita and Its Commentary in the Writings of Medieval and Modern Rabbis (Hebrew)", 10, 57.

9. The occlusion is more severe in the English monograph because the work is more explicitly policy-oriented.

10. To be sure, Feldman maintains his reading of the beraita as advocacy throughout. But it is difficult to remain consistently within this viewpoint as he gets further involved in the task of reading the post-Talmudic responsa literature. This creates an inconsistency within the work that I diagnose as the problem of trying to do critical work while participating in the discourse.

11. Sometimes it seems that Feldman loses control of the compartmentalization himself as when he says Feldman, "Three Women Are Employing a *Mokh*: The Beraita and Its Commentary in the Writings of Medieval and Modern Rabbis (Hebrew)", 10. that though the use of a *Mokh* is acceptable, the practice of *coitus interruptus* is prohibited because of wasted seed. Feldman must be presuming that though the beraita's compositional intent is health advice, the debate between R. Meir and the Sages is understood against a backdrop of wasted seed; the Sages object to the mechanics of *coitus interruptus* because of its explicit and male initiated wasting of seed. Feldman must be presuming that though the contextual intent of the beraita is health advice, the debate about that advice is driven by extant prohibitions and is descriptively useful regarding those prohibitions.

12. This is not to say that Feldman ever fully forgets his initial insight into the beraita. He sometimes uses traditional viewpoints to support this reading. But by submerging himself within a traditional discourse that presumes things about the beraita that go against his own insight, Feldman effectively ignores his own observation much of the time.

13. Michael L. Satlow, "Wasted Seed: The History of a Rabbinic Idea," *Hebrew Union College Annual* 65 (1994), Michael L. Satlow, *Tasting the Dish: Rabbinic Rhetorics of Sexuality*, Brown Judaic Studies; (Atlanta, Ga.: Scholars Press, 1995), 232–64.

14. Though Satlow, "Wasted Seed: The History of a Rabbinic Idea." does not explicitly make Feldman his straw man, it is this relationship that explains Satlow's thesis; Feldman's reading wasted seed into the tannaitic literature is what makes Satlow's observation such an intervention. Feldman is the explicit straw man in Satlow, *Tasting the Dish: Rabbinic Rhetorics of Sexuality*, 232.

15. Satlow, *Tasting the Dish: Rabbinic Rhetorics of Sexuality*, 232.

16. Satlow hints to this when he says: Ibid., 262. "What (2) is not is a *condemnation* of contraception, a theme entirely absent from any attributed tannaitic source (emphasis mine)."

17. That rabbinic law often develops from the moral to the legal is already treated in both Jeremy Cohen, *Be Fertile and Increase, Fill the Earth and Master It: The Ancient and Medieval Career of a Biblical Text* (Ithaca: Cornell University Press, 1989) and David Daube, *The Duty of Procreation* (Edinburgh: Edinburgh University Press, 1977).

18. Satlow, "Wasted Seed: The History of a Rabbinic Idea."

19. A more cautious (and in my view more defensible) thesis that the Stammaim are responsible for turning this notion into a redactive program is relegated to Ibid.: no. 113. In his new book (David Brodsky, *A Bride without a Blessing: A Study in the Redaction and Content of Massekhet Kallah and Its Gemara* (Tübingen: Mohr Siebeck, 2006).) David Brodsky argues that Massekhet Kallah and the first two chapters of Kallah Rabbati are Babylonian early amoraic compositions. One of the core texts for Brodsky's argument is a passage that appears in parallel at Kallah Rabbati 2:15–19 and Bavli Niddah 13. Since this source contains the texts cited in the Bavli regarding wasted seed, it provides further evidence that the Stammaim may have been responsible for some of the programmatic commitment to wasted seed, but did not originate the idea entirely.

20. This is a highly simplified reading of this part of the Sugyah. I hope to return to this material in another context.

21. This notion of the Stam's function echoes one that I have been developing within the context of my treatment of Bavli legal narrative. See Barry Wimpfheimer, "Talmudic Legal Narrative: Broadening the Discourse of Jewish Law," *Dine Yisrael* 24 (2007).

22. That the moral opprobrium does not fade in this context with the evolution into legislation is evident from Maimonides, Yad Hahazaqah Issure Biah 21:18 "It is prohibited to emit semen in vain. Therefore, a man should not thresh inside and winnow outside and he should not marry a minor unfit for childbearing. But these who are adulterous with their hand[s] and ejaculate semen not only is it for them a great prohibition, but the one who does this sits in condemnation and about them it says, "Your hands are full of blood," and it is as if they killed someone."

23. See Keith Bradley, "Wet-Nursing at Rome: A Study in Social Relations," in *The Family in Ancient Rome: New Perspectives*, ed. Beryl Rawson (Ithaca: Cornell University Press, 1986), Gail Labovitz, "These Are the Labors: Construction of the Woman Nursing Her Child in the Mishna and Tosefta," *Nashim* 3 (2000).

24. Abraham Weiss, *Al hayetsra hasifrutit shel ha-Amoraim* (New

York: Horeb: Yeshiva University, Lucius Littauer Foundation, 1962),
176–231.

25. Bradley, "Wet-Nursing at Rome: A Study in Social Relations."

26. K.R. Bradley, *Discovering the Roman Family: Studies in Roman Social History* (New York: Oxford University Press, 1991), 28–29, Bradley, "Wet-Nursing at Rome: A Study in Social Relations," 216ff.

27. Daube, *The Duty of Procreation*, 18–34.

28. Boswell, *The Kindness of Strangers: The Abandonment of Children in Western Europe from Late Antiquity to the Renaissance*, Catherine Hezser, "The Exposure and Sale of Infants in Rabbinic and Roman Law," in *Jewish Studies between the Disciplines*, ed. Klaus Herrman; Margarete Schluter; Giuseppe Veltri (Leiden/Boston: Brill, 2003).

29. Philo, *The Special Laws*, trans. F.H. Colson (Cambridge, Mass.: Harvard University Press, 1929), 3.116, pp. 547–49.

30. Boswell, *The Kindness of Strangers: The Abandonment of Children in Western Europe from Late Antiquity to the Renaissance*, 149.

31. For a more detailed analysis of this phenomenon see Hezser, "The Exposure and Sale of Infants in Rabbinic and Roman Law."

32. Aulus Gellius, *The Attic Nights of Aulus Gellius*, trans. John Carew Rolfe, The Loeb Classical Library (London, New York: W. Heinemann; Putnam's Sons, 1927), XII.1, 353–61.

33. For the literature about such couvade tactics see Daniel Boyarin, "Jewish Masochism: Couvade, Castration and Rabbis in Pain," *American Imago* 51, no. 1 (1994).

34. Satlow, *Tasting the Dish: Rabbinic Rhetorics of Sexuality*, p. 233.

35. Ibid., 233.

36. Shabbat 129b; Yevamot 72a.

37. Compare the very brief responsum of R. Moshe Feinstein *Iggrot Moshe: Yoreh Deah* 2:49 on cigarettes which cites this same theological fiat in defense of status quo against consensus.

38. Jacob Neusner has famously critiqued the reliability of rabbinic attributions, especially for rabbinic biography. Neusner's critique has been resisted by a number of scholars. Nevertheless, it is possible that the various issues associated with R. Meir are attributed to R. Meir because of a literary assumption about R. Meir's relationship with nursing. If this is the case, then my observations are to be transformed from historical claims about the tanna R. Meir to literary claims about the later tannaitic redactors of Mishnah, Tosefta and Bavli Beraitot.

39. Eruvin 47a, Yevamot 42b, Ketubot 60b.

40. The relevance of this position attributed to R. Meir for reading the

birth control beraita is magnified by its appearance within this small tractate of nursing in Tosefta Niddah.

41. This position also appears within this nursing tractate in Tosefta Niddah.

42. Tosefta Niddah 2:3.

43. The Palestinian Talmud presumes that R. Meir's position vis-à-vis the Niddah issues is motivated by a scientific (Galen) understanding that connects the lack of menstrual blood to nursing. This does not undermine the possibility that there is additional motivation for this position. The existence of a disputant makes it apparent that the science was not uniformly accepted.

44. Bavli Yevamot 42a borrows the language of the birth control beraita to justify this decree of R. Meir, thus connecting the two laws as based on the same public health rationale.

45. Labovitz, "These Are the Labors: Construction of the Woman Nursing Her Child in the Mishna and Tosefta." Labovitz's thesis is that there is a programmatic difference between Mishnah and Tosefta in this respect. I do not fully accept this thesis because: a) as Labovitz struggles to extract herself, there is a passage in Mishnah Sotah (referenced above as one of R. Meir's reforms) that reflects the best interest of the baby and b) there are not enough sources in parallel to make this claim. Since the treatment of a topic is largely determined by direct context, it is not surprising that the Ketubot sources reflect the discourse of marital rights and responsibilities. Nevertheless, I credit Labovitz with the observation that the small nursing tractate in Tosefta Niddah is remarkable for its thematic commitment to the newborn's wellbeing.

46. Solomon Gandz, writing in Himes, *Medical History of Contraception*, 73., is the only writer to talk about this evolution and assumes the transformation is driven by the need to transfer responsibility for the contraception from the man to the woman.

47. Feldman, *Birth Control in Jewish Law: Marital Relations, Contraception, and Abortion as Set Forth in the Classic Texts of Jewish Law*.

48. Michel Foucault, *The History of Sexuality*, 1st American ed. (New York: Pantheon Books, 1978), 154.

49. Yevamot 12b infers from the beraita that it is possible for a minor to conceive and give birth while Yevamot 100b, Ketubot 39a, Nedarim 35b and Niddah 45a employ the beraita to buttress a question that it is impossible for a minor to be pregnant.

50. Satlow, "Wasted Seed: The History of a Rabbinic Idea," 152, Satlow, *Tasting the Dish: Rabbinic Rhetorics of Sexuality*, 234.

51. The phenomenon of Tosefta text modified by the Bavli is fairly common in MS Erfurt as Lieberman has noted. It is less common in MS Vienna, but it does happen. The preference of the *editio princeps* over MS Vienna here leads to the possibility that the pre-history debate was not about nursing specifically. Satlow recognizes this, but notes the grammatical evidence. If R. Meir initiated all three categories of the beraita and suggested *coitus interruptus* to deal with these categories, the above discussion of R. Meir remains unchanged except for the notion that R. Meir is responsible, then, for the notion of risk in all three categories.

52. The fact that the response in the beraita is one of opprobrium and not of legal prohibition is picked up on in Jacob Z. Lauterbach, "Talmudic-Rabbinic View on Birth Control," *Yearbook of the Central Conference of American Rabbis* 37 (1927): 373.

53. I am puzzled by Satlow's non-treatment of Genesis Rabbah 85. As a source that connects Onan with wasted seed, albeit without focusing necessarily on the spilt seed per se, it is relevant for dating the origin of wasted seed as a rabbinic concern.